FINDING VENICE

Smyth & Helwys Publishing, Inc.
6316 Peake Road
Macon, Georgia 31210-3960
1-800-747-3016
©2024 by Scott Hughes
All rights reserved.

Cover image created with the assistance of Midjourney

Library of Congress Cataloging-in-Publication Data

Names: Hughes, Scott (Joseph Scott), 1957- author.
Title: Finding Venice : (I hear it's nice this time of year) / by Scott Hughes.
Description: Macon, GA : Smyth & Helwys Publishing, 2024 | Includes bibliographical references.
Identifiers: LCCN 2023040048 | ISBN 9781641734691 (paperback)
Subjects: LCSH: Cerebrovascular disease--Religious aspects--Christianity. | Caregivers--Religious life. | Cerebrovascular disease--Patients--Religious life.
Classification: LCC BV4910.6.C47 H84 2023 | DDC 248.8/19681--dc23/eng/20231109
LC record available at https://lccn.loc.gov/2023040048

Disclaimer of Liability: With respect to statements of opinion or fact available in this work of nonfiction, Smyth & Helwys Publishing Inc. nor any of its employees, makes any warranty, express or implied, or assumes any legal liability or responsibility for the accuracy or completeness of any information disclosed, or represents that its use would not infringe privately-owned rights.

Advance Praise for *Finding Venice*

Most honest stories embody confident, joyful strides keeping company with hesitant scramblings through dark nights of the soul. Scott Hughes captures the chaotic struggle found in living authentically within each footfall. A father's and family's day-to-day trek alongside a daughter bent low just as young hopes set out invites us to journey in our own deep doubts whispering prayerful protests. Scott gives light for the path when best-laid plans falter. He tends our tomorrows as he discovers daily practices in taking one more step.
—*Chaplain David Blackmon, MDiv/MHA*
Asheville, North Carolina

A rare and unapologetically honest account of trauma, anger, grief, and rehabilitation by a stroke victim and her immediate family. Storyteller Hughes privileges the reader with access to personal confession, family frustration, and medical intervention amidst a crisis of faith and patchwork healthcare system. Besides telling a captivating and tender story, Hughes offers hard-earned wisdom for any family facing drastic loss and the death of long-held dreams. Just like his relentless daughter, Hughes shines uncommon light on the blessing to be found along an unanticipated and unenviable journey.
—*Casey Callahan, Associate Pastor*
First Baptist Church, Asheville, North Carolina

In *Finding Venice*, Scott Hughes unflinchingly tells the true story of the worst thing a parent can experience—the suffering of their child. Rather than being paralyzed by pain, Scott has crafted this book for other parents and caregivers who find themselves shoved off the road they thought they were traveling. I hope this book will find its way into the hands of those who could benefit from Scott's experience, practical advice, and most of all, his compassion.
—*Rev. Dr. Jenny Lee, Minister of Word and Sacrament, PC(USA)*
Pastor of Pocket Presbyterian Church, Sanford, North Carolina

Finding Venice is not for the faint of heart, and it shouldn't be. If you need to be an advocate and cheerleader for a loved one in crisis, this is the book for you. Thank you to Scott Hughes for putting to word the experiences of the Hughes (and Miller) family around Megan's stroke. Our prayer is that it will help many others going through a health crisis to never give up hope and celebrate baby steps along the recovery way.

—*Jon & Kim Miller*

Scott Hughes is one of the finest people I've been privileged to know. To be his friend and to experience his integrity, faithfulness, thoughtfulness, and good humor are gifts I cherish. This book is an honest account of a harrowing but also hopeful journey that Scott and his wife, Linda, have traveled—and continue to travel—with their remarkable daughter, Megan. Scott is candid about his nagging doubts and expresses gratitude for his persisting faith. He tells us about his questions and shares with us his hard-earned wisdom. He lets us see his tears and hear his laughter. He bears witness to the importance of community and the power of love—human, divine, and canine (!).

—*Guy Sayles, writer, speaker, and consultant*
fromtheintersection.org

As an eyewitness to the incredible journey recounted in this book, I can wholeheartedly confirm both the unfailing fortitude of Megan Hughes and the deep faith of her father, Scott. The skill, transparency, and inspiration of Scott's words in telling their story make this book truly compelling. To all who have experienced an unexpected change in their life's destination, he tells unflinching truth, offers vulnerable identification, shares first-hand advice, and gives a powerful faith witness.

—*Clark Sorrells, Minister of Music*
First Baptist Church, Asheville, North Carolina

A Medical Memoir

FINDING VENICE

(I Hear It's Nice This Time of Year)

SCOTT HUGHES

*To my darling Linda,
our entire family
and all who find themselves in the daunting role
of an unexpected caregiver*

Contents

Prologue	1
Chapter 1. Sweet Megan	5
Chapter 2. Life . . . You Never Know What You're Gonna Get	13
Chapter 3. Pokes, Prods, Pain, and Scans	21
Chapter 4. I See You (ICU)	29
Chapter 5. Losing Direction	39
Chapter 6. One Step Forward, Two Steps Back	49
Chapter 7. Nailed It!	63
Chapter 8. Ice Cream, Pudding, and Panthers	69
Chapter 9. Finding Rehabilitation	79
Chapter 10. Almost Intermission	89
Chapter 11. Atlanta's Calling	97
Chapter 12. Assessing Miss Megan	109
Chapter 13. Quashing Hope	119
Chapter 14. Being Right	127
Chapter 15. The Caregiver	135
Chapter 16. All Therapy All the Time	143
Chapter 17. Zero Gravity	153
Chapter 18. Discharge Day	159
Chapter 19. The Power of Prayer?	165
Chapter 20. The Power of Music	173

Chapter 21. Are We Covered?	181
Chapter 22. Meet Shepherd	189
Chapter 23. The "Mental" Part of Brain Insult	197
Chapter 24. What's Next?	205
Chapter 25. Saying Goodbye to Some Things	213
Chapter 26. Lessons Learned	221
Chapter 27. The End?	231
Epilogue	239

Prologue

Our meager existences often seem insignificant when measured against all of humanity. For most of us, it lasts something under a hundred years or so. But the time we spend living our one human life is dwarfed when we consider the millions of people who have lived before us and those that will live long after us.

But to you and to those around you, the moments that are significant and truly meaningful are often of limited duration and often result in life-altering experiences. They usually remain with us for the rest of our lives and are a benchmark for measuring most other experiences. Each of us experiences significant days with fear or elation or sometimes both—a first kiss; the birth of a child; the death of a parent; marriage to a soulmate; the suicide of a friend; that first broken heart; a significant illness for you or someone close to you. None of these are easy, but some are harder than others.

All such events require adjustments. All will leave some mark indelibly on our souls. All will place a bookmark when we review the entire contents of our life's work. With each event comes other significant changes, and the ultimate outcome is never completely assured. So it is in this "crazy, tragic, sometimes almost magic, awful, beautiful world."[1]

Each of us starts out in life with dreams and hopes, expectations and ideas of how to live, and we set off trying simply to reach the goal of success and then live out our days in our perception of comfort and peace. And to some people, those days come easy with few impediments. Some even carry a large contingent of groupies and wannabes on their backs along the journey. To others, life seems a

---

1. Harley Allen and Darryl Worley, "Awful, Beautiful Life," *Darryl Worley*, DreamWorks Nashville, June 2004.

constant struggle, a fight for every achievement, with elusive success and hope just out of reach. And for many of us, life is a blend of both. We live in times of success and failure, hope and despair, ease and struggle—and usually with very little control over when or how that tide changes.

The most intense events that we live through often do not happen specifically to us but rather to those we know and love. Any parent will tell you they would gladly trade places with a sick child, gladly accept the punishment for actions that land that child in trouble, gladly give anything they have in this life in order to prevent that child from feeling pain or suffering loss. The intensity of that passion is easy to imagine, painful to observe, and almost impossible to experience firsthand.

This is the story of a series of events that, in a long life of struggle and some accomplishment, seem to me as significant and difficult as anything I have experienced in life so far. Such experiences realign the cosmos in a way that alters everything that comes after. Everything else must further realign. My hope is that these words somehow bring hope and encouragement to all who face illness and its trials.

A longtime mentor told me in my youth, "Anything that doesn't kill you will only make you stronger." After living through one of the most challenging periods in my over sixty years, I have learned that being stronger sounds fulfilling, but the analogy is not actually honest. I do not see myself as "stronger" but rather as "changed."

Much of this work was initially written late in 2018, which was about two years after Megan's stroke. Writing served my needs to document the journey and offered an intentional outlet, which brought its own catharsis. It is my hope that these stories and observations will bring you hope, give you tools to face your life's obstacles, and provide a gift and perspective of faith that has served me and those who helped form my character and intellect. I believe that if we are honest, there is little original thought in the cosmos. We have shared similar experiences but have experienced them with different perspectives.

My faith is simple and trusting, and some of these lessons may be controversial to some. We are a product of our own individual experiences and our own circumstances. They are all formed from our perception of who God is and our willingness to learn, our willingness to grow, and our willingness to change. I pray that as you read about these events, you take something from our pain that brings you comfort, enhances your faith, and helps you grow from the lessons we have learned in the last couple of years.

I can only speak for me as to what I felt. Those around me may have different recollections or memories or thoughts. I know that there are events and content that I simply did not get to or maybe didn't get exactly right. As you read, know that in some cases I have only hit the high spots and also just the low-hanging fruit from a tense and overwhelming period. My goal is to convey some communication of hope from tragedy and miraculous healing when we had no initial belief that such healing was possible. I also offer a few object lessons we learned that might help you in your journey.

I offer one other disclaimer regarding my occasional use of colorful language. While my use of such verbiage is not the norm for me, I am admittedly weak and human. During the days I bring before you to explore, I wanted you as the reader to sense the intensity and rawness of these events. I apologize in advance for that content, but I accept that in most cases these are a fair approximation of my thoughts, feelings, and personal pain. I would take them all back if I could. If I had my preference, though, their use would have never been necessary to begin with. They are what they are, so I apologize in advance. Please judge them accordingly. *So we begin.*

Chapter 1

Sweet Megan

From the moment I laid eyes on her I was smitten. Our firstborn. A tiny seven or so pounds of absolute beauty, joy, huge eyes—and lungs to match. In fact, the extra days in the hospital due to Linda's C-section were welcome. They allowed us a little time to discover how inept we really were as new parents. We figured out that breastfeeding was not for us. Cloth diapers were not for us. We also figured out that patience may be a virtue, but a screaming child at 1:30 in the morning causes exhaustion to take over, and as a result patience goes out the door.

On that first night at home, 1:30 a.m. came, and Linda got up to try to console our baby's cries of hunger. I awoke to the cries of this bundle of joy turned possessed demon from hell. I arose to help and found Linda reduced to tears, suffering from postpartum exhaustion. I told her to get some rest, grabbed my little girl, and headed out to the sofa. Parenting is like practicing medicine—it is all practicing until you learn what works and what doesn't. We had no idea what worked for our child, so everything was an experiment.

I stuffed a warm bottle in her little mouth, and after a couple of sips the cries began anew. I laid back on the couch and put her tiny head on my chest. I had heard someone say the heartbeat of a parent brings comfort to an anxious child. And it did initially seem to help, at least for a moment, and then the writhing began once more. Even though her little ear lay right on top of my rapidly beating heart, I felt more and more hopeless that I would get her comfortable. Add to that a new twist: as she lay on my chest, she began to grab handfuls of chest hair and tug with all her might, which for a five-day-old was amazingly strong. But the cries continued.

Just as I was about to move to a chair to try plans F, G, or H, I heard yet another unique sound and then felt the moist eruption of a very messy diaper. I jumped up and ran for the changing table, the baby's cries still being voiced, and I did my best imitation of a diaper change. Those first ones were most uncomfortable for me and for her.

But to my amazement, when I sprinkled powder she quieted, and for the first time in what seemed like hours, our house was calm again. I found our baby's new best friend "binky"—her pacifier—wrapped her in the blanket her Nana had made for her and sat down in a chair in the living room. She sucked on that binky and batted those gorgeous eyes at her old man for the longest of times, and my love and pride welled up within me. Soon she began to drift away into baby dreams.

In order not to wake Linda, I moved to the couch, laid the baby on my chest once again, and covered us both with an afghan. She slept until almost morning, and I slept myself for a few hours. That first night home, we questioned everything, particularly if we were qualified to raise this precious gift. But the moments of frustration, fear, panic, and even terror were equally matched over the coming days by joy, love, and delight as we got to know our daughter.

Linda and I were late starters among our peers; I was twenty-nine and she was twenty-eight when Megan was born. For a while, having a child had seemed like another challenge during a time when life was just beginning to hit full stride. Careers had evolved and would soon evolve once again. I left my first job in an accounting firm to take a position with one of my best and biggest clients in an industry that I am obsessed with . . . cars. Just as I accepted that job, Linda and I figured out that we were expecting.

We had planned it. We were thrilled, and we thought we were finally ready to begin a family. Just as we approached the third month of pregnancy, I came home to find Linda not feeling well and then suddenly encountering unexpected spotting. A visit to our obstetrician the following morning brought uneasiness and concern as to the viability of the pregnancy, and the following evening Linda miscarried after several long hours of symptoms and a lengthy trip to the ER that lasted until the next morning. I was amazed at how attached we had become to this tiny life that ended before it really had time to begin. We experienced loss that was hard to get past.

So, when we found out that we were expecting again, it became a time of occasional joy with regular intentional medical care. Now we were categorized as "high risk," so Linda spent hours hooked up to monitors and non-stress tests. And this time one of our defensive obstetric folks quipped that she was not convinced we would have this child either. Linda was already a bit fragile, and this comment sent us over the edge. Every potential symptom was stressful, every OB visit a time of fear.

But as the Scriptures say, "the time came that she should be delivered" (Luke 2:6). And then it passed. In fact, we went two weeks past the planned due date, so our OB said, "Let's go to the hospital and do some tests, and if we have any questions, we will go ahead and induce." We were scared. But after more monitors and other tests, Dr. Davis, a wonderfully kind and caring healthcare professional, said "Let's do this," and several hours later when normal labor was getting only minimal results, he said, "It's time to opt for a C-section. I would rather not take any further chances; it's time for this little one to be born."

An hour or so later, Megan came into this world calmly and even quietly and with very little fanfare. She only cried when provoked because she seemed a bit timid about her new surroundings. And when smacked she found those wonderful lungs until a nurse wrapped her in a blanket and plopped her in my arms.

This daughter of ours was always a gift. One we fought hard for and one who filled our lives with joy from the first week. We learned all the lessons and tricks of parenting from our friends of child-bearing age. We fought the earaches and the tummy aches, the gas, and all those two o'clock feedings. She survived the bumps and bruises of childhood and welcomed with open arms her little brother Jeffrey, who became her "bestie" before there was such a thing.

Megan grew up in daycare with one of the true "saints" providing daily love and care. Willena was one of the best friends to our kids that we and they have ever known. Fortunately for us, Linda's job at the time had all the employees' kids in one place. Through it all they learned to talk, to sing, and even potty train, then moved on to gymnastics, spelling, math, and how to be good friends. They explored Girl Scouts, American Girl dolls, Cabbage Patch Kids, Power Rangers, and Beanie Babies, and soon it was time for school and kindergarten to divide that daycare tribe for the first time.

Our involvement at First Baptist Church in Asheville, North Carolina, allowed for an easy transition into children's and eventually youth activities, along with one of the finest music development programs in any institution, religious or secular. We were blessed by the saints of that time who taught our kids the lessons we were incapable of teaching.

Parents raising kids these days are already so overwhelmed by the demands of simply existing. Working long hours and climbing the corporate ladder all too often mean that Mom and Dad work all day and then work all night at the more important job of being a parent. In my mind, the power of a strong support structure of family, friends, and faith are all that have kept our children's generation from flying completely off the tracks.

It is no wonder that our kids are so different from us as they reconsider the need for *more* and the value of a simpler, less frivolous life of *me* and *mine* and *stuff*. It is a bit of a silent rebellion that has gathered steam and resulted in doing with less and having more time for quality of life. The reality is that our kids are doing this much better than we have. These kids are smart, and they innovate in ways that we gray hairs say will never work. Yet they do.

Megan's high school and college years were where she truly blossomed. In grade school she was an average student with a good deal of untapped potential. But in high school she began to open her mind and apply her intellect. And when she went off to college at the University of North Carolina at Greensboro, she came into her own. UNCG tapped into her unique talents to "out-think" those she could and "out-work" all the rest.

There was little doubt that Megan would never follow in the steps of her accountant Dad, and in fact neither would her brother Jeffrey. But just because she did not want the hours or overtime of tax season does not mean she did not have the drive and commitment to achieve. She found her calling of early childhood and pre-K education and became a fearless voice for the appropriate education of our youngest minds.

She graduated with honors and began her career of touching one life at a time. She spent a year in Greensboro teaching for a local childcare provider, and as the year came to a successful close, she decided that the classroom was not a long-term career in and of itself. Instead, Megan felt called to improve the "big picture" of early childcare. To do that meant she must seek out higher learning once again, and so she received a working scholarship at UNCG to complete her master's degree, which she did with amazing speed and grace.

When she completed her master's degree, she made another choice that made me proud by returning to Asheville to continue her career. Over time, she found her way to the Buncombe County Partnership for Children, a wonderfully innovative organization that seeks to help childcare providers of all sizes to achieve better ratings through licensure in North Carolina. Her job was to help teach the teachers and administrators of the facilities, many who struggled for resources and who struggled with the complexities of providing this incredibly important service to families and their children.

One of my favorite lessons from my daughter is the constant correcting when I misspeak the educational world's vernacular. I could do no right, it seems. "Don't say daycare; say childcare," Megan said. And then there was her outrage and indignation at my use of the word "retarded." I had to learn a new way to communicate because she was as committed and passionate about her field of study as I have ever been about accounting. It humbled me and made me so proud that Megan was on her way to great things in education. I began to learn that my daughter was every bit the "type A" personality that I had been for decades.

Megan began to put down roots in her childhood neighborhood. She bought her first home and did all the legwork of arranging her mortgage and finding her favorite "shabby chic" décor to decorate this charming three-bedroom home that was on three levels. It was an incredible buy, enhanced in part by the financial crisis of 2008, the decline in property values, and the over building of the years before. She bought this little townhome for a fraction of its true value and had monthly payments that were less than rent for anything close to that size. And on those occasions when Mom and Dad dropped in, we found our little girl obsessed with her newfound love of HGTV and the Property Brothers along with Pinterest and consignment shops as she turned her pride and joy into a tasteful, thoughtful space on a budget.

She shared that space with her newest friend and First Baptist's just hired youth minister, Jenny Lee. They were truly birds of a feather, and together they invested themselves into enjoying life, which went hand in hand with reenergizing the eighteen- to thirty-four-year-old population of our church. For most churches, that entire generation has taken an intentional sabbatical from organized religion. To attract them, congregations have had to find ways to integrate relationship and friendship back into their core values.

Jenny and Megan hosted Tuesday nights out at restaurants and pubs, where those of that age who had become disenfranchised among our congregation felt safe and encouraged. Most important, here these young people did not feel judged by traditional Baptist congregations that spurned an occasional beer or watching the game in a pub or bar. Jenny and Megan were willing to challenge the standards and cause conversations to erupt about things many felt uneasy about.

The innovation and willingness to think creatively brought new life to a stagnant sector of our congregation and helped open conversations that might have been taboo in years before—about issues this age group finds important including gay rights and faith as well as other less controversial issues about what faith looks like in this postmodern world. Megan became the youngest woman ever ordained by our church and never shied away from any subject she felt strongly about. Her passion once again helped to change the environment around her. Megan is a person of action, and she shows that through her everyday life.

During her college years, our daughter became a ravenous football fan and fell in love with our own Carolina Panthers. She never missed a game, could quote statistics and game plans better than most sportscasters, and fell in love with one player, Luke Kuechly. In fact, she and some friends drove to Concord and test drive a GMC vehicle in a dealership promotion just to meet Luke and have a picture taken with him. She had one of her friends drive it for a second time so she could meet him twice that day. She is a nut, loyal to a fault, and fearless when it comes to things that are important to her, particularly when there is a little risk involved.

In 2015, shortly after her roommate Jenny Lee got married and moved away, Megan decided it was time to redo her kitchen, so she ordered new stainless-steel appliances around late fall and took an online teaching gig through UNC-Greensboro that would help pay for her new equipment. Her Nana gave her granite countertops for Christmas, and all this was delivered and installed in early January right after her twenty-ninth birthday. The final touch was a subway tile backsplash, which we helped her buy over the last weekend of the month. While she shopped, Linda and I spent the weekend at our beach house in Holden Beach, North Carolina, with our close friends Jon and Kim Miller.

Jon is my best golf buddy. Linda and Kim grew up together in Asheville and graduated from Appalachian State. Fate brought us back together early in our married lives, and their kids and our kids are about the same ages. We have been through so much together over the years.

In 2007, Jon and Kim's middle daughter, Katie, suffered a traumatic brain injury after being hit by a car. It was a terrible time, and we did our best to be there for them. Our friendship was always important to us, but those days of pain and stress and fear allowed us to cement family relationships that will forever stand the tests of time. They are among our best friends.

When we returned home on Sunday night from Holden, I texted Megan about getting together to see what she had bought and to plan for when the two of us would tackle the tile installation. She had plans for that night, so we decided to have dinner together at Chili's on Monday to catch up. It was good to be back and to see my little girl. I remember thinking about how Megan's busy life was beginning to mirror my own.

When dinner was over, we walked to the car with plans to finish the final touches of her beautiful new kitchen on the weekend, and I knew we would see her at choir practice that Wednesday night. It was nice to be home and even better to be with our little girl, if even for only a few minutes. She headed home to 17 Union Chapel Road, and we pointed our cars to 37 Nichols Hill Drive as the start of my thirty-seventh tax season would begin in earnest the following days of that week. Life was good, and the future seemed promising as Linda and I enjoyed the downhill slide of our careers while Megan began to ascend to the pinnacle of hers.

Sweet Megan and her dad in December 1987

Chapter 2

Life . . . You Never Know What You're Gonna Get

The following morning started like any other day. The alarm went off at 6:30, Linda headed to the shower, and I finally stirred and turned on the local TV news. Then both of our phones "dinged" together as they sometimes do. "Must be a morning traffic alert," I thought, and I got up and headed for the bathroom to shower and shave. As I passed my lovely wife, I said, "Your phone dinged," then jumped into a hot shower. Later, I started putting on my clothes and just happened to pick up my cell phone to check for texts.

MEGAN HUGHES
2/2/16 6:42 AM
Yum and Magazineggggggguuuuuuuu
I'm nilly questions
Eng

MEGAN HUGHES
2/2/16 6:51 AM
When not
OAfp the best

"That's odd," I thought. Linda looked at hers and it was similar. I hurried to text our daughter.

SCOTT HUGHES
2/2/16 7:15 AM
You ok?

MEGAN HUGHES
2/2/16 7:15 AM
When call

And with that simple text exchange our world changed. The thirty-minute gap between the first text and my 7:15 response still brings me guilt that we might have reacted sooner. It is a "parent thing" to find ways and reasons to feel guilty. But that was Tuesday, February 2, 2016. That was how it started, and it quickly went downhill from there, at least for a while.

I immediately dialed Megan, and the phone was answered quickly, but the sounds I heard on the other end were almost otherworldly, like a wounded animal yelling for relief.

I cried, "Megan!" and the moans and wailing became more urgent. "What's wrong?" I pleaded. The sounds from the other side were loud and panicky, half crying and half something else. All I knew was that if this was Megan, she was in trouble and needed our help. My mind raced in a dozen directions. "Should I dial 911? Has she been assaulted? Is she overdosed on some kind of medication? Is this some experiment with drugs that has gone horribly wrong? Is she sick? Has she fallen?" Oh my God, the possibilities—and none of them good. I did not even know for sure that she was at her home.

I handed my phone to Linda and barked "keep her talking," which is oddly humorous now, since to that point Megan had yet to say the first word. I threw on my pants and slipped on shoes, grabbed a coat and my cell phone, and told her, "Honey, I'm on my way. I'll be there in five minutes." And with that I ran to my truck, once again barking to Linda, "I'm on my way over there; I'll call when I know something."

I jumped in the truck and sped toward my daughter's condo some three miles away. I was not very courteous when I came up on other drivers. I admit to breaking about every rule one could break on a Tuesday morning during rush hour. I made the left turn through a completely red light at Reems Creek Road and drove over the traffic island with lots of loud thumps and screeches, and I cut off a service vehicle for one of my client's repair services.

I know there were many epithets offered at my expense that morning, and the strongest likely came from the driver of the pickup truck who literally had to lock down his brakes to avoid being hit by this crazed accountant on a mission. In my mind, my red lights and sirens were blaring, but unfortunately that was only in my mind. After a skidding left-hand turn onto Union Chapel, suddenly I was there, pulling into the small parking pad in front of her condo. I was absolutely frightened out of my mind with what I might see.

I fumbled through my key ring looking for that Kwikset key among the six other Kwikset keys, and finally I felt the knob turn and the door push open. I listened briefly for sounds, and from the bedroom at the top of the stairs I heard muffled cries that silenced briefly when I yelled, "Megan! I'm here, honey."

When I got to the top of the stairs, I was completely crushed to see my little girl lying on her bed, struggling to push herself up on her left arm. Her face bore the runny makeup and bloodshot eyes of the torment of a struggle that had obviously gone on for some extended time. She was completely naked, and the room was a mess. Clothes were strewn around the bed, the nightstand askew, with the lamp turned over toward the wall. The expression on her face was sheer terror and tears, coupled with incoherent moans and total panic. I then noticed that the right side of her face drooped a bit as if almost frozen in time. My heart fell. I thought to myself, *A stroke? How?* She is only twenty-nine. Surely it is something else.

I embraced her and helped her lie back down as she did her best to try to communicate with me using gestures and sounds that only made sense somewhere deep in her injured brain. I covered her with the sheet and reached for my phone and told her, "Honey, I'm calling 911." I held her head in the crook of my arm and told her, "Megan, no matter what this is, no matter what has happened, your mom and I are going to be with you every step of the way, whatever that means." Those words were no sooner spoken than she closed her eyes and almost instantly dozed off, exhausted.

I listened as the phone rang, and the man on the other end said, "911—police, fire, or ambulance?" I replied, "Ambulance," and he said, "Sir, what is your emergency?"

I explained as best I could that I had found my daughter in her home exhibiting stroke-like symptoms. My mind still raced uncontrollably as he asked his list of questions. And as I looked at that sweet painted face that was so different from the beautiful young woman whom we had left the night before at dinner, I wondered "How can this be happening?"

My drifting thoughts were rattled when the 911 operator asked, "What is your physical address?" I drew a blank. I said, "17, uh, 17 . . . oh, it's the road that goes to the golf course at Reems Creek."

I know that address better than I know my own. To my delight, he threw me a lifeline and said, "Union Chapel?" and I said "Yes, yes, that's it." He said, "The ambulance is on the way. I'll stay on the line until they get there." And with that, suddenly there were just a few short moments of silence.

In that brief time, I saw the rapid pulse of my daughter's neck pounding away. Then I heard my own broken heart hammering like a jackhammer. And in those few seconds I realized she was alive, and maybe I got there in time. I prayed my first prayer in those moments and asked God simply to be there and keep us safe. Then I heard the gradual sounds of a siren turning onto Union Chapel, and I told the kind man on the phone that his crew was on scene and that I was going downstairs to get them in the house. He wished us good luck and I thanked him.

I woke Megan when I pulled my arm out from under her head, and I told her I had to go let the paramedics in. She grabbed the sheet and pulled it up, and then I noticed that she could only use her left arm and leg. The right lay almost limp and had no motion as she struggled to rearrange herself on the bed.

I went down the twenty steps to the front door and met the ambulance as it stopped just ahead of my truck. The crew of four young men, most about Megan's age, grabbed their appointed gear like a fine-oiled machine. Each had a box or device to carry. I explained once again what I had found and told them the gurney they were unloading would likely do them no good because of the steep steps and the way the stairs turned ninety degrees at the top.

At about the same time, Linda arrived in her car. I told her what I had found and what she was about to see.

When we got the whole group to the bedroom, the crew set up and the lead paramedic introduced himself to Megan and asked for her name. She looked at me as if to ask permission to speak, but no words came out. He asked, "Can you tell me your name?" and she mouthed words that never came out. Then to our surprise she said "Yes," and he asked again "So what is your name?" She looked at him and said softly "Yes" one more time.

In life, we all at some point face individual moments when we realize that we are no longer in control. The circumstances surrounding us are way outside our ability to alter, improve, or fix. The reality that we believed we were in just moments before is forever and completely changed.

I am one of those dads who "fixes" things. That is my job, my station in life, and I had up to this point been comfortable with it. Just moments before, I had told my daughter that we would find a way through this, but now with the things I had just seen and heard I knew that this was serious and perhaps life threatening. Our daughter was in real trouble.

The paramedics checked her vitals and tried to get her to move her arms and legs. The one thing that I, as her father, held out hope for was that I believed it was obvious that she knew she was naked in front of four young men about her age. She was not going to let go of that sheet.

The young lead paramedic was very professional and knew his stuff. He examined Megan as thoroughly as any physician I had ever seen. He tried to break the tension with kind words and attempts at humor. But as I studied my daughter's face, I could tell that she had no clue what was being said—or anything else for that matter. Her face looked simply bewildered, helpless, tormented, and panicked.

As they began moving toward transporting her to the hospital, she was obviously at least somewhat aware of her lack of clothing in front of these paramedics. I was proud of Linda because she showed amazing composure and strength as she helped Megan find underwear and a shirt so they could transport her to Mission Hospital.

These fine young men of the Reems Creek Fire Department got to us in less than five minutes, and now, some fifteen minutes later, they helped Megan into an upright chair with handles. They strapped her in and carried her down those twenty very steep steps to the waiting gurney just outside the door.

By the time we got downstairs, there were at least ten people gathered around the front door, all helping put things where they belonged and keeping traffic moving on the street. They transferred our daughter into the ambulance and started IVs in each arm. The lead paramedic, proving his kindness, knew just how shattered we both were. He told us they would transfer her to Mission and that she would get excellent care. He then said we should come to the emergency room as quickly as we could. From there they would get us to her when we arrived.

I will not soon forget what he said next: "Don't try to keep up with us; we will be running lights and sirens." The lump in my throat once again doubled in size.

We got into our cars and waited for the ambulance to pull out. It sat there for another few minutes as they worked with Megan and reported what information they had gathered. I began dialing the phone but struggled for a moment with whom to call first.

I told Linda to take her car to a local Ingle's grocery store and drop it off so we could ride together, since we were nearly at the peak of morning rush hour. We both left and saw the ambulance crest the hill in front of us at a quick pace. I began to check off one by one the long list of folks I needed to notify. I remembered that I had an 8:30 meeting with one of my partners and a prospective client, so I called him and let him know our circumstances and that I would not be there. I could hear his concern, and I could tell that my vulnerability pushed him to try to say something encouraging. "Scott, be strong," he said. That was my first experience of hundreds to come with friends and associates who did not know what to say and were simply shocked out of their minds by this turn of events.

Next, I called my brother Bud and told him we were on the way to Mission with Megan. His shock and disbelief were as I expected, and his response was one of love and compassion. Then came the first of dozens of questions we would hear over and over: "What can I do?"

I asked him to call several folks, including our church ministerial staff, to let them know. And with that I began to sob uncontrollably, if only for a moment. He said, "What else?" I responded, "At this point I just don't know, Bud." My mind spun uncontrollably. What if she dies? What if she can't ever be the same? What if . . . what if?

We pulled into the Ingle's parking lot. Linda hurriedly jumped in my truck, and we headed to Mission, even if at only a slightly slower pace than my trip earlier that morning. I grabbed her hand and held it like a vise. We traveled in almost stunned silence, occasionally verbalizing things that we needed to do. And almost like a blurred vision, once again we were there, dreading what we were about to experience. I dropped Linda off at the emergency entrance and went to find a place to park.

As I headed toward the entrance, I saw Megan's ambulance already parked in the side lot. I felt as though I were walking through a tunnel into a place that was dark and cold and uncertain. My mind continued its tormented spin.

Chapter 3

Pokes, Prods, Pain, and Scans

As I walked through the emergency entrance, I was suddenly reminded of the fact that I hate hospitals, particularly when coming through this entrance. We had spent weeks with our friends the Millers, which all started from this entrance. Their daughter Katie's initial injury to her brain was identified and diagnosed, and then she was sent on for further treatment and emergency surgery from this very spot. Entering the hospital through these doors comes with an emotional price that is impossible to repay even if the ultimate result is positive. Entering this giant structure through these doors is hard, incredibly hard, and I knew to a degree what likely lay ahead.

After I parked the truck, I literally ran to the emergency entrance and saw Linda waving me back to the security area. I thought, "My God, here I am trying to get to my little girl and wasting precious time getting a security badge while having to give a bunch of information about who we are and whom we should allow to know we are here should they come to visit." We went through enormous automatic doors, and soon we came face to face with "medical people," all looking at us as if they knew something we didn't, trying to be professional, and directing us where we needed to go to be with Megan.

As we walked into the small examination room, I remember thinking how clinical and impersonal everything seemed, and then there she was, our Megan, lying on a hospital bed, wrapped in a hospital gown, hooked up to monitors and IVs, and surrounded by nurses and aids. Her eyes were open, and her face looked almost blank.

I expected fear, but what I saw was something different, whether being confused or being overwhelmed or even perhaps being somewhere else. I grabbed her hand and held it tight, as did Linda, and for only a moment, we felt like the parents at the ER with the kid who skinned her knee or sprained an ankle. But the difference was that in those previous experiences, there was an underlying confidence that everything would be okay. A stitch here or there, a cast or bandage, a prescription for the drug store, and then home we would go. Not this day.

From the door we heard the inquiring voice of a confident but compassionate doctor. "You must be Mom and Dad." "That's right," we stammered, and with that she said, "We are going to take Megan for a CT scan in just a few minutes. Can you answer a few questions?" And with that we began reliving the previous hour moment by moment in graphic detail. Questions led to other questions, and the focus was to get as much detail about what was going on around Megan during those early morning hours.

We soon realized that we had done a poor job of observing her surroundings, and we immediately felt as though we had failed her. But to be honest, my God, I could not remember what street we were at much less whether we had observed any open medicines or any evidence that would give us an idea of exactly when her struggle began.

I turned around to see what expression was on my daughter's face and how much of this she was taking in. Megan usually has an opinion about everything, so I hoped she might be able to add something, visually or otherwise, but her sweet face still looked almost blank, still drawn, covered in runny mascara with the right side elongated and drooping and without expression, only occasional eye contact and completely emotionless. Once more my heart sank. We did the best we could to give information and felt all the while totally inadequate. The doctor offered no assessment of what this was but instead focused on getting every bit of information we had to offer.

Finally, a friendly face or two began to appear as we moved to the central area outside the exam room, waiting for Megan to go to CT. My brother Bud walked in, as did Megan's former youth minister and our dear friend Eddie Morgan.

Eddie has always been someone who can cut through any circumstance, say what needs to be said, and then fold into a tearful, emotional heap for a moment or two before starting again. He is more than friend, more than a pastor; he was and is someone we depend on to direct us toward the center. He is someone whose compassion always leaves us better than when he found us and someone whose judgment we rely on, usually without question.

Eddie walked in and hugged Linda and me, kissed Megan on the cheek, grabbed her hand, and asked, "How are you doing, gal?" Emotion gradually filled his voice as he slowly went through the many probing questions that we all wanted to ask, but as only Eddie could. "What happened to you? Have you taken anything? Anything recreational? Do you know why you are here? Do you know who I am?" And in the midst of all those questions, Megan, for the first time since Union Chapel Road, whispered, "Yes."

We did not know which question she was answering, and we soon found out that "yes" could mean everything from "no" to "maybe" to even "go to hell." This was her new vocabulary for now. She would soon learn to emphasize "yes" with raised eyebrow, increased or decreased volume, and saying it as if it had several syllables. But for now, it was her only tool to communicate all the pain, fear, and angst she was feeling. One simple word. "Yes."

The technicians then showed up to whisk her away to her CT scan, and we continued our conversation with the neurologist and with our dear friends and ministers who were beginning to arrive. And now the endless telling of the story began in earnest. Each person who came wanted the whole story, and soon we began to understand that we would spend the coming days telling this same painful, private, raw, excruciating story over and over and over again, and as time went on it would grow in length and details.

We went from the hallway back into Megan's exam room and tried to make phone calls to continue to keep information and work and the "obligation" plates spinning in the air. We asked God to help us and asked for wisdom as we made decisions. Then, after what felt like only a few short moments had passed, the neurologist came back into the room, asked to speak with us alone, and said, "Well, I've just seen the first images from the CT, and your daughter has suffered a significant stroke on the front left lobe of her brain. It is a big stroke. Is there any history of stroke in your family?"

I tried to answer her, but my mouth simply would not work, and I realized that I was spouting some type of gibberish. Did I just hear what I thought I heard? Our speculations, even hopes for Bell's palsy or something seemingly less serious, were now shattered.

The doctor, seeing that our minds, heads, and hearts were spinning dangerously out of control, said most sincerely, "I'm sorry. I've just given you some really hard news. Perhaps you ought to take a few minutes or so to process this, and I'll be right back."

In that moment, Linda and I looked at each other in disbelief, and then we both folded into an embrace filled with tears, incredible pain, otherworldly gasps, and sobs that seemed to come in uncontrollable waves, one right after the other.

I am not sure, but I believe that I had not cried, really cried, since the death of my father thirty-five years before. Eddie and Bud and David Blackmon, another of out pastoral staff who is almost family as well, came in and wrapped their collective arms around us and allowed us to release this time bomb of emotion. Our hearts were broken.

As our emotional meltdown eventually began to settle, the doctor returned and said, "Listen, I know this is a lot to absorb, so I am here for you. What questions can I answer?" I remember asking the obvious: "What kind of treatment options are there? What is impacted? Is she in danger? What is the cause?" None of the answers registered except for the fact that the doctor wanted us to speak with a neurosurgeon, who would explain further treatment possibilities and might be able to explain the impact in more detail.

She introduced us to the tall, slender neurosurgeon, who was all business. He introduced himself as a member of the neurology surgical team that would take care of our daughter. He then explained that our daughter's stroke was "severe," and the reason he would be involved was that with young people suffering brain injuries, the brain is more likely to swell. That swelling, if unabated, would cause the pressure in her skull to build and further damage the brain.

Unchecked, it could result in death. His job was to intervene should that happen by removing a section of her skull to relieve the pressure and perhaps save her life.

His next words stung yet again. It was his opinion that it was not a matter of *if* Megan would need this surgery; it was a matter of *when*. He further explained that the normal window of risk for this type of "insult" was from five to seven days and that he would not perform the surgery until she exhibited symptoms that the pressure was becoming dangerously high.

Once again words would not come, which is most unusual for me. I uttered the only question that made sense to me considering the hard words he had just spoken. "When you say 'severe stroke,' what exactly does that mean?" He then said, "Come to the computer screen and I will show you."

The doctor pulled up large black and white image of a human brain, and the information label at the top of the screen said, "Hughes, Megan Leigh—2/2/2016." It looked like a photo negative being displayed on a screen. He gave me guidance for what I was looking at, and although some of the technical names and descriptions of lobes and arteries did not initially "stick," what was apparent was the large area toward the front of Megan's brain that was obviously much darker than the rest of the image. "Oh, my God," I thought out loud. "That area is huge!" He did not disagree. I then asked my next stupid question, which was, "Where is the clot?" He pointed to the approximate area. And once again I felt the tears welling up inside.

"This can't be happening," I thought. I asked, "What is in that part of the brain? Will it heal? Can it be treated?" The tall, slender man said, "Listen, my job is to do surgery. These are questions for your neurologist." With that, he was gone and we returned to the room.

By this point Megan had come back to her room, and we sat down once more with the neurologist. Hanging on to every hope and the little bit of medical knowledge I had accumulated over fifty-eight years on this earth, I asked our ultimate question: "Is there anything else we can do? What about the clot buster drug TPA?" The doctor asked us questions concerning what we knew about the onset. She indicated that the drug is only effective if delivered within three to four hours of onset, and if administered after that it could be detrimental or even deadly. After exploring what we knew, once again our hopes were dashed when she concluded that Megan was not a candidate for TPA. My question of "why" was met with "hospital speak" that basically said, "We have a hard and fast rule that if someone was not with the patient when the stroke began and we can't verify the time of onset, we will not administer the drug, period." There came the tears again.

I couldn't stop the questions in my mind. Can this really be happening? Is my daughter going to have to endure this seemingly unending list of horrors? Will she ever speak again? Will she ever walk again? Will she know who we are? Will she end up in a nursing home for the rest of her life? Will she ever teach again? My God, will she even survive? Am I going to lose my daughter? The questions came one right after the other, and our world was crashing in and collapsing all around us. We were completely in panic.

For the next few minutes, we simply sat with Megan, holding her hand, unsure of what she understood. But we were comforted by the fact that her left hand held on for dear life and her eyes, when open, scanned the room for us. These were simple gifts that kept us away from the cliff.

After a variety of other tests, we were told that as soon as a room was available, they would be moving Megan to intensive care. When the time came to go, they would send us ahead to a different floor in advance of a team of folks that would take her there the back way.

We rotated Linda and me out of the room when other family or ministers came by to see our baby girl, and it was during those brief moments that our ministers loved on us, tried to encourage us, and tried to stir the flickering flames of faith that would be so important in getting us through what was to come.

To be honest, the words did not matter; the hugs and presence and just being together were what held us up. "Devastating" is a word often used, but its meaning is very different when the circumstances involve your own child.

I am an accountant, for God's sake; I plan for a living. I am accustomed to being in control, with a plan and a backup plan, and a backup plan for the backup plan. I was already in "what's next" mode, and I could not come up with anything that made sense. I could not just fix this.

On that first morning, one of our other dear ministerial friends, Clark Sorrells, offered important advice that still applies after a long journey that at that point was just beginning. He said, "Scott, you have to stop thinking and planning for days or weeks out right now. You can't allow yourself to plan for more than just today. So tonight, you will start planning for tomorrow. Only one day at a time."

I am not sure where in Scripture that comes from, but I know Clark's life and his family's own challenges that have taught him the lessons of caregiving. And in the relative stillness of those moments, he gave me a life lesson that has *had* to become a part of my "personal mantra."

Live for only today; tomorrow will come soon enough.

Our doctor interrupted and told us a room was now available, and we would be moving upstairs soon. Our support team gathered our things, and we transferred the flag to the next stronghold, the intensive care unit. Although our time in the ER had been relatively short in hospital time, the change to our lives that began there would be of much longer duration and more transformational.

The future remained uncertain and promised challenge and more obstacles to overcome. All I could think consistently was, "This can't be happening."

But it was.

Chapter 4

I See You (ICU)

As we arrived on the fifth floor for the first time, we were introduced to the charge nurse who helped us acclimate to our new surroundings and its rules, protocols, and procedures. A huge marker board in Megan's room listed our nurse and aid for the day; we also observed that this was a large room with lots of high-tech, imposing equipment including a lift and a life support component. It did have a recliner that converted to a sleeper, and for that I was grateful.

Our vigil was just beginning, and there was no way I would be convinced to leave this precious child until I knew she was out of the woods. We were told that for now the focus was to monitor Megan for signs of further brain trauma and perform an in-depth assessment of the potential sources of the clot that caused her injury. We would begin therapy as she could tolerate it to assess her abilities to eat and otherwise regain function.

We met the first of many shift nurses and tried to figure out their personalities and styles. That first day we were vulnerable, afraid, quiet, and tearful. Those wonderful people treated us as if we were in a five-star hotel. Megan's needs came first, but our needs were a close second. And we stood and hovered and held her hand and held each other. At times it was like having lost our way in the woods. Nothing was familiar or reassuring. We didn't know where we were going.

We were not aware then that outside in the waiting room a large group of folks had gathered and held vigil there as well. They were Megan's friends, our friends, church members, work friends. Our good friends Jon and Kim Miller arrived and pretty much took over, making sure visitors were acknowledged, keeping up with any messages we needed to be aware of, and sending messages if they thought we would want to know someone was there.

That first day we were going nowhere. We were absolutely scared to death. Megan was sedated to a degree and the constant line of doctors and nurses, X-ray techs and MRI techs, and even lab folks seemed almost nonstop. We were constantly being briefed, questioned, updated, or asked to sign yet another release. It was overwhelming, and there is no way to be prepared for anything like it.

About four o'clock in the afternoon, we were told that the doctor had ordered the installation of a "PICC line," a long, skinny tube inserted into one of the veins in her arm that would allow for the injection of medications directly into her blood system and also let them take blood without continually sticking her, which to this point seemed like a never-ending hourly process. We of course agreed and signed that release, and then we were asked to leave the room.

That was difficult for me, control freak that I am. There would be many such moments to come. It was not that I did not trust them to do their jobs; I just needed to be there in case she woke up or missed us.

I could not bear the thought of Megan not understanding what was going on and waking up alone and afraid or among perceived strangers. I had promised to be there. I could not break that promise.

They let us know that we could return to her bedside after the installation procedure, and soon the parade of MRI machines began again. They scanned her arms; they scanned her legs; they scanned every inch of her body over the first couple of days. I finally asked one of the techs, "Why all the hardware and scans?"

His reply startled me a bit when he said, "We are looking for additional clots. Actually, we are looking for the source of the original clot." To that moment, I had not even considered that there could be more clots waiting to break loose and do more damage or worse. Chills ran down my spine and dread came over me yet again.

That afternoon we were visited by a cardiologist who explained he was there to look at Megan's heart. He wanted to do another echocardiogram with a "bubble study." We did not have a clue what that meant, but we trustingly said yes and signed another piece of paper. He indicated that they would get it scheduled.

Megan would rouse occasionally and want to see who was in the room, see what was going on, and occasionally pull herself up to get comfortable or reposition. She showed little emotion other than occasional frustration. We were not sure if it was discomfort or pain or fear of not being in control. She is my daughter, after all.

In the emergency room, my brother Bud told us that when his daughter Lindsay, who is a teacher in Durham, found out about Megan, she walked out of class, requested a substitute teacher, and jumped into her car heading toward Asheville. Lindsay is like a sister to Megan. They are peas in a pod. When they are together the whole world knows it, and they are each better for the presence of the other.

When Lindsay arrived and walked into the ICU for the first time, she leaned down over Megan and hugged her with tears in her eyes. Megan soon realized who it was and made some noises, trying to form words, then said "yes, yes, yes" and even began to weep as well. They embraced emotionally for a long time and Megan grabbed her hand and would not let go. She soon nodded off, and Lindsay slipped away but promised to return as soon as she got settled at her parents' house.

Another of the hardest parts of this never-ending day was the need to communicate what had happened to our family, friends, coworkers, and church members. It was incredibly constant and painful. It never got easier, and depending on our relationship with the person we were telling, it took a significant toll on our emotions and mental state. The stream of telephone calls, texts, emails, and people just showing up was constant if not overwhelming. Over time, we knew we would have to find a way to get information to folks that still allowed us to do the other things we simply had to do. Megan's needs had to come first.

Bud and Dianne asked several times whom we needed to contact, and they did a wonderful job of telling as many as possible the life-changing news we were getting on this very different day. None of those communications would be harder or more painful than telling my eighty-eight-year-old mother, Megan's "Nana." I simply could not fathom having that conversation in the mental state I was in, and they graciously agreed to go to her home in Weaverville to deliver the hard news in person.

My already broken heart shattered yet one more time as I knew they were there shattering her fragile world as well. My mom is the family matriarch who embodies the soul of this strong-willed band of mountain people turned citified folk to all we know and can keep fooled. She was a child in a large Depression-era family who were dirt poor but joined at the heart. That is the way we are as family. We argue with each other often, throw political stones and Baptist barbs. But if you say something bad about one of us, you will have to fight all of us.

Despite that strength, the delivery of this kind of hard news would take a significant toll on anyone. I knew it would be devastating for my mother. But we knew that in these days of the text and email and Facebook posts, news travels faster than the speed of light, and she needed to hear it from family. It must be part of some mountain code somewhere.

Later in the afternoon, I was sitting in the recliner as Megan napped. Linda had stepped out to the lobby for a moment. I happened to look up, and there stood my dearest friend and spiritual mentor Guy Sayles, who was our former pastor. He had found his way into the ICU as only clergy members seemed able to do. There must be secret passages, I guess.

Guy was fighting his own significant health battles with multiple myeloma. The odd circumstance of being ministered to by someone whose own struggles demanded my attention and compassion was not lost on me. My friend, however, wrapped his compassionate arms around me, and his words provided comfort and hope even though the clouds of uncertainty were still thick in that somber room.

We talked for a good while and had a good visit. I told the same sad story once more to my dear friend. Through tears and trembling, the visit finally had to end, and in one of the most profound moments of that day, he asked if he could pray. He put his hand on Megan's arm and spoke words that helped restore just a smidgeon of courage and faith when he said, "Megan, you are a child of God, and God takes great delight in you, and God is giving you all you need to be all

God wants you to be." And with a final hug, we went back to nurses and doctors and techs and monitors, IVs and beeping alarms, one very troublesome bedpan, and continuous injections and needles.

Things were moving so quickly that the process of treatment did not allow much time to dwell. And when it became apparent that the constant stream of white and blue coats was slowing down, we started to be aware that this vigil would be ours to deal with for some time to come. Figuring out a schedule and doling out responsibilities would be necessary. Linda and I began trying to figure out the tasks that had to take place. Most tasks involved the essentials, including getting a few basics for Megan and us and then determining who would do what when.

Family once again gathered belongings and essentials for Megan that we thought she might need or want—toiletries, a toothbrush, lip balm, underwear, and a robe. Aunt Dianne and Lindsay went to her home to dig through the mess and mounds of clothes we had left on the floor.

I was so glad they did that because the thought of going back into that condo nauseated me and would for weeks to come. It was too fresh and too raw. And to me, the prospect of going there was like returning to a crime scene where my lovely daughter's future had been violently assaulted and stolen from her.

Later in the evening, Bud and Dianne came back and said, "You all go get some dinner." At first, I said, "I'm not hungry," and at that point we had a "planned" conversation for my benefit: "You will be of little value to your little girl if you don't attend to your own physical needs." Good advice, but I still did not really want to leave.

Linda and I headed out to the waiting room together, and the number of folks still there was amazing. It was almost eight o'clock, and the room was still relatively full. When we walked in, everything got incredibly still, and every eye turned to us. I did not know what to say, but I think I mumbled something about us knowing how to make an entrance. A little gallows humor usually helps people breathe a bit easier.

We made the rounds for a few minutes until we could not tell the day's story anymore. Then Kim and Jon grabbed us and said, "Have you eaten?" Of course, we hadn't, so they said, "Let's go." I think that first night we made our way down to the cafeteria. It would be the first of many meals that were part nourishment exercises and part psychotherapy. The value of simply allowing our shoulders to fall a little brought a bit of calm and release that had not been present since early that morning.

In those first days, it was the gift of friends and ministers, family and relatives that allowed us to find our way through the fog and pain. I've always struggled in circumstances like these when I was the one trying to make a difference, feeling the need to say something wise or profound or encouraging or perhaps memorable.

But, from this perspective, the words are seldom as important as the hug or the touch, the handshake or the simple "How are you doing?" That is what means something in these times. Just knowing folks care calms the soul. The words don't matter so much. Simply being there or being available matters. Listening also matters. What is most helpful initially is to listen, react, and love.

An hour flew by like a moment, and we soon figured out it was time to go back. Our friends hugged us and said, "We will be back in the morning." We did not argue. It was reassuring to know that true friends were there for us. They loved us unconditionally, warts and all, and they lifted us up when we could no longer stand on our own. The significance of the gifts given during days like these can never be repaid and will never be forgotten.

When we got back to the ICU, we again assumed our stations and began the conversations about who was staying and who would go home. I knew I could not leave; there was no sleep in my future. The tension and anxiety and fear would not allow it. My mind could not relax. We decided Linda would go get some sleep, take care of the house, and return in the morning. I would stay the night.

Bud stayed with me for a while longer and finally went home to see Lindsay. Eddie also snuck in around ten and of course razzed me about his "guessing there was no way that Megan's overprotective dad was going to go home and get some rest." I emphatically said once again, "No, I'm here and plan to stay until she is better." Wrong answer, and certainly not assured at that time. But he expected it, and it had to be okay for that night.

Our nurse brought blankets and pillows, and I prepared for what I knew would be a sleepless night as my little girl became more agitated, more disconnected, and more distant. Sleep came and went for her, but times of confusion, anger, and discomfort became more regular and more complex.

She would pull herself up with her strong side and begin moving with one arm towards the end of the bed as if trying to escape out the door. Even with only half her strength, she was still a force to contend with. But upon defeat at the hands of her keepers, Megan would finally lie down and gradually fade off to a drug-induced slumber.

There are very few places in life that seem as dark or intimidating or just plain scary as this part of the hospital. The sounds of machines and oxygen being dispensed and alarms going off cause the heart to race or jump each time something changes. I watched the monitor and observed that Megan's heart rate and blood pressure varied constantly and widely. I also knew that during the times when she was sort of awake and agitated, what I saw in her eyes was almost distant, a mind in torment. She was confused, angry, and uncomfortable. She knew this was not a familiar place, and she longed for the sanctuary of her bed and her townhome. She needed the familiarity of home. She didn't want to be there any more than we did.

Her attempts to escape became more regular and always ended the same way with me saying, "Where are you going, baby girl?" She would get to the bottom of the bed with her weak side folded under her, wires and tubes stretched to their limits or even past.

The night nurse was less patient and suggested restraint might become necessary. I pushed back and insisted, "No, we aren't there yet," and I was usually able to get her to lie down again. I would also wipe her forehead with a cool compress, which seemed to comfort her. Then soon the drugs would win for a while, and she would drift off to something like sleep one more time.

I would return to my chair, choke down the tears trying to escape, and then turn on my computer. I began to respond to the dozens of emails of well-wishers. Each response, including many I sent in the wee hours of the morning, was returned almost instantly with additional requests for an update. I soon figured out that keeping those close to us informed was impossible. We would have to find a way to keep people informed without trying to respond to each message.

As midnight came and went, a tall, gray-headed figure appeared at the door. It was our good friend and fellow church member Buddy Corbin, a volunteer chaplain for Mission Healthcare. Buddy came in and gave me a big hug that seemed to last for a long time, and then he asked the first question everyone asked, "How are you doing?" As time went on, I realized that if I were totally honest, I did not know how to answer that question, no matter who asked it. I tried "As good as can be expected," and "We are doing okay," but then I ended up settling on "We are okay for now." We figured out quickly that things change so fast in the ICU that you can be okay one moment and not very good in another.

Buddy then said, "How is she?" And with that the tears again flowed. I responded honestly as best I could by saying, "I don't know." I added, "Buddy, I am so very afraid." We sat together in silence for a few minutes, and he put his hand on my shoulder and said, "You know we are here for you and for her." I told him some of "the story," and then the time came that he needed to be other places. He promised to return.

As he left, he went to Megan's bed, bowed his head, and put his hand on her head as if to bless her. There he said a prayer. Then he quietly slipped out on his way to his other families in need. During that night, Buddy came back to our room no less than three or four more times, just to check on us. During those darkest hours just before dawn, his friendly face was a welcome sight.

About 4:30 in the morning, a tech came in and did an additional MRI. In the quiet of the evening, I asked him if he was continuing to look for additional clots and he said, "No, I'm looking at her heart. We are trying to see if she has any heart abnormalities."

I asked, "Her heart? I don't understand."

He said, "One of the hospital cardiologists will be by in the morning, but they know that in some of these cases there is a connection between the heart and strokes in young patients."

Her heart? How is that possible? The stroke is in her brain. Soon the relative calm of night gave way to an early morning with the return of a host of caregivers, all charged with a particular task assigned by someone else.

And the morning and the evening were the first day.

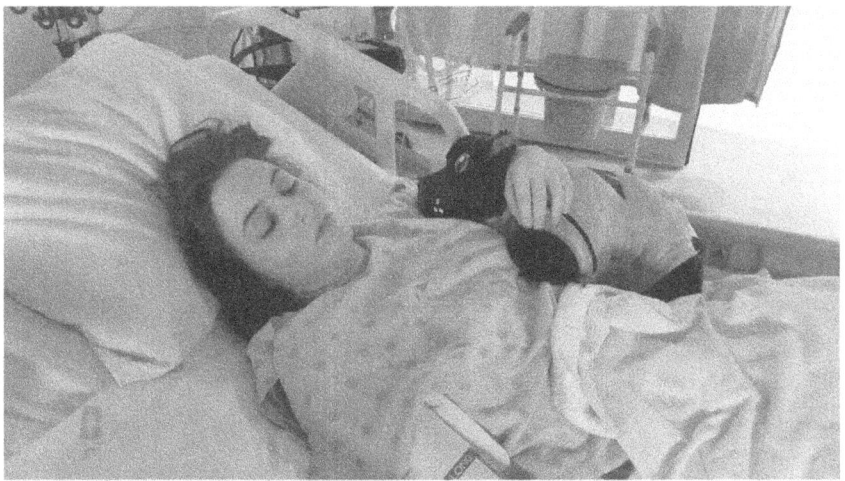

Comfort in intensive care from Sir Purr for this ultimate Panthers fan.

Chapter 5

Losing Direction

In writing or even reading a book like this, the heavy content can quickly become like an anchor around the necks of readers. It seems way too heavy, way too real, and just downright depressing if not at least discouraging. Where is the happy ending or at least the path to it?

To this point, I have tried to tell a story that includes a glimpse of a profoundly happy young woman, living her life to the fullest, enjoying being a twenty-something and exploring this world while building herself a promising career that could positively impact the future education of young children nationwide. Megan was on her way to being a political activist in particular support of children's issues and women's issues and matters of justice. She was someone of faith who believed that her God was bigger than any of the "pigeonholes" and sexist descriptions fundamentalist interpreters of Scripture seem to want to corner people into. She was a free thinker, an old soul, a modern progressive. And after only one day and a few thousand words, the events of that Tuesday already have me writing in past tense.

A single medical event seems to have taken her future from her and made all her marvelous investments somehow moot. But the story is only beginning. That is what we didn't know. At this point, despite Megan's distant scary haze, she was fighting like hell, as always. Every waking moment she was struggling to regain awareness, perspective, and context.

No one begins one of life's specifically important days with the expectation that the day will be any different than the last. Life has a way of causing us to lull ourselves into complacency. And then life changes, suddenly, radically, and sometimes completely.

In the short cat naps of early morning next to my daughter's hospital bed, the thoughts and intense memories of the day just past wafted over me like a curious reminder of the pain and angst we had all experienced. The realization that yesterday was a bad memory was emphasized by the further realization that our lives were significantly changed and the "what was" was missing if not gone.

And to be totally honest, there was dread and fear of the coming day as if waiting for the other boot to fall. All of us experience that realization in this life. Perhaps it's the death of a loved one or a fire or storm or other such catastrophe. Perhaps a divorce, infidelity, or sickness. All such events transform the soul and psyche in a way that deflates the spirit and causes us to question and then challenges us to "go on."

On the night my father died, the intensity of the evening's events forced us to wade through our grief, do what was required, and perform the tasks necessary to begin moving from "what was" to "what is." We fulfilled our duties, which included calling the funeral home, notifying those close to us, and arranging to sleep on the couch simply because we couldn't force ourselves to go back to the "room where it happened." Our bodies had to renew, even if only for a short while.

When exhaustion finally won out, we all crashed where we were. But what is profound about the morning after a crisis is that even though the early moments of awakening may bring a sense of comfort, as if the weight of the world is off your shoulders, the sudden remembering and realization of "what is" comes with an overwhelming feeling of grief and loss. You cannot pull yourself up from the depths, and life doesn't go on. It actually "stands still" for a time of grieving and adjustment. It may be natural, but it is unforgettable, hard, and incredibly painful.

But our situation was different even from that because each day was inextricably tied to the last. The resolution of the initial insult took much longer and required much more effort. The silence of the moments when Megan slept and attempted to heal allowed the demons of those who loved her to speak loudly and caused already exhausted and troubled minds to go down the paths of questions with no answers and expend great energy without being helpful.

Those first days, I spent so much time trying to avoid the "why" question and the "how" question. I asked myself, "Am I or are we being punished for something? Did we do something to deserve this? Did we fail our daughter in some capacity by not being more involved in her personal health decisions?" Somewhere in my mind in the stillness of those few quiet moments, I allowed self-pity to show its face and I asked, "Why me?" and "Why us?" and "Why her?" My denial of the circumstances would not allow me to face the fact that my Megan could die from this.

It became important that I not allow myself to "go there" on the questions to which I had no answers, because the energy I had left needed to be invested in the immediate circumstances. We had to stay present in the moment until that moment passed. But the exact timeframe of when the moment would pass was anyone's guess.

The feelings of days two through four were similar. Opening eyes gave way to confusion, panic at the realization that yesterday actually did happen, dread, fear, pain, and loss. In those first calm moments of this new day, the heartache was almost debilitating.

Megan's eyes occasionally popped open, and her actions and attempts at letting us know she was still in there somewhere would again make Mom and Dad hit that next gear. Once more, those other feelings would be put on hold as the crisis of the event continued and slowly emerged into a different struggle.

Linda walked in carrying a bag of the nectar of the gods (Diet Coke) and a container of McDonald's oatmeal with fruit. For a few moments, the two of us were family again, choking down the drinks and shoveling the oatmeal into our mouths as folks began to arrive. The first texts and emails started coming around 5:00 that morning. By 7:30, there was no hope of responding to them all.

About that same time, the tall, slender surgeon arrived, talked with the nurse right outside our unit, and then entered to begin his evaluation. I felt my stomach sink and that damned lump in my throat began trying to make its way forward again. He attempted to rouse Megan, shined a light in her eyes at which she protested, recoiled, and pulled away. He poked and prodded, moved and pushed, and then he came over and simply said, "Not today. The pressure is elevated but it isn't life threatening. They will contact me if things change. "

He then asked if we had any questions, and Linda and I couldn't get them out fast enough. We had tons. "How did this happen? What can we do? Where is this going? What comes next?" He held up his hand as if to shush us and responded, "Mr. and Mrs. Hughes, I am the surgeon. I have one responsibility, and that is to operate. Your questions will need to be addressed to someone else."

I must admit that I apologized and felt a bit like the poorly dressed geek who used the wrong fork at the fancy dinner. But to be honest, I was getting mad as hell. At what point were we going to be given the answers we needed to calm our minds and allay our fears?

We returned to the remains of our gourmet Mickey D's and Diet Coke, and we each breathed a short sigh of relief. And then the lights came on, the carts rolled in, and the tests and parade of techs started their constant attack on this unknown culprit. Needles and electrodes, EKGs and echocardiograms, MRIs and more CT scans. Each saying, "May we?" or "We are here to _____."

Who in the hell is ordering all of this stuff, and is it necessary?

Megan seemed more and more agitated. Her face had become puffy from all the fluids, flush and red when awake and pale, frighteningly pale, when at rest. I drove home quickly to grab a shower and came straight back. I cried all the way home and cried all the way back. I spoke out loud behind the wheel of the truck, talking to God. I voiced my fears, I asked for strength, I railed at the injustice of the whole thing, and to a degree I felt I was being heard.

I said, "I can't" But I heard, "You have to." And deep down I knew that to be true. My promise to my little girl could never, ever be broken as long as I had breath. We were and are in this together. My prayer was that God was offering the same promise to me.

A simple verse popped into my mind that held hope: "I will not leave you nor forsake you" (Heb 13:5). I parked and began to trudge through the cold morning air toward that lobby and, after speaking to the friends gathered there continuing to hold vigil, through all those hallways and out of the elevator into the ICU.

Family and adopted family continued to minister to us and sat with Jenny at times so we could grab lunch or dinner and take quick breaks. The day moved quickly with so much to discuss and decide.

For the first time, we met John, who was an incredibly funny man with a sharp sense of humor. John would change our lives and give us our first vestiges of hope. John was the speech therapist. Speech therapists are an interesting lot. They are charged with so much more than just speech. Did the stroke impact your throat, they ask, and if so, can you control your tongue, can you control your head, can you swallow, can you chew, can you sense what is in your mouth? This sounds simple until you realize you have to eat and drink to stay alive.

On that first visit, John did some basics. Once he roused Megan enough to harass her, he asked, "Can she respond to basic commands? Does she understand what you are asking? Can she speak?"

Oddly enough, for whatever reason, even though Megan was in some other place at least partially, she responded to his funny ways. She said "yes" several times, even when the answer should be no. He briefly tried to teach her "no." She bonded with him almost immediately, and their eyes connected if only for moments.

John saw something there and tried things to see "what she had." To our amazement, she did respond to his efforts by emulating him. If he stuck his tongue out, she would try to do that as well. His games quickly became therapy, and before he left, he put an ice chip in her mouth to see if she would attempt to move it around. She did.

He then gave her a sip of water, and she took a sip and swallowed, even though it was awkward. John indicated that he believed she would be a candidate for a "swallow test" and that perhaps in a day or so they might try to give her some pureed food.

Baby steps . . . the very first.

John promised to return the following day with more to do, and he kept his promises to us the whole time we were there.

Shortly after John left, the cardiologist showed up with a nurse and began looking at computer images from previous scans. He came in the room and abruptly announced, "I am Dr. T, and I need to talk with you about your daughter's stroke." He said, "We think we have found a likely source of the blood clot that went to your daughter's brain."

He showed us video on a computer screen of a black and white image that looked like screensaver art. "The gray area is your daughter's heart," he explained, "the colorful circles are bubbles, and this circular area is a hole in her heart commonly known as a PFO. As you can see, the bubbles appear to be traveling through that opening, and that opening leads directly to your daughter's brain. We think this is where the clot crossed over."

I felt like a third grader immediately thrusting my hand into the air with my questions. I had a million.

"What the hell is a PFO? What caused it? Can it be treated? What happens to the bubbles you just shot into my daughter's brain? How does this impact her?" He pushed right past the questions and said, "I want to do a TEE (trans-esophageal echocardiogram) to determine the size of the hole and whether it needs to be closed. We can do that one of two ways." And he launched into a verbal explanation that was dizzying. He turned and looked at me and saw the tear coming down my cheek and how beet red my face was. He stopped mid-sentence and said, "Are you okay?" Wrong question!

I launched into about a three-minute diatribe about "my concerns over the healthcare system, this hospital, and all of its doctors." I said, "I'm convinced that no one here has my daughter's back. Someone over the internet is sending robots to stick needles in my daughter, poke cameras and other strange devices in her mouth, ears, and every other orifice on her body. One crazy son of a bitch wants to remove her skull, and after two full days, not one damned doctor has given us any idea of what the hell they are doing and where this is heading." My first attempt at advocacy on behalf of my daughter just blurted out. Let's say I launched my whole arsenal in one fell swoop.

Dr. T put his arm around my shoulders and said, "You are upset. Let's go somewhere and talk." With that, he took Linda and me to a small conference room with a table and chairs and said, "Sit down and let me see if I can answer at least some of your questions." For the first time since we'd arrived at the hospital, that good doctor talked to us in cornbread language and drew pictures of the human heart on the back of a napkin, complete with a PFO among the various chambers of the heart.

He explained that to know the size of the PFO and the risk of Megan passing a second clot, we needed to get a better look at it. They would do this by pushing a device down Megan's throat to the area just behind her heart and then using that to do another echocardiogram directly over the PFO. "How big is the tube?" I asked. He showed me his thumb and said, "About that big." I asked, "Will you sedate her?" and he said, "Perhaps."

I objected based on what our neurologist had said about the possible negative effects of anesthesia on a brain already insulted by a stroke. He indicated that they would first try it without sedation. Knowing my daughter, I asked if he knew what overactive gag reflex was. He smiled and said, "Without this we won't know how or if to treat the PFO."

I was immensely grateful that this kind doctor had taken the time to address at least some of our concerns and answer some of our basic questions. For that he has my admiration, my sincere thanks, and my appreciation.

These first encounters, though, highlight what I think are some of the most significant flaws in our medical system. First, getting relevant information to families and caregivers and decision-makers takes time. It requires explanation at a point when time is not your friend. And I get the fact that the docs are trying to weigh the family's ability to process information during an emotionally trying situation. But as for me—and I may not be normal—I wanted to understand.

Second, in these situations, doctors in different specialties are often trying to solve different problems. Sometimes the treatments conflict with each other. We needed a referee. When we spoke to our neurologist the following morning, he indicated that that closure of the PFO was controversial and likely would not be done until treatment of the stroke had progressed. However, after further consultation and discussion, the decision was made that we should allow them to do the TEE to assess the size of the PFO. "Neurology" was not thrilled about the prospects of additional sedation. "Cardiology" indicated they would not sedate unless she couldn't tolerate the tube.

The first series of decisions happened, but they changed the game a bit with some unintended consequences. During this whole negotiation, we took our eye off the ball and forgot that we were still in the window of brain swelling and had just agreed to another procedure.

The cardiologist brought in a release form for us to sign, and when we had signed it, we were asked to go sit in the lobby for a while, yet again. They started the TEE, which took about forty-five minutes. They came and got us, and when we got back to the room, the doctors were huddled and having an animated conversation of their own.

When we got to Megan, she was obviously out and sedated, and her face was flush and still puffy. In a few minutes, the neurologist came in with Dr. T. They explained that the TEE was done, but Megan had been unable to tolerate the tube. He held it up. I swear it was the size of a garden hose. They had ended up giving her sedation to do the TEE, and it was more than they had anticipated. The neurologist said we should try to rouse her and get her more alert as soon as she began waking up.

Of course, I got angry. My perception was that they had rushed the test and were heading down the path toward heart surgery. So later in the evening when the neurologist stopped by, we talked pointedly about our concern, and he indicated that it was potentially valid.

I told them no more tests that aren't medically necessary. Let our daughter heal for a while. Look for clots, do what you need to, but let's slow down a bit until we get past the swelling threat. The following day, we found out that the TEE had irritated her throat, already weakened by stroke, and that set us back for the swallow test for fear that fluid might get into her lungs and cause pneumonia.

My anger was becoming a problem for me and those around me. I was a bullet looking for a gun.

That night was the most problematic we had experienced thus far. Megan tossed and turned and was agitated, possibly because of the drugs and the swelling. By the end of the day, I was nearing exhaustion.

Bud's daughter had arrived and offered to spend the night to allow us a night in our own bed. I objected. Let us get through tonight, I told her, and then if everything went okay, she could stay the following night. Once again, I didn't feel that I could leave. We left for a couple of hours for dinner and therapy with our friends, and I returned to ICU around ten. Once again Linda went home to take care of our pets and plants, and I held vigil next to Megan.

She was out of her head. Fits of anger and agitation led to more attempts at leaving her bed. And we had "that" nurse—a control nut (worse than me) who tried to use threats instead of encouragement. She and I locked horns in the first ten minutes, and I let her know I wasn't intimidated.

I got Megan to lie down, and once again she drifted off for a little while. Up to this point, Megan had emptied her bladder using a catheter that had been inserted the previous day. About three in the morning, she grabbed the left rail and pulled herself up with such force that the IV rack went rolling and alarming with beeps and buzzers.

I jumped up out of a semi stupor of tormented sleep and caught her right at the bottom of the bed. I said my normal, "Where you going, sis?" and I swear she smiled that crooked smile and then handed me her fully inflated catheter that she had pulled out without even a whimper. She wasn't through, and she wanted out.

Enter "Nurse Personality."

"Little gal, if you don't lie down, I'm going to put restraints on you!"

Megan looked at me and looked at her, then she took her good arm and pointed toward the nurse's nose and said emphatically in significantly increasing volume, "Yes Yes Yes Yes YES **YES YES**!"

And with that she flopped down on the bed. She pulled her pillow over her head and slammed her good arm down. She was more than a bit emotional and exhausted.

I turned to the nurse with a certain parental pride and said, "Young lady, if I had to interpret that, I would conclude that you have been 'cussed out' using only the word 'yes.'"

At that moment, the patient advocate in me popped out, and I continued, "And if you ever threaten my daughter with restraints again, I'll be on you like 'white on rice.' Don't ever do that again whether I am here or not."

It's funny now, but that would be the last night we had "that" nurse.

I pulled my chair up next to Megan's bed, and for the first time we held hands a bit. After a few moments to calm down, she briefly stared into the dark of space and soon fell asleep for most of the rest of the night, as did I.

Chapter 6

One Step Forward, Two Steps Back

Exhaustion and emotion greeted Linda and my gourmet breakfast of bacon, egg, and cheese with Diet Coke that she again delivered. God bless McDonald's and the Coca-Cola Bottling Company. And God bless the Carolina Panthers. During the few periods of time in which Megan was focused and alert, our nursing staff attempted to do things that might seem a little more normal. For a few moments the previous afternoon, Jenny, one of our favorite nurses, had asked if we wanted to try to transfer Megan to the recliner for a few minutes while they changed her bed.

We were excited at the prospect; even the smallest things like sitting up or in a chair or even transferring to a potty chair were welcome momentary lapses in the tension and overcast ambiance attached to this intensive care room. When we transferred her to the recliner, complete with IV tubes, monitor cables, and transfer belt, she rallied a bit and tried her hand at watching TV, which I had turned on for the first time since her stroke.

And there it was. On the screen was the whole outside world that surrounds this dark place, even though we had put our connection to that world on hold for a while. Most of the time in the chair, Megan nodded or slept. But for a fleeting moment or two, she took the TV controller in her hand and scanned it, trying to remember how it worked.

Another particularly normal occurrence was when she identified the button that caused the channels to change. So off she went channel surfing. She stopped initially when she found HGTV, but then she really stopped when she found ESPN. They were running a story on Cam Newton of her beloved Carolina Panthers, whose

Super Bowl appearance was three days away. Her obsession over the Panthers still seemed to be there. It was at least familiar.

When they interviewed Cam, she looked at me, and I saw what seemed to be that crooked little smile for just a second or two. I asked her if we were going to have our Super Bowl party in the ICU, and she looked at me with additional animation. "Yes" slipped out once more.

Those first real interactions indicated that Megan was in there at some level, and for the first time we focused our hopes on things that were obviously there, even though the communication was still with periodic "yes" responses. She was content to watch TV for a few moments before sleep, or the multiple medications that she continued taking, robbed her of her focus and once again forced her to slip into that slumber and haze of uneasy rest.

I kept very few pictures of these first days. I have none of the first two days except for a picture of her health insurance card. But of the ones I have, it is still amazing to me that in every single one, Megan's eyes are closed, and her face is swollen and red, and half is drawn and appears almost frozen in time.

Nurse Jenny was a young nurse who was likely close to Megan's age. Jenny treated her differently from how the other nurses did. She tried to engage her. She spoke to her as a friend. She would sit on her bed and simply brush her hair. She would make a ponytail or try to engage her by talking "to" her rather than talking "at" her. She could often get Megan to do things that no one else could.

Jenny would also spend rare extra moments with us. We found out that she was a travel nurse who provided extra resources to hospitals by serving thirteen-week temporary assignments. She said it allowed her to travel and see the country. Although she was originally from Charleston, South Carolina, she loved the Asheville area. She also told us about her time working in a large rehabilitation facility for patients just like our daughter.

Rehab was becoming a point of discussion, and we knew we would have decisions to make if things continued to progress without setback. Jenny was unassuming, humble, and genuinely interested in the care her patients were getting.

I have developed a newfound appreciation for those in the nursing field. It is an incredibly hard job to serve people when their lives are in such turmoil and to have to deal with trauma both physical and emotional.

But Jenny was like having another daughter in the room. And she would soon play a key role in our daughter's long-term treatment plan by giving us simple, honest opinions about treatment options considered in the perspective of a twenty-nine-year-old.

Our speech therapist John returned mid-morning and wanted to continue where he left off the previous day. He started with ice chips and a small cup of water. He put an ice chip in Megan's mouth, and she moved her tongue slightly and sucked on the ice. She acted as though she wanted another, and John obliged. John said, "I think she is doing well with the ice, and if you all want to give them to her from time to time that will probably be okay."

At this point, Megan had not eaten in almost four days, and John said, "We have to begin addressing her nutritional issues soon." Then he said, "Well, let's try a sip or two of water." He put the cup to her mouth and instinctively she grabbed the cup and tried to guzzle. The results were predictable. She lost a good amount of it out of the weak side of her mouth, as if in the dentist chair after being "numbed." The part that made it down her throat caused her to choke. We rushed to pat her on the back and sit her bed up taller so the water might come back up, which it did to some degree.

We did not understand the significance of these events until we spoke to John after the attempt at hydration. This *was* the swallow test that he had mentioned, and obviously she had failed it.

Of course, Dad kicked in and I said, "Let's try it again with a little preparation." I held the glass, and when Megan attempted to take control, I pushed back a bit. She looked puzzled but allowed me to pour some fluid into her mouth. John watched and felt her throat, and she seemed almost amused that we were staring at her intently as if to say, "What in the world are you all looking at?"

John asked her to open her mouth, and at first she didn't comply, but when he touched her mouth and said, "Open up," she did. I thought she had long since swallowed the water, but to my surprise a fair amount was still in her mouth. And it came out of the weak side when she opened up.

John said good job and transitioned to a few speech activities to try to test her responses. She began to look tired, so he said, "Enough for today." She lay back down and was asleep within moments. John said, "Let's go over here and talk."

He said, "Mr. and Mrs. Hughes, I'm not going to be able to approve Megan for pureed foods at this point. Her ability to swallow appears to be pretty significantly impacted by the stroke, and although she is able to swallow, I am concerned that she can't clear her mouth and therefore there is increased risk that fluid will make it down her windpipe, choking her, which can cause pneumonia and bacterial infections. It is my recommendation that we insert a feeding tube to address her nutritional needs immediately."

"Dammit!"

Have you ever had a moment when someone tells you something, but while you hear what they are saying, you still disagree intently with their reasoning based on your knowledge of the issue, even though they certainly have you "outgunned" with knowledge and experience?

For whatever reason, I said, "I'm not ready to go there yet. I know my daughter and what she has been through over the last days. I know that she had no problem ripping out the catheter you all inserted, and I suspect she will do the same with this feeding tube. I also think that going this direction will break her spirit and cause her to give up."

John said, "I know how emotional this is for you both, but my focus has to be on her safety, and my opinion is that allowing her access to fluids and food will be detrimental to her health or worse."

"I appreciate your perspective," I said, "but you have known her for twenty-four hours and I've known her for twenty-nine years. I know my daughter, and this will set her back weeks."

I then "practiced medicine," which I had absolutely no right to do. But I knew that I had to advocate for Megan if I could. I asked John about whether the reduced ability to swallow might be tied to the TEE that they had performed the previous afternoon. He looked at his notes in surprise and said, "TEE?"

Caregiver's lesson number _____ (you fill in the blank): Do not ever assume that those taking care of your loved one know everything that has happened or have read all the notes in the file or even know what has happened recently. Even if he had known those facts, John was not present and didn't experience the post-procedure recovery from sedation. He meant well and was doing his job, but it was my new job to express my concern. If you have any doubt, tell the story again. It may save you a lot of heartache.

John first indicated that he did not think the TEE would have had an impact, and I didn't really buy that. I asked, "Do you understand what they did to her in performing the TEE?" He said, "Yes." And then in my stern voice I asked, "So you don't think sticking a garden hose down my daughter's throat and then yanking it back out might have an impact on her ability or desire to swallow less than twenty-four hours later?"

Ouch. I had no right to say that. John's heart was always in the right place. He truly was concerned about Megan's well-being, and I am immensely grateful for that. But on this issue and treatment being proposed, we did not agree.

To my surprise, John said, "I need to look at that and talk with her doctor. Let's just leave things where they are for now; she is getting nutritional supplements through her IVs. I'll come back by this afternoon, and we can talk again." John did as he said and came back later in the day. He told us he thought we might want to wait until Monday to make a final determination. He still believed a feeding tube was warranted and would be beneficial, but we would wait to see if a few days made any difference.

John became a dear friend, and I never, ever questioned that he wanted what was best for our Megan. He gave an angry, emotional, arrogant, overbearing parent a wide berth and allowed me to advocate even though I was way over the line more than once. He was and is one of my heroes in this whole experience, and our family will always be grateful for his outstanding care even when I was particularly hard to love.

Another frustration of the hospital environment was the fact that in four days we had seen four different neurologists all employed by the hospital. It made sense to me that having at least some continuity of care, particularly within the primary specialty responsible for treatment decisions, might be a good thing. But that is not how modern emergency medicine works.

I know that if you ask five accountants about a particular tax issue, you are likely to get five different iterations of the issue, and all will conflict in some regard. I personally doubted that medicine was much different. But what I did know was that today, that tall, slender surgeon had not been by, and our "doc of the day" indicated that the swelling was still there but had not gotten worse. That was a more promising sign.

That "doc of the day" also indicated that she believed Megan's cognitive issues were not only expressive but were also "receptive" and that they would monitor her, but they were not sure how much communication was "getting in." In other words, this made her recovery much more complicated and difficult. Once again, our hearts sank, even though they did not have much further to drop.

For the first time, a physical therapist came by. She wanted to do initial assessment of the stroke impact. We knew Megan's ability to use her right leg was severely affected, as were her right hand and arm. But we did not understand why or what this meant. The PT came in and helped Megan sit up in her bed, and of course when the only word you can say is "yes," the PT takes advantage of that by asking questions beginning with, "Would you like to try _____?" If the answer is "yes," you become an overachiever. But that was okay.

PT immediately brought Megan a significant amount of joy for just a few minutes and gave us hope that some of her weakness might be overcome. She stood up for the first time with help from the PT and an assistant. They then tried to get her to take a step. But things did not quite work at that point.

She stumbled and bumbled a bit and was obviously unstable on her feet. The PT also tried to get her to move the arm, but Megan looked at her arm, grabbed it with her good arm, flipped it upward, and then shrugged as if to say, "Not much there, Dad."

I watched carefully, searching for any evidence that communication was going into that brain, even if it was not coming out. I admit that it was a mixed bag. Her response to certain stimuli resulted in typical Megan expressions. But with other stimuli, it was as if she wasn't significantly present in the situation. She has always been a bit stubborn, but I concluded that this was not her pushing back or ignoring the request; it just seemed that she did not understand.

When she sat back down, we got our first lesson in stamina. She lay back and was asleep in seconds. Our girl was beat.

The nurses were constantly cleaning the PICC line and taking blood and giving meds. But that afternoon, Megan slept for more than three hours yet again. She was exhausted after this first effort, and so were we. Our Megan was a mess, and any hope of a quick rebound seemed almost unimaginable. I looked for any sign of encouragement or progress, but during those days, there simply were none.

"My God," I thought, "the troubling news keeps on coming and just doesn't end." I sat in the chair and stared into space. I thought my broken heart would explode, and the thoughts that ran through my mind were painful, constant, and multifaceted. I feared that Megan would end up in a nursing home or worse. I feared that her condition would eventually wear her down. I worried that she might have another stroke. The PFO is still there, I reasoned.

Online statistics said people who have one stoke are often 40 percent more likely to have a second stroke. I also feared that we would be ruined financially and that her insurance would not cover much of this. The nightmare of bankruptcy and financial ruin would get us even if the disease did not.

And the world, our world, still wanted to know how she was doing. Overwhelmed? You bet we were.

One of Megan's closest friends and one of our ministers dropped by to get the day's news, and we talked for a few minutes. The minister said, "Listen, you all have enough to deal with. Let us handle the information distribution." I said, "But they are coming to us still for news, and I'm not sure that will stop. Also, folks have been so wonderful, I just don't want to hurt anyone's feelings." He said, "What about a Caring Bridge site?" Eureka! I had not even considered that.

We decided that such a site would work, so Bud's daughter Shanna, who lives in West Virginia, quickly set it up and emailed us the password. That night between 10:30 and 1:00 a.m., I wrote the first of many posts. Caring Bridge is a web-based information repository for folks going through medical crisis or treatment to share their experiences so that you do not keep retelling the story. It allows readers to post encouragement and remains there as long as you like. It is apparently nonprofit, so there is no charge to the user, which is an immense blessing.

That first post took about three hours to write, mainly because I am a perfectionist and there was so much to tell. I was also afraid of saying too much, but I knew that if I did not give an honest and complete account, the questions would continue to come. My post was perhaps a bit too honest and a bit too detailed, but it was true and real, and folks got the gist of what we were living through. I tried to post at least every third day, and that was enough.

A side benefit was that it was therapeutic and cathartic for me to write. I had to consider my thoughts, and that helped me think through things more thoroughly, more positively and hopefully. As a result, I would not be quite so blunt. My initial anger was tempered a bit.

Writing also helped me recognize how lucky we were to have such a support group of friends, and it allowed them to talk back. For every post, we could expect fifty or more responses from people we may not have seen in years. The service also connected us to folks hundreds, if not thousands, of miles away. People we loved and who loved us. Caring Bridge was relatively easy to learn, it was a great tool that helped us get through the hard days, and it also did a good job of documenting the journey. We highly recommend it.

That evening just before shift change, nurse Jenny stopped in and said, "I know this whole nutritional thing has you all concerned, and I know it was frustrating for you. I have a friend in that department who is my age and I asked her about it. She said she would like to stop by and check on her this weekend. If the circumstances have changed, she might be able to move things along sooner. Would that be okay?" Linda and I blurted out, "Absolutely!" Jenny was off on Saturday, but she said she would arrange it.

The path back to "what was" had become obscure and faded even in just four days. But on such days, all one can do is look forward. I knew in my heart that my life outside of this crisis was stacking up. It was early in tax season, and my client responsibilities still existed. But my firm's partners and staff were incredibly supportive. When clients had demands that had to be addressed, they found a way to make it happen. They insulated us from so much, and they gave us glimpses of how they were cheering Megan along and lifting us up.

A typical tax season this would not be, but how could we simply survive it? On Friday afternoon, I slipped out for the first time and went by the office. I had dreaded this moment. The emotion of seeing those close to you for the first time is hard.

We generally spend more time with our coworkers than we spend with our families. I slipped into my office and punched the message play button on my phone and found that I had over thirty messages. I hung up and did not listen to a single one.

I felt the familiar tears rolling down my face and looked up to see five of our good staff at my office door. I wiped my face quickly, hoping no one had seen, and they in unison asked, "How is Megan, and how are you?" For the next hour, I got almost no work done, but instead I was hugged and loved on by my second family.

I confessed to my managers and partners that I was panicked about the fact that work was not happening and was not likely to happen any time soon. One of my favorite partners said, "Don't worry about it. We've got this." My IT folks forwarded phone calls and emails to others within the office. I went back to the hospital with orders to forward anything I thought worth responding to and to "focus on what was important."

I have been a workaholic for thirty-six-plus years, and there have been many times when my family has taken a back seat to work. Never again. I may be slow, but even I understood that life had just changed, and Megan's care would have to come first. My promise to her on Tuesday morning made everything else secondary.

On Friday night, Megan's former roommate and dear friend drove in to spend some time. Jenny Lee is an incredibly smart, well-studied, professional minister. She is about Megan's age. Seeing her expression the first time she saw Megan, I saw her broken heart and shaken faith, even though she had put on her best "I am in control, I am a trained professional" face and vocal tone. Jenny also did her best to minister to us and to love on Megan. But even I could tell that this young minister would forever be affected by the days we were all living together.

One more day ended the way it began, with that haunting transition to night care and a look backward at the day's progress. Our nurse Jenny sent us word that her friend in speech therapy would come by in the morning to evaluate Megan's swallowing. The evening was still restless for Megan, but the activity of the day made the hours a bit more restful.

As if we did not already have enough to deal with, our nurse informed us that Megan was presenting an elevated temperature. They had ordered tests, and we suggested that a UTI was a likely cause, given the trauma of ripping out an inflated catheter. We were told that this assessment would be included in the cultures they were "growing." So once again, hurry up and wait.

Megan's cousin Shanna stayed overnight, and I went home to sleep for the second time. By this point, "hospital fog" was beginning to settle in quite severely. Each day was filled with the same things, and the things that changed were usually stressful and intense. Our friends and family continued to hold us up when we fell, and our little girl had shown signs of improvement. But what was evident was that our lives were forever changed by the events of the week.

Both Linda and I wondered in our hearts if this was the beginning of a new phase in our battle. In our simple minds, to date, the enemy we were fighting was almost a malfunction in Megan's cognition and expression, but somehow the doctor's use of terms like "insult" and "injury" were very different from "being sick." And now, with Megan's fever, we were venturing into the uncomfortable area of infection—of being "sick," not necessarily being "injured," and we knew this could also kill her if it was not controlled.

As Linda and I went home to rest and feed the cat, we both again expressed our frustration through silence and tension. Our focus on the process, the problems, and the questions kept each of us wrapped in a blanket of pain, hurt, fear, and a shroud of those questions good Christian folk are not supposed to ask. And again, if I am truly honest, we simply didn't know how to care for each other without taking our eyes off our daughter. Our relationship was suffering because we were not focused on what we each were feeling.

An important bit of advice that I can give to any family that goes through something like this is that while the focus should be on the patient, the love expressed must be spread around a little bit more. During these events, everyone has needs. Ignoring those needs will damage relationships for a long time to come if you get and keep a certain patient tunnel vision.

It is not abandoning the critical needs of the patient to care for another loved one's needs. It is important and necessary to retain a healthy family dynamic. Loving those around you, close to you, important to you, even when you do not feel like it, helps maintain appropriate perspective. It preserves what has not completely changed. It allows you time to feel something other than pain. It secures the bonds that must remain if, God forbid, things are not to go well. And it is also incredibly hard to do when your world is falling apart all around you. It is hard to take your eyes off your precious patient.

Case in point: A friend said to me that in reading my blog posts, he could not discern whether the story I was telling was about Megan or about me. Initially I felt embarrassed by his words because I was not the one directly stricken, other than emotionally. But over time I realized that we each tell our own stories of such events. The perspective is so brutally personal that it sounds like our story when in fact we hurt so completely that we take on the pain of another and do our best to cure it, share it, and heal from it.

An experience this painful and personal creates a different story for each participant. We were all living it, but each of us had our context and content. The stories interconnected but were driven by our sweet daughter. Make no mistake, Megan was the one most significantly affected, and it is her life that will continue to be affected long after I am gone.

But what we each feel and felt is our own to bear and tell. It is an experience shared, and together we fight the common enemy using whatever ammunition we can find on the battlefield of disease. What I feel and perceive is different from what Megan and Linda each feel and perceive. At some point, though, the stories must be reconciled, and communication is the sole key.

We each must communicate what we are feeling and find a way to unify our concern or emotion, or the moments and growing pain will rip us from each other. That reconciliation is at best challenging and seems never ending. But it is necessary. It restores the bonds of family and unifies the application of combined resources needed just to survive. It pours a new foundation for old relationships that can be used to support progress and healing, both physical and mental. Without communication, disease wins yet another battle in this consuming conflict. It is like letting go of one emotional bomb while trying to defuse a second one. Unfortunately, both can destroy their target.

Regularly take a breath. Step away. Say a prayer. Show love and gratitude to those you hold dear or those who minister to you. Then, when your head is clear and your heart isn't racing, go back to your patient and look specifically for some fragment of hope, and hold on to it until it is no longer there.

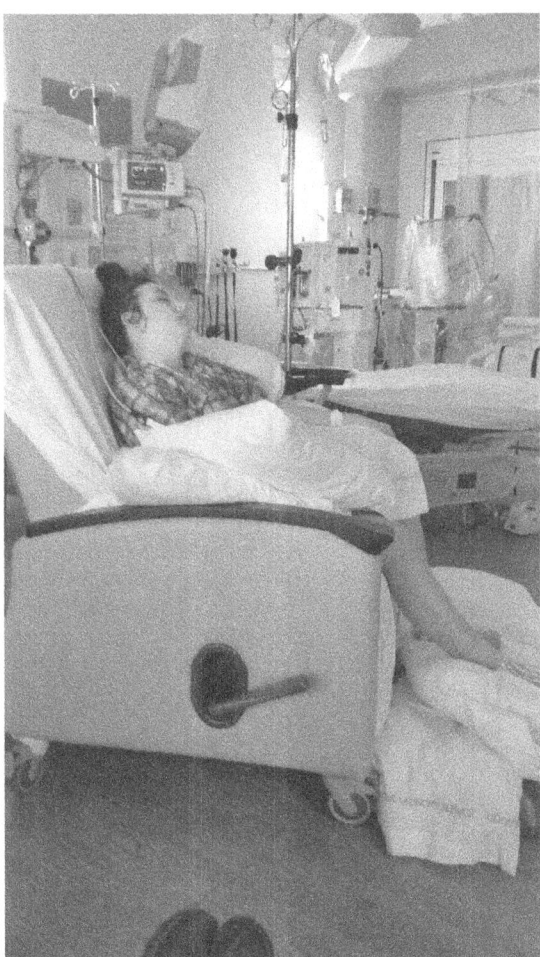

A few minutes out of the ICU bed and into the recliner still result in "nodding off" after only a short time of watching TV.

Chapter 7

Nailed It!

The hospital is an odd place on weekends. On weekdays visitors show up early because most must leave to go to work, but on Saturdays the visitation cloud happens a bit later. Most of the patients who can go home are discharged by Friday, so those left over the weekend are the sicker of the population. Showing up at six o'clock on Saturday morning is still a bit slower paced until you enter the ICU. Not as much difference there.

Shanna indicated that Megan had a better night with fewer episodes of attempted "grand escape." Our hope was that this might be a sign that the brain swelling was improving. Unfortunately, her temperature was continuing to rise. Our nurse indicated that the doctor had prescribed antibiotics among other medications to try to stem the additional challenge of infection.

As Shanna headed home for some well-deserved sleep, we began the day's rotation of doctors and tests. Since this was day five, we hoped we could finally conclude that the tall, thin surgeon would not be removing part of our daughter's skull to make room for her brain to expand. Enter the neurologist of the day: the husband of the neurologist we had seen the day before. When I learned of this unusual element of our hospital's neurology staff, I thought of all sorts of things, not the least of which was, "What do a husband-and-wife neurology team discuss around the breakfast table? What are their most intimate moments like? Do they tell intellect jokes?" Alright, enough of that.

The doctor was engaged, animated, and verbal, which was an unusual set of skills to this point. He tried to get Megan to respond to basic commands. She was exhibiting common symptoms of stroke patients that include emulation. Enough was "getting in" that she sensed someone wanted her to do something, but she was unclear about what it was, so she copied the command.

If we said, "Look at the television," she would look where we looked. But this guy was creative. He played face games. He said, "Megan, touch your nose," and he touched his. To my surprise, Megan touched her nose. He said, "Touch your ears," and she struggled until he touched his and she did likewise. My eyebrows went up a bit. And then he played the bad joke. He said, "Megan, touch your eyes," but touched his nose. Megan touched her nose.

He motioned me outside the room, and we talked for a few minutes. He asked, "Do you have any questions?" Once again, I said, "I have dozens, but no one will stay around long enough to answer them." He said, "Let's go down here." I didn't need a list, but I sure wish I had taken a pad to write notes. I started with "How is she doing?" And his response was honest and brutal.

He said, "There isn't a lot of change, it doesn't appear." He discounted her responsiveness and reflex movements because he and his team believed she had significant cognitive failure. He didn't think much was registering with her brain regarding communication. His encouragement was, "Look, it's very early, and this is a marathon, not a sprint." I was learning to hate that phrase.

I asked if we were in the clear for the brain swelling that we had feared for so long, and he indicated that the swelling appeared to have peaked, but still the risk of surgery would need to be monitored for two more days.

Then I got to the questions that had been formulating in my tired brain for days. Finally, I had someone who took more than a few moments to address the various concerns of a frightened father. I asked, "So what happened to the clot that caused the stroke? I am an accountant, not a doctor, so what happened to the clot? Will you go in to remove it?"

What he said next haunts me even now. He pulled out a pad of paper and drew some arteries and such and explained that when the clot went to her brain, it blocked an intersection or split in the plumbing of that sweet brain and stopped the blood flow to that area. Restoration of blood flow to that part of the brain didn't happen, and unfortunately, he said, "That part of her brain is dead. It won't be coming back."

Gulp!

I realized at that moment that my mouth was incredibly dry, and I was having trouble swallowing. On top of that, I was about to choke on the lump in my throat. I asked the "dumb layman accountant" question: "What happens to that part of the brain?" His once again brutally honest reply was, "It kind of breaks down and will ultimately drain away or be absorbed by the tissue around it."

I felt sick.

He saw my despair and turned the table a bit and said, "Look, the bad news is she is twenty-nine and the good news is she is twenty-nine. If she were fifteen years older, we would be talking about what long-term care facility would best fit her needs. But I believe she will be a good candidate for rehab. Younger patients have plasticity in their brains that allow them to relearn. However, that goes away as we get older. My hope is that she will do well."

I think this was the first comment from a doctor that gave me real hope that our daughter would survive and could perhaps have a future that allowed her to come back to us at least in some form.

We talked for a long time, and his encouragement gave me hope that I could share. Not every doctor, nurse, or specialist could offer us hope during our days at Mission. But there are a few to whom I will always be grateful, as much for their care and education of us as parents as for their incredible care of our Megan.

I returned to the room to find that Linda and nurse Jenny's friend had arrived, and they were talking to and engaging our daughter. The freedom and anticipation I had felt just moments before turned again to anxiety and fear because I felt the results of the swallow tests could either move us forward or significantly set us back.

Over the next moments, this young speech therapist worked thoughtfully and intentionally to see what Megan could do. She started with the ice chips. "Check!" She opened Megan's mouth to see if the water was there, and to our surprise and delight it was gone. "Check!" She had Megan manipulate the ice chips from one side of her mouth to the other. "Check."

Then the moment of truth. She took a cup and, without letting Megan hold it, gave her two sips of water. Each time she instructed her to swallow and felt her larynx, and to her delight she said, "She swallowed it." Opening her mouth confirmed it.

"Well done, Megan," she said. "I want to talk to your mom and dad for a minute."

She smiled and said, "I am going to order a barium swallow test for this afternoon. I think I can get that done. Megan has passed the swallow study, and I think she may be able to go to a liquid and possibly a pureed food diet if this goes well."

I had a "redneck" moment—did a fist pump and yelled, "YES!"

Of course, the "day" nurse stuck her head in to see what the commotion was and to give me "the look." We parted with our new favorite therapist and anticipated the afternoon's next step. We gathered around Megan's bed and hugged a bit and even shed a tear of joy.

Saturday visits were a cloud of folks. Those who worked through the week came out. Linda and I made a few visits to the waiting area and allowed close family and friends to share some time with a more alert and less agitated Megan. While her periods of awareness happened more often and were perhaps a bit longer in duration, she would also quickly drift off to sleep. But time spent with Megan was encouraging and precious to those who were able to have short visits at her bedside. It reminded me a bit of the first days of a new baby, with everyone wanting to hold her.

The afternoon came, and Megan even spent time watching ESPN as they spoke of her precious Carolina Panthers and her heroes Luke Kuechly and Cam Newton. Everyone was predicting that the Panthers would carry the day. No one thought the Broncos could play with them and win with the old man Peyton Manning at the helm.

One of the most touching moments of our stay in ICU was the mail run, when a small box was dropped off. We opened it and found a Panther mascot plush pillow in brilliant blue and black. I held it up, and Megan reached out and made a noise. It was familiar and soft, and to our amazement she wrapped it around her good arm and snuggled with it and immediately went to sleep. For the first time, I had the presence of mind to take a phone picture.

Moments later, our nurse came in and said she had heard from the speech pathologist, who asked that she bring Megan and one guardian to the x-ray lab for a barium test. They unplugged her bed and put everything else on the rolling pole, and off we went. It was way across the hospital, and the trip took several minutes as we pushed her bed through the halls. Megan lay quietly but attentive for the entire trip.

When we arrived, our speech therapist friend met us, and they wheeled us into a room barely big enough to hold the bed and the two of us with a fluoroscopist. He hooked her up and moved all sorts of things to get the pictures and angles he wanted. Soon he said, "We are ready." He started with clear liquid and had Megan swallow water once again.

On the screen I could see, in real time, the inner workings of my daughter's throat. I could see the fluid go past the windpipe and down the throat. I was amazed. They repeated the test over and over with different materials, and each time Megan did what she was asked, even if it required some extra emphasis and encouragement. And then it was time for the barium.

The technician came out with a cup of the most awful mix of milky-looking pudding I have ever seen. I got a whiff, and it was noxious. I was convinced that Megan would gag, but when the time came, she put it in her mouth, grimaced a bit, and swallowed it three separate times. I wasn't totally sure what I was seeing on the screen, but I knew something bright was making it down.

The speech folks and the x-ray folks met for a few moments, so we waited in the hall with our nurses. The speech therapist came out with her best poker face on and said, "Well, I am encouraged. Megan, we agree that you are swallowing and clearing thick liquids, so I think it's time you had something to eat. You passed!"

I couldn't hide my delight; once again the tears came, so I did what dads do: I hugged this young professional with tears streaming and said over and over again, "Thank you, thank you, thank you!"

We waited in the hallway for a few more minutes, and for a moment it was just me and sweet Megan. I realized that she was fixated on me and that my tears were troubling to her.

I leaned over and got almost nose to nose and said, "Baby girl, do you know what you just did? You probably just cut your rehabilitation by two months by passing that swallow test. I am *so* proud of you; you nailed it!"

I stroked her hair, and to my amazement she showed that little crooked smile and whispered, "Nailed it."

The world stood still for just a moment. For the second time in one day, my heart leaped for joy and the tears flowed even more. Words that didn't revolve around yes.

Emulation? Yes. Appropriate in the moment? Yes.

There are few things in life that stir the emotions of our souls the way having the tension of the most stressful and intense times somehow be suddenly and specifically resolved. Oh, there remained questions and fear and so much more to come, including all the other ongoing emotions of the circumstances. But a win is a win is a win.

We made the long trek back to ICU, and I conveyed the results to Linda and our close family. The results were relief and excitement all in one. To add to the jubilation of the moment, our nurse let us know that they would be moving Megan to a private room within the hour. For the first time in days, I felt my shoulders slump and relax. I not only allowed myself the hope that I was more convinced that Megan would survive; I also began to embrace the prospect that she might make a remarkable recovery.

Chapter 8

Ice Cream, Pudding, and Panthers

About 4:30 on Saturday afternoon, the nurse came in and said, "I have a room number; Megan will be moved to room 515. They are on the way to transfer her now. If you want to gather your things, you can head that way because we will take her a different way."

I looked around and realized that we had accumulated so much stuff over the last five days that we would need help and probably some boxes, so we gathered folks from the waiting area and began to send what we could to the new room or to the car.

When we arrived at the room, we walked in and found a recliner and a tray table. I swear I thought we were in a closet, but this was the room. I wasn't sure the bed would even fit, and if the goal was to keep visitors out, the size of the room would certainly help with that.

As we tried to find a place to store things, we found a closet that was less than two feet wide and would barely hold our coats and Megan's few personal belongings. We decided, "The car it is," and took the first load of get-well cards, teddy bears, socks, signs, handmade signs from her Sunday school kids, coloring books (*yeah, I know*), and other "best wishes" items from her adoring fans to the covered truck bed.

And you know what? The size of the room didn't matter. It was heaven.

No fishbowl feeling, a bigger TV, and the nurse's station and snack room were just outside the door. It was lit, and it had a marvelous window and view, even though the bleak midwinter was in full force with temperatures in the teens and snowflakes flying from time to time. I looked at Linda, hugged her, and told her this almost feels normal. She said, "No it doesn't feel normal, but it sure does feel better."

About that time a lady walked in with a tray and said, "Nutrition." When we lifted the lid I saw a bowl of broth, applesauce, yogurt, a cup of gelatin, coffee, tea, and utensils. I laughed. In all of that, I knew that there was nothing that my daughter even pre-stroke might have intentionally eaten.

We heard "knock-knock," and a bed was at the door, complete with entourage of nurses and aids, IV poles, and a lady with a laptop computer taking notes from an ICU nurse. We of course exited to the waiting room while they got Megan settled, which took a good long time.

When we got back to the waiting room, even after five days, people were still coming and going. We grabbed a couple of hugs, and the nurse came out and said they were almost done. Our new unit had an "information station" at the entrance, and they wanted to chat. They asked, "What about visitors?" I hadn't anticipated that one. I asked, "What are our options?" She said, "We can keep folks out if that helps, or you can set times. It's up to you." We decided that for now we would be selective to protect Megan's dignity and say no visitors unless we came out to guide them back.

When we got back to the room, Bud and Dianne had already arrived and the nurse was introducing herself and Megan's LPN. They said the speech pathologist wanted to be present when she was ready to try her dinner. And about that time, she walked in. She asked Megan, "You ready to eat?" Megan's face lit up like a sparkler.

We started with yogurt. One by one, we were each allowed to try giving her a spoonful, very specifically placed to aid in her swallowing. With each spoonful her face grimaced and there was a hint of gag. Then we tried the applesauce, and the first bit had a touch of "sour face," but once it went down, she tried to sit up and obviously wanted more.

From then on it was spoon, sip, spoon, sip. She ate the whole "meal," and we watched in amazement and delight. We had to apply control to get it all down without her choking or allowing it to go down the wrong way, but for first attempts, it was a wonderful success.

Even after this, Megan was obviously still hungry; after all, the child had not eaten in five days. Our floor nurse said, "Dad, let me show you something," and we headed to the "snack" room down the hall. There we found a refrigerator with various shelves stocked with yogurt, vanilla and chocolate pudding, and little ice cream cups. I suspected once again that there wasn't much that wouldn't make Megan turn up her nose. But I grabbed the pudding and yogurt and another applesauce and off we went.

We first tried a strawberry yogurt, and she took one spoonful and wasn't sure, but the second bite got pushed away. She looked at the other things we had requisitioned and tried chocolate pudding. Sure enough, that did the trick, and she ate the entire cup. By then she was obviously getting tired, so we dimmed the light and turned on the TV, changing channels until we found ESPN. She focused on the TV until her eyes gently closed and she drifted off.

No matter what the successes, there were always things to worry about next. At this point, her speech consisted of a lot of yeses with an occasional "no" and very little else. Many times, the answer didn't fit the question. She continued learning to say "yes" a hundred different ways with inflections and a hint of nuance.

We were now facing more difficult decisions, and things suddenly seemed to be moving so fast. Of course, everyone wanted to know "what is next" as far as when she would be ready to begin rehab.

Rehab. What did that mean?

Although we had known this would come, we never expected the transition to happen so quickly. That night we had a conversation with Bud and Dianne and found out that Shanna, their eldest daughter, who was also a talented occupational therapist and qualified to help us weigh our options, had been spending a lot of her time researching rehab possibilities. I must admit that this was one of those helpful gestures that made me feel like we were somehow being treated as grieving parents and therefore left out of a more technical decision loop. In my mind, but not in reality, I wasn't in control, and others were trying to guide or direct decisions without our input thus far. That sort of pissed me off.

Of course, there was no such intent, and I should have been simply grateful. But after five incredibly stressful days in which we were focused on basic survival and continuous attempts at sustaining life, now we would have to quickly make the transition from crisis mode to "taking back our daughter's life mode." To my surprise, I became painfully aware that I was still carrying around a lot of anger and frustration. We truly were a mess.

Sleep for me was elusive. The nights at the hospital contained short naps at best. The nights we went home, I fell asleep almost immediately but would awaken in fits and starts usually around three in the morning. I was in the shower by five and at the hospital by six most days. We were exhausted, and, quite frankly, I was being an ass.

I said we would look at the information the next day and make decisions then. Dianne wanted to stay that night and we said yes with gratitude. Linda and I went home and immediately began looking online at the places Shanna had identified. She was most focused on the Shepherd Center in Atlanta, Georgia. Her analysis was based on outcomes, patient mix, and other stuff I didn't have a clue about.

In my mind, we weren't going anywhere. CarePartners was here in Asheville. As far as we knew, it had an equally great reputation, and if we sought treatment here our support network would be close by. And it was still tax season, and I had work that I needed to do. I couldn't be away for an extended period. That was out of the question.

I didn't sleep much that night. The more I read, the more confused I became. Then it hit me: it was Sunday morning. It was the first Sunday since the stroke, and I wouldn't be going to church, nor would Megan or Linda. On top of that, it was Super Bowl Sunday, and Megan's beloved Panthers would soon take the field. That melancholy reflection allowed sleep to slip in, and I was soon out.

Sunday morning proper began with showers for me and Linda and the hurried trip to Mission where, to my surprise, Dianne was sitting up with our girl, who had an obvious chocolate moustache.

I said, "What's going on here?" Dianne laughed and said, "Don't sleep in that chair (the recliner); you will freeze."

It was quite cold outside. The glass wall on that side of the bed offered an incredible view but allowed in lots of cold drafts. Dianne continued, "And this girl is eating us out of house and home," to which Megan let out a loud "Yeah!" That expression of delight continues to this day as her "go-to" expression. My redneck friends would precede the "yes" part with "hell," spoken with three syllables.

I looked down and there were two separate ice cream cups completely empty. I said in amazement, "You ate ice cream!" and Megan said, "Yep."

"You hate ice cream," I protested, and she grinned that little crooked grin.

Megan never ate ice cream before the stroke; she detested it. But in her new state, ice cream became a staple, particularly in milkshake form. We concluded that the cold and the sweet brought pleasure and familiarity, and it was filling for one struggling with weakness, difficulty in swallowing, and an apparent lack of sensation in her face and mouth.

For a dose of emerging enthusiasm, the experience seemed much more familiar than any my daughter had participated in over the last several days. We finally had the opportunity to start a day with hope and promise.

Shortly thereafter, the sound of a tray being delivered to the words "food service" were followed by the tray cover being raised with a clang. Under it was, of all things, a waffle, eggs, grits, and sausage. All were puréed but cleverly formed to look like the real thing.

Megan looked at it and said "yes," to which I replied, "You want some?"

"Yes" again as she tried to pull herself up, pushing down with her good arm.

I pushed the tray table over her bed, and during the next several minutes she began a process of re-familiarizing herself with a form of partially solid nourishment.

We tried the waffle, and it was an immediate hit. In fact, she wanted to go too fast, so I had to be the dad and slow down on the delivery. But in only moments she had completely eaten the waffle and moved on to the eggs.

After a few bites she pushed the fork back and pointed to the sausage. We tried a bite and she immediately grimaced. She pointed to the apple juice and straw, so I put it to her lips. As she drew it in, it trickled down her cheek, so we removed the top and began with sips once again. She did get some down, even though the result wasn't nearly as successful as the waffle had been. Thin liquids would be an obvious challenge.

The whole meal took less than ten minutes but felt much longer and fulfilling. At that moment, I became aware that this was the first exercise in common life that made me feel as though our Megan was still in there. Oh, her pointing was more primal and included only involuntary attempts at selection or choice. But there were moments when the eye contact and expression were Megan. She was animated and expressive, if only for short bursts. I was hopeful because our daughter took in nourishment over a period of hours after several days of not eating. More importantly, at some level she expressed a new form of joy and perhaps her own understanding of hope.

This was a first step toward "normal," whatever that would become. And such first steps made the journey into rehab something to be anticipated and not dreaded.

Since the first night in the new room had been long on food and exploration and short on sleep, the morning after was filled with vitals and removing IVs and such. And that meant the complete laundry list of drugs Megan was taking would have to find a new way into her system. We crushed everything from antibiotics, which taste horrible anyway, to antidepressants and everything else into a single cup of applesauce. With a little encouragement, she was able to get it down through a few grimaces and sour faces. She was pretty responsive to most commands related to her health and seemed to be able to understand the difference between eating and taking her meds.

Since it was Sunday, as soon as church ended folks started to show up, and we had to make decisions about who to let in. I was convinced that Megan recognized and knew faces, but we weren't sure how much more she understood, and we didn't know how folks her age would respond to her condition.

I remembered the looks given to a grade school friend when bandages revealed scars and bruises, and how that friend melted into tears at the reception of friends who were not prepared for what they were about to see.

Linda and I agreed that we would prepare the closest of her pals for short-duration visits, telling them to keep the emotions positive and encouraging. But try as we might, there was an occasional friend who could not hide the deer-in-the-headlights look due to that first shocking view of a friend very different from whom they last saw. In those visits, we tried to deflect and encourage and control the positive nature of the conversation, even if a bit forced.

Megan was quiet for most of the initial visits, and after it was apparent that even her closest friends were talking more to us than they were to her, we decided to delay the contact until we felt more comfortable that she was not feeling embarrassment or stress. At this point, we couldn't really tell what she was feeling.

As the afternoon progressed and naps became the order of the day, we let close friends sit with Megan, and Linda and I had conversations with family and others whose opinions we treasured about the hard choices we needed to make regarding rehab. The prospect of going two hundred miles away for an extended period was like adding insult to injury. I was absolutely committed to getting our girl the best care available, even if we had to mortgage everything we had.

What we found was that each facility we considered had an incredible amount of information about their programs and outcomes. The local provider CarePartners, which is a sub-function of the Mission Healthcare system that has the hospital, treats more stroke victims than the Shepherd Center in Atlanta, which was the other facility that had skyrocketed to the top of the pile. I felt almost convinced that staying in our home area was best for us all, but I knew that others in our family thought that was a mistake.

It is a difficult process to discern what is best for someone you love more than life itself, and at the end of the conversation, there is probably no truly right answer. I knew that the two options we were settling into would both give Megan a fine chance at rehabilitation, but that didn't ease the tension. The Shepherd Center would require a commitment that would change our lives for the foreseeable future and remove our one comfort of having family and friends nearby.

Linda and I simply didn't know what to do. We prayed, we talked to anyone we thought had knowledge that we didn't, and we weighed it all. Once again, it was an angel of unexpected origin that pushed us past our indecision.

Late in the afternoon, we heard a familiar voice. It was nurse Jenny from ICU. This young woman had already won our hearts and given us hope that no one else had been able to deliver. She even reminded us of our daughter.

She said, "I had to come check on you and see how my girl was doing." And with that she sat down and began to brush Megan's hair as she had done in the ICU. Her unassuming comfort put us at ease and obviously endeared her to Megan.

She looked at us and said, "Okay, so what's next? Have they talked about rehab yet?" I felt tears well up a bit, and she said, "Tough subject?" And we said, "Yes."

We told her the options, and she seemed interested that we were considering Shepherd. Jenny told us she had been in a rehab facility that would be similar to that program. She said it would be more intense than here, and for someone Megan's age that was a good thing. She talked about rehab in a way that made us know she had experienced it firsthand.

We eventually asked her what she would do if it were her family member. Jenny said almost unemotionally, "You need to get her somewhere with people her same age. You will be doing this for a while, and it's important because people your same age push you. It's the peer pressure, and it will motivate her."

Finally, we had an opinion spoken without anything at risk, and it made perfect sense. We still didn't like the choice, particularly the distance and the loss of our support network, but we couldn't deny the wisdom of this late twenty-something. For the first time, the haze began to clear and focused us a bit. The tension went out of our shoulders. Jenny said, "Well, I gotta go," and we asked her for her phone information because we wanted to stay in touch.

I called Bud and asked him to have Shanna initiate contact and find out what would be involved in getting Megan admitted and transferred to Atlanta. Later that afternoon, we had our first contact with a representative of Shepherd who lived in Chattanooga, Tennessee. We signed releases for them to access medical records, and from that point things moved even faster . . . until the insurance company got involved. I will save that story for another chapter.

As the Super Bowl kickoff approached, Megan was sitting up in bed and out of the blue took off toward the recliner with huge thud. I yelled, "Megan!" but she slid herself into that chair with much more ease than I was comfortable with. The one remaining IV was just enough to set off an alarm to the nurses' station.

Megan was focused on the pregame show, and she hardly noticed the scolding from her nurse or anyone else. The nurse gave in pretty easily because she simply looked comfortable and a lot more normal, particularly since she was now dressed in a Panthers tee shirt and warm-up pants. This would become the uniform of Team Megan for the coming weeks. Waiting for kickoff, we enjoyed pizza that was delivered along with Megan's evening food service of all things pureed.

Megan enjoyed her evening meal although it was nowhere near as exciting as that waffle had been. The one staple that became an immediate favorite that night was mashed potatoes and gravy. She didn't eat much else, but the potatoes never lasted long. There is a good dose of Lewis (Linda's family) in those genes after all.

The game began, and the Panthers couldn't get much going early. Turnovers would bring groans of discontent from Megan. The football was familiar, and her Panthers were still important. More initial steps toward normal. It was welcome and comforting.

It had been a good first day out of ICU, and we were so grateful. Before the first quarter was over, the nurse brought Megan's meds, including her sleep aid. It was early for that, but since she was in the chair and not the bed, there was a move toward getting her back into bed by halftime. The sleep agent took its toll, and Megan slept through the second half but woke up to see Cam throw an interception that put the Panthers down for good.

The nurses helped move her to bed, and shortly after the third quarter the Panthers once again stumbled.

Megan rolled over on her side, pulled up her covers with her good arm, and pulled the sheet up around her head. She closed her eyes and said with recognizable disgust, "*Yes*." I was amazed at what I was seeing, but with that she resigned to the defeat that was obviously coming and went to sleep.

The parallel between the past several days and the whippin' Denver put on Megan's Panthers was obvious. The Panthers had almost gone undefeated in the regular season, and no one thought the Broncos had a chance.

Megan's life just a week before had her and her close friends planning a celebration Super Bowl party that she would host. A time for joy and celebration of a season no Panthers fan would ever forget. Victory. Boy, did those plans change in a hurry. No one expected this day to be as it was.

I wondered as she drifted off to sleep what impact this additional insult might have. I once again felt the pain of unrealized opportunity on behalf of my little girl, but I admit that the reality established by simply being "promoted" to a private room made the sting of the football game pale in comparison.

Finally, it was a victory worth celebrating . . . just not the victory we had planned for.

Chapter 9

Finding Rehabilitation

Monday morning came, and the comments of our friends who had come by were of gridiron condolences, concerned over how Megan would react or understand what had happened to her Panthers. To our surprise, her uncle Bud asked, "What happened to Cam?" and the sneer that she presented suggested disappointment but continued loyalty and a gloomy "yeah." She wanted her Panthers T-shirt to wear that day, but the particularly motivated morning medical staff only had limited time to chat Panthers laments.

Her neurologist and one of our particular favorites began the day with his assessment of our patient, and for the first time he said it was time to begin planning for Megan's discharge. He said, "I believe she is an excellent candidate for rehab and should do well." He then said, "I assume you folks will be going to CarePartners." "Well, we haven't totally decided at this point," we admitted. He said, "Oh really? Where else are you looking?" We rolled off two others that we were considering, and for some reason I let it slip that we were leaning toward the Shepherd Center in Atlanta . . . total silence. The doctor then asked, "Why there?" We listed several things, including the fact that they had a much younger patient median age.

He continued his evaluation of Megan and offered that he was convinced Megan still had significant cognitive limitations and that he was not sure how much she truly understood. I knew that her response to some commands was puzzling to us. He would ask her to point, to wave, to do simple commands, and almost invariably she would look to me as if for some type of prompt. He was easily able to mislead her, and while he spent only a few minutes each day with her, his comments held weight and brought concern and doubt just when we were beginning to feel that Megan was truly making progress. He reminded us that she was only now really beginning to heal, so her recovery was barely underway. Emulation was common, he said; she would take her lead from those around her and be prone to repeating what she saw and heard. That didn't mean she understood. There went that pit in the bottom of my stomach one more time.

He then most compassionately said something helpful but frightening based on our circumstances: "She is young and will soon be healthy again, that is amazing, and with good rehabilitation her brain has the ability to relearn what has been taken. As I said before, please understand that if Megan were older right now, we would likely be making decisions about her long-term care. Youth is on her side."

As he left the room, he asked one more time, "So really, why would you go to Atlanta? All they have is a big reputation, but based on my experience, the care you would get here would be just as good and a lot easier on you both." We assured him that we knew CarePartners was a quality facility and was here at home. I said with tears in my eyes, "I just want what is best for my daughter, and that includes her care and the environment." It is funny how, when pushed about our daughter's care, the tears were always just below the very thin surface and quickly returned without much effort. But our doctor understood that we did not take this decision lightly, and he backed off a bit, saying, "Folks, there is no right answer here. I am pleased that you all are taking this decision so seriously, and Megan will do well wherever you go because she has such strong support." We were flattered, but the discussion was still uncomfortable. Were we making the right decision?

If I am honest, the decision of where we would do rehab was to that point wrapped up in facts, but once again we had just heard someone whose opinion was independent of our own, someone who had so much more technical knowledge than we would ever have, say, almost jealously, that the Shepherd Center had a "big reputation." I did not see that as an impediment, but rather I wanted Megan to be somewhere with a storied history of positively changing people's lives.

At this moment, we were looking for the "hail Mary pass" even though the road ahead seemed long and winding. This discussion made our conversations with nurse Jenny and our decision to pursue Atlanta appear much more reasonable. It was one of the scariest and most difficult decisions we had faced. It was way past overwhelming. But later that morning, my cell phone rang. It was the lady from Chattanooga, who said, "I'm glad to tell you that we have reviewed your daughter's records and we have accepted her for inpatient treatment. We are working with your insurance carrier, and we think we will have a bed as early as Tuesday."

Tuesday? That was tomorrow. How could we possibly be ready by then? The great equalizer was that last part about the insurance company. We were about to find out that the insurance carrier uses warp drive when they think it might save a buck and the Yugo motor when they are approving anything significant and are always looking for alternatives.

While I was on the phone, John our speech therapist had arrived and brought all sorts of materials. I wasn't sure how he would feel about the swallow test, but to my surprise his questions were on point, including, "How did she tolerate eating and drinking?" We were honest and told him about the experiences, warts and all.

He was supportive and helpful, and Megan focused on him in a way she didn't with others. He was funny and animated, and that invited Megan to appear to engage. Her interest wasn't lost on John, who immediately said, like a gameshow host, "Megan, point to the TV," and to our surprise she looked at us and then pointed upward in the general direction of the TV.

Finally, the room was empty and quiet. John closed his big book and said, "Megan, I want to try something with you." We sat quietly and watched in amazement. John said, "Megan, I am going to count to ten, and I want you to say the numbers with me as I say them." He began, "One," and then said, "Two," and I noticed Megan's lips were pursed as if forming words. He said, "Let's do it again. I'll start. One . . . two," and to our delight Megan said "two" with him and went all the way to ten. "That's good, Megan." Never missing a beat, he said,

"Let's try the letters of the alphabet. I'll start and you join me. A . . . B . . . ," and on B she joined and went all the way to P.

Once again, I wiped tears away and happened to catch Linda's gaze as she did the same. John said, "Megan, I'll be right back," and he motioned us outside for a consult. He said, "Let me work with her alone for a little while. I want to see how much is still there." I surmised that he also needed to remove the emotion and distraction of having loved ones there, particularly Megan's far biggest source of any visual prompting—that being me, her dear old dad.

We sat there with friends for a while, and after what seemed like an eternity John came out with papers and various aids he had used. He said, "Your little girl is amazing. She said the alphabet, she counted to twenty, and she said the months of the year, all of them." He said Megan had a wonderful foundation for rehab. I asked about what little I knew at that moment, which was, "So how much of this is her memory and how much is emulation or rote?" He said, "To me it doesn't matter; the fact is she has that part of her brain intact. How she accesses and expresses it is the issue."

I asked, "What does that mean?"

And this dear, sweet man said what mattered most to Mom and Dad. "I think it means that a lot of her learned knowledge is there; she just has to learn how to access and use it."

"So you think her school and work knowledge is there?"

He said, "I do. Just remember this is going to take time, a lot of time, but you should see this as encouraging." We were elated, and for a moment the possibilities seemed endless and hope filled.

Now, there is a fine line in this type of illness between "rehabilitation" and "recovery." I never knew that such a big part of medical treatment depends on the semantics of the words being used. But I was about to learn that "rehabilitation" is the process of learning, remembering, recognizing, and applying.

"Recovery" is that unattainable goal at the end of the rainbow. Recovery is what you end up with. That is the best way I can explain it. Doctors and therapists seldom talk of recovery; they talk about rehabilitation, the interim benchmarks and goals that are a part of the bigger process. And the process is filled with different phases and steps.

I began using the term "baby steps" almost from the outset, but now that mental image was our new reality. Each problem solved was a "baby step" toward recovery, but recovery is a place far, far away. We aren't there even now. And in those early days, we did not even know if we were going in the general direction of that "place."

We left our friend John and headed back to Megan, where we found her talking to and working with her physical therapist, who also had showed up for a little workout. I watched as she maneuvered Megan here and there, each time with a transfer belt. I asked about the belt, and she said it would save our backs and keep Megan safe as well. If she fell, falling on one of us would injure us and might injure her. Without the belt, we couldn't possibly catch her from behind without going down too. With the belt, we gained leverage and control over her movements because we could lift if need be. The therapist then prophesied a bit when she said, "You guys will get used to seeing and using this."

Again, no truer words were ever spoken. That belt soon became a means by which Miss Meg would gain some initial freedoms and mobility. But just as quickly, it would become a never-ending frustrating symbol of her plight. Just stopping to put it on was an interruption and a source of pain that her wide eyes and her "mad face" scowl would soon reflect.

When they finished, I could tell Megan was exhausted; it had been a busy morning, and she was having trouble holding her eyes open. Food service dropped off her lunch. It was unrecognizable except for mashed potatoes and gravy, and, being my daughter, she ate every bite of the potatoes. But nothing else got touched, except for the vanilla pudding and applesauce. The great state of Idaho saved our daughter by keeping her nourished over those first weeks with their mashed spuds.

I hoped to hear Megan use some of the words she had offered to John, but most of her attempts at communication still involved "yes" or "yeah" or a few two-word phrases. Occasionally, I could tell that her mind was working, and she would look at me and try to initiate a question. Finally, that afternoon late in the day after straining and several grimaces, she said it.

"Why um . . . ?" and then she couldn't get any more out. Why? That was the question I dreaded most. For me and for her. I prompted her with, "Why did this happen?" and after a moment she said "Yeah."

I put on my best "wise Dad" face and began trying to explain what we knew to this point. "Well, it looks like you were born with a PFO in your heart that let a blood clot go to your brain, and that caused part of your brain to not get oxygenated blood, resulting in part of your brain being injured." (We didn't learn until later that PFO means "patent foramen ovale," or a hole in the heart.)

The expression on her face did not change. Her right eye drooped slightly, and the right side of her face almost looked frozen in time. It was unreactive and expressionless. It entered my mind that her face looked as if she were only half there. I felt the hair on the back of my neck bristle a bit.

Normally, my daughter has one of the most animated faces in all of God's creation, and now even that had been taken from her. We sat and stared at each other for the longest time, and then she yawned as only she can. I said, "But honey, it's going to be okay. You are on your way to getting better." And with that she used her good left arm to roll on her side and almost immediately nodded off.

Linda and I looked at each other as we had hundreds of times over the past week. Ducking the obvious pain of what had just happened, I asked rhetorically, "How in the hell are we going to get ready to go to Atlanta by tomorrow?"

We transitioned to making lists once again. "You need to go to the house and pack some clothes. I need to go to the office and let them know and figure out how to make this work." We left Dianne and friends with Megan while we tried to put things in motion to accomplish the next scary phase that had just been thrust upon us. What we did not realize was that over the coming two days, we would be disappointed twice that the insurance had not given final approval for the transfer.

Each time we heard from Shepherd, we heard from Mission that *today* was the day. In one instance, Mission had already called the transport vehicle and had to cancel it. Finally, our case worker came in Thursday morning and said, "I still haven't heard anything, but I think it may be Monday now because Shepherd doesn't typically want to do intake going into the weekend since Fridays are typically alternative therapy days." I didn't know what that meant, but we would soon learn.

We were way past frustrated, and I began looking for the insurance company phone numbers to get rid of some internalized anger and at least vent. Megan continued doing the therapy that Mission could work in, and we were introduced to our newest challenge, Coumadin, and the testing required for this blood thinner.

Coumadin is the brand name for a drug called warfarin. Its original use was as a rat poison, but it is an effective, inexpensive blood thinner that has a known antidote, unlike many of its more modern counterparts. Vitamin K is the antidote. Each day or so, they drew blood for a test called an INR that would tell us how much of the drug was in Megan's blood. If it was within limits, she was pronounced "therapeutic," and that is what we wanted because at that level her blood was unlikely to cause clots that might cross over her PFO and cause another stroke. The part we didn't know or understand was the fact that blood thinners have significant side effects.

A nosebleed is a big deal, her period would be a big deal, and a hemorrhagic stroke would be devastating. Megan would be on this drug until either the PFO was closed or for the rest of her life. This is a much bigger deal than it sounds, particularly for a twenty-nine-year-old. On top of that, it required changes in her diet. No foods that were rich in vitamin K, so no salads or leafy greens. But for now, she was therapeutic, and that was all that mattered at that moment. We would save the additional battle for down the road.

About ten in the morning, the nurse came in and said, "I just got the approvals from insurance and Shepherd, and you guys are heading to Atlanta about 2 p.m. You will get there after the staff has already gone, but they have you a room and they will save Megan something to eat."

We called our families and some friends and let them know. Our friends Glenn and Sandy Pierce dropped what they were doing and headed for Atlanta to be with us that first weekend. Other dear friends, Mike and LuAnn Nelson, owned a hotel within twenty miles of the Shepherd Center and said, "You have rooms for as long as you are there; just send a text when you need one."

God is good and so are our friends. Those are gifts we can never possibly repay. It was like we were going to a distant world, and I admit I was frightened to tears. I made a quick trip to my eighty-eight-year-old mother's home for a hug, a kiss on the forehead, and an update. "Nana," as Megan calls her, was having an incredibly hard time with all of this. But she put on her best face as we shared a few moments of joint pain and greater hopes for what this might do for "Meggie," as my mom calls her sometimes. Leaving my mom was hard because it meant that now her care would be secondary to Megan's, even for the near future, and Mama was by no means in good health. But we both agreed this is what had to happen. So, with a few parting tears, I headed back to Mission one last time.

We carried more "stuff" that had again accumulated in Megan's room and stuffed it into the bed of my big Ford truck. Our nurse came in to say, "They are here." We transferred Megan onto a gurney in a warmup suit, with her tattered childhood blanket. We met the ambulance at the emergency entrance for the three-plus-hour trip to Atlanta. I did the math, and it looked like we would probably make it to the city around rush hour. Nice. We found out that regulations prevented us from being able to ride in the ambulance with Megan; only one of the crew could do that, so we would ride together in the truck. Megan seemed oddly engaged in all the activity going on around her now that she was outside of the place where she had been bottled up since that hard morning nine days before.

I told the young driver that we would be "glued to his fanny" the whole way down I-85 and for him to keep an eye out for us. He promised he would. With that, we nervously took a giant leap of faith that we were doing what was best for our daughter's future. Staring at the back of that big green and white ambulance allowed my mind to wander among all the problems we needed to solve and all the emotions we could not control or even partially deal with.

In our own minds, we were convinced that this was the right thing to do, even though it was incredibly hard. We looked for courage and took hold of our faith and watched as all we knew and all we were comfortable with slowly disappeared in our rearview mirror.

At least for now.

Chapter 10

Almost Intermission

The concept of faith and the mental state of my daughter are interestingly combined by the articles of faith that her stroke dictates. Megan has the interesting focus that allows her to hear bad news, dwell on it for only moments, and then dismiss it with an almost resigned statement of "oh well." In subsequent days she has added "sucks for me" or "sucks for you." The awful, terrible part that Linda and I can't seem to get past is an acceptance we find hard to tolerate. Megan still has difficulty staying on task and staying focused. It is almost a defense mechanism that serves her and spares her the pain that we as her parents and caregivers can't seem to find resolution for. We wrap our minds around the unfairness of this insult that has been hurled at her and we continue to rail and yell, and yet she seems almost at peace with her burden and continues to be focused more than anything on the potential tools we (and she) identify as having any measure of promise for positively impacting her circumstances.

During these days, I have often focused on the Scripture that has always been a source of unending stress for me: when Jesus tells the disciples not to worry. It goes like this in the King James Version that I originally committed to memory:

> "Consider the lilies, how they grow: they toil not, they spin not; and yet I say unto you, that Solomon in all his glory was not arrayed like one of these. If then God so clothes the grass, which is today in the field, and tomorrow is cast into the oven; how much more will he clothe you, *O ye of little faith*? And seek not ye what ye shall eat, or what ye shall drink, neither be ye of doubtful mind. For all these things do the nations of the world seek after: and your Father knoweth that ye have need of these things. But rather seek ye the kingdom of God; and all these things shall be added unto you." (Matt 6:28-33, my italics)

I am so terrified at the continuing impact this stroke has had and will have on my sweet child, yet her faith at some level is stronger than my own. We were and are kindred spirits. Before her stroke, she was Type A; she worried about everything; she was subject to depression and sought the approval of those she respected. And, she had strong opinions about everything. This child was already dealing with our family nemesis of depression and had already sought medical treatment and counseling. But if there is something positive to be learned in this, the stroke to this point has apparently not overwhelmed her with the fear of what is lost or of what might go unrealized in the future. She sees that our circumstances are unfortunate—yes, they suck—but life goes on, we have things to do, and the worry of the day, while present and painful, does not overwhelm her the way it sometimes does us.

I admit that my faith has been shaken to its core over the events of this crisis. And though at this date in which the months post stroke total just less than two years, I struggle as much now or perhaps even more than in the days just after the stroke. I called on the name of God for help and strength and patience and comfort, and to be honest I still do almost daily. The mornings are still the hardest.

But Megan offers a much more stoic view from her perspective that does not involve the constant unending worry and stress that her family feels. Oh, there are days and even weeks in which her situation is much more manageable and less debilitating than on other days. But even when I am most susceptible to the fear and worry, it is my daughter and her little sweet dog friend that pull me from despair and lift me up. Megan is always aware and appreciative of the care Linda and I provide. She knows at some level that her attitude in addressing hard days helps to right our ships and provides new winds for our sails as we proceed on this journey together.

I have often said that there is no instruction book on how to go through such an event as this. I wish there were, and I suppose this is my attempt at a start of one. But to me, if there is advice we can offer, it starts with taking control of your loved one's treatment. It includes taking care of yourself as a caregiver and taking the advice of friends that the terms of this journey will happen over a longer period than you would prefer. It is essential to relieve the pressure on a regular, planned basis, even if those periods involve short, simple stress-relief activities that can only reduce the pressure in that situation and do little to eliminate the source. Our wonderful friend and doctor at the Shepherd Center told us on our very first day, "A stroke changes a family as well as the patient." Again, truer words have never been spoken.

The emotional jungle you will encounter in this type of situation is something no one is prepared for regardless of the previous station in life. It is intense, incredibly personal, raw, and painful. Sharing your thoughts provides some immediate relief from the stress of a particular day, but my experience is that care should be exercised when you consider whom to tell. We made the mistake of talking with all who were concerned and willing to listen. It was a tonic to share the stress with those expressing love and concern.

The reality is that the words spoken in times of stress, pain, and bewilderment become the foundations for actions by those who are equally stressed by the painful situation. Those actions may often go against your desires if you are unprepared to express these desires outside of the events you have become invested in. It's not that good people necessarily do bad things; it is that sometimes asking for help without structure may take you down paths that waste time and energy in a period when you have little of both.

Further, those around you sense your pain, know of your heartbreak, and sincerely want to help. They approach everything you are experiencing with a desire to solve the problem. Unfortunately, there are multiple problems, and the problem they want to solve may not be the one you find most pressing. And the solution they reach may not be what is best or what you would want.

The best first steps in any health emergency should include identifying your team and establishing communication. They are your most trusted advisers, those who accept you for who you are without judgment or question. They act when asked, offer advice without insistence, and can be trusted not to share conversations with others without thought or consultation. This core team of advisers will be the folks you share and consult with first, and the first to wrap their arms around you when the news is not good. These are the folks who will pick you up off the floor if it all goes badly. They do not latch on but instead function as a buffer of compassion and protection. They wrap you in a warm, loose-fitting blanket of love and concern. They are there without asking and pray without telling you they are praying for you. These are your truest friends and family.

Establishing this team may take time. And depending on age and location, the pool may be shallow. In those instances, reach outside! Linda and I were slow to engage in the various associations and nonprofit resources, but lately those resources have become more valuable and worthy of investigation. Their resources are often available online or through agents. Listen to anyone, and accept what you can verify, but trust must be earned, and that requires time and an investment on their part.

What about your church or family of faith? That is personal and a choice for each to make, but we would not have survived the first hours and days had it not been for that network of God's children. As our story has already exposed, the shock and complete devastation of sudden-onset illness overshadows everything else that is going on. As the situation evolves, you must find time to establish your support network. The good news and the bad news are that you will spend a lot of time "waiting," so use that time wisely.

- Take notes.
- Talk to others and penetrate those initial walls of discomfort and profound emotion. This will help you identify those who might assist you and those who are afraid of being in the eye of the storm.
- Do not apologize for asking others to make your situation survivable and livable, and do not lose sight that your goal in the process is to meet the needs of your loved one.

I've always heard that parents will do anything for their kids, and that is true even before catastrophe happens, but my experience is that parents will offer superhuman efforts when events like this take place.

What about the guilt that I began with in this chapter? No matter how you approach these difficult days, there is no way to avoid some guilt. It is hard at times to differentiate between the emotions of guilt and the emotions of regret. You will continuously have questions. The why and how and what are ruthless.

For weeks, I felt significant guilt that I wasted thirty minutes between the time when Megan first texted us that morning and the time when I read the five lines of gibberish and responded with "You ok?"

In my mind, those minutes might have made a difference. I certainly could have ended Megan's distress thirty minutes sooner. In my mind and in those moments, I experienced guilt because initially I wasn't sure if my actions might have prevented the possible administration of the drug TPA. I felt guilty because in those first moments of stress and panic and fear, I didn't have the awareness to assess Megan's home to determine if the stroke had happened that morning or the night before.

I fell into the emotional trap of convincing myself that I had failed my daughter by not finding answers to the questions surrounding what happened. And in fact, it was two months before I learned information that convinced me that those answers were not present in anything to be found at my daughter's home that morning. Further, Megan herself knew in her tormented mind that the stroke had happened or at least begun the night before. Due to those facts, the use of TPA would have likely further injured or perhaps even killed our little girl.

It is only natural that when bad things happen, we as humans want to find a source for our anger and distress. We desperately need someone to blame, or, to use a more politically correct phrase, we need someone to "hold accountable." Unfortunately, it isn't that simple. When we run out of targets to aim for, we inevitably turn our only remaining weapon on the only remaining person in the room . . . ourselves. Guilt is our response to a circumstance that we cannot control and one that is so unfair, so unfortunate, and so troubling that it demands a response, even when we can find no one else to blame other than ourselves. It must be someone's fault. Guilt places the responsibility on us.

We make it ours to bear. We must be to blame somehow. We didn't act quickly enough. We didn't intervene in a situation when we could have. We didn't warn the person about things we knew could be potentially negative. Thus, we dwell on the "what" that could have been, not on the "what" that truly is.

My advice? Don't waste your time!

In the movie *The Martian*, the central character utters a truth that I have recently begun to paraphrase as, "You start with a problem and solve it, and then you turn to the next problem and try to solve it. Solve enough problems and you get to go home." In our case, solve enough problems and you get to live, you may get to walk, you might get to speak, and it's remotely possible you might be able to use your right hand.

Not one of those problems involved determining whose fault it was and then holding them accountable. I'd be lying if my mind doesn't occasionally go there, but once again I aspire to be like Megan. It "sucks for us," but it won't help. "Oh well."

Our energy must be invested in progress, not revenge.

Finally, time is often not your friend when it comes to "treatment." But when it comes to "healing" from a stroke, time is the only friend you have. After a stroke, you'll hear many platitudes, but few have absolute truth.

Well-intentioned friends told us they had heard that what you recover in the first year after a stroke is all you will ever recover. That isn't true. While it is true that the largest amount of recovery happens in the early months, research now suggests that stroke victims can continue to regain function for many years to come. It all comes down to effort and therapy.

My point is simply this: Don't rely on hearsay. Do the math, read the materials, solve the problem. The internet is a wonderful tool if you use it wisely. Information from the National Stroke Association, the Shepherd Center, our own Mission Hospital, and many other sources brought encouragement, hope, and motivation.

Recovery is multifaceted and complex, and no two stokes are exactly alike. Each is unique, and recovery depends on where the stroke occurred, how much brain tissue was damaged, and what type of stroke it is—I have learned there are two, ischemic and hemorrhagic. Learn all you can about the malady that your loved one faces and use that gift of knowledge to learn more and to help make decisions about future treatment.

I admit, I'm an accountant, not a doctor or speech therapist, but in nineteen months I have learned to be a helpful assistant and caregiver. We have had to do things we were not trained to do, and it has been hard. But the results and the connection to how hard my Megan has worked is another shared experience. Her successes are our successes.

As we began to transition from the lifesaving, life-stabilizing staff at Mission Hospital in Asheville, we knew that those days had to come to an end and rehabilitation had to begin. The next six weeks would be truly life changing.

Chapter 11

Atlanta's Calling

After four hours of reflection and being incredibly frustrated that we were only going the speed limit behind that green and white ambulance, which is an uncommon occurrence in most of my vehicles, we made the turn onto Peachtree Road. Within moments we saw a towering facade with large block letters that said *The Shepherd Center*. We turned into that campus from one of the busiest thoroughfares in all of Atlanta. It was so much bigger than we expected, and the ambulance immediately came to a stop under a canopy. A guard instructed us to continue to the parking deck and to then come to the second floor. I dropped Linda off to accompany Megan into the facility and then complied with the guard's instructions. The fear and excitement and angst all came together in a moment of panic as I exited the truck after having parked it in a space labeled "compact car." It fit (barely), and I was in a hurry to get to my family and see the place that would now be our home for the near future.

The first "aha!" moment I encountered was that this facility was unlike any place I had ever been before. Every door was automatic, and each was grossly overstated as far as width and size. Soon I found out why. This place provides healing and hope to people with all sorts of brain and spinal cord injuries, many of whom are in large, imposing wheelchairs that can be guided in numerous ways, whether by joystick or mouthpiece or even head and eye movement. These devices are immensely expensive and intimidating to those of us who are unfamiliar with the needs and limitations of their patient occupants.

Many of these good people are profoundly injured, and these massive machines give each of them various gifts that include mobility and physical, mental, and even digestive support. Each is fitted to its recipient. Every time you go from one area to another, they are a constant part of the scene. This is one of the gifts of the Shepherd Center.

As someone just getting used to assisted and adaptive living, I suddenly realized that I had accumulated years of bias and uneasiness of being around "adaptive living." I soon began to see and understand the beauty and opportunity of a place that uses whatever is available to empower people who have experienced bad things to live the life they yearn for. In doing that, it allows them to reclaim portions of their lives that illness or injury might have taken from them.

As I walked through those big, imposing doors and rode that extra-deep elevator (one of four, and that is seldom enough) up to the second floor, I was met with my first obstacle. I faced a locked door that I could see through into an area that housed nurses and clinicians, all at a large central station, and none of them were noticing me. I meekly tapped on the glass, and a person in scrubs waved and reached over and "buzzed" me in.

I struggled with the door a bit but finally figured out how to push and where, and then I came face to face with an imposing band of organized, busy people. "Can I help you?" came the response of a technician who was obviously balancing a full plate of tasks.

I said, "I am Megan Hughes's dad," and she looked at me like I had two heads. I continued, "We just got here from Asheville." Then another tech said, "Oh, they put her in 237." I said, "thank you" and walked away, as if I had any idea where I was going or where room 237 actually was. I followed the walls and the numbers and soon came to 237, and as I went in the door, I was met by an older lady wearing the most colorful sneakers and lab coat I had ever seen. She said, "I am Miss Dorothy, or at least that is what everybody calls me. Who are you? Are you Dad?" And I said, "Yes ma'am."

I knew from the outset who was in charge, and as I looked at Linda, she was grinning—as was Megan. Miss Dorothy told us what we needed to hear. It was an initial, valuable, miniature orientation in less than ten minutes. We had a dozen things to do, and it was already after seven o'clock, and we were late for everything. The doctor had gone home, and Miss Dorothy was rattling off things we needed to know. I knew there was no chance in hell I would remember anything being said, but I nodded my head affirmatively.

Miss Dorothy saw our distress and looked at Megan and said, "Child, have you had anything to eat?" and then she looked to us. I said, "Not since 2:30 this afternoon when we left."

She said, "Well, let me find you something." We explained Megan's dietary limitations, and she indicated that it should not be a problem. "Mom and Dad," she said, "you need to go downstairs to get checked into the dorm apartment next door." Then she asked, "One of y'all staying in here tonight?" I said, "That would be me." She wryly smiled and said, "Not my first rodeo," and we all laughed. She asked Linda and me, "Have y'all had anything to eat?" and I said, "No." "Well, the cafeteria is likely closed," she said. "There is a Chick-fil-a and a Ted's up the street. Y'all go and do what you need. I'll take good care of your girl."

And for whatever reason, my complete lack of trust with almost any other new care provider up to this point was thrown to the trash heap. This was like going to summer youth camp in Kentucky, and we were all there for a common purpose.

I trusted Miss Dorothy from the first moment we met her. She was a complex mix of trained professional, Sunday school teacher, and Mama all in one. She was focused, not much nonsense, but filled with compassion in a very matter-of-fact delivery. She met our needs, understood why we were there, and did everything she could to make us feel welcome given the limitations that an already long day had dumped on us. I liked her and would grow to love her because she would grow to love our Megan and embrace our desire for Megan to "get better."

Linda and I unpacked the truck and got sheets on the two twin beds this two-room apartment had to offer. We contacted Glenn and Sandy, who got checked into the hotel our other friends had offered across town. I then grabbed some "dinner in a box," and that was fine as we nervously began to transition into our new surroundings. We spent a lot of time going over meds and foods and new needs, and these good new friends showed me how to set up a big chair and ottoman that connected to make a pretty fine place to sleep, given the recliners we had used for the last week and a half.

And then Megan began to crash. They found all of her meds except two and would get alternatives for those before the night was over. We explained her "meds in pudding" approach, and they made it work with ease and a positive spirit. This truly wasn't their first rodeo, even though it was ours.

Linda headed back to the apartment with a promise to return early since we knew the assessments of the coming day would be long and arduous, with much paperwork to fill out, much to learn, lots to get to. We had already figured out that things happened pretty quickly down here.

We got Megan ready for bed, brushed her teeth, and she even used the bathroom. She also used an "appropriated" wheelchair to maneuver in her large single room. I then received a two-minute crash course in how to operate the bed and TV and located the schedule for the next day on the massive marker board near the nurse's station, listing the sessions and times for every patient on the ABI (acquired brain injury) floor.

Shower would be at 6:30, and they would be in to give it to her. That would be her first part of the initial assessment, so the occupational therapist would be there to "assess." Then breakfast would be at 7:30 in the gym. That was another "aha!" moment. Gym? Not the cafeteria?

We got Megan in the bed. I then received sheets and a blanket and pillow for the chair, and we watched TV for a few minutes until Miss Dorothy dimmed the lights. And with that we both crashed, completely exhausted.

The nurses checked in about every hour but were not obnoxious about it. Around five o'clock in the morning, our first visit of many from the lab tech happened with vials, needles, and elastic tourniquets along with latex gloves. There was also a blood pressure machine that looked like one they used when my dad had cancer surgery. We would see and hear it every morning as well.

About 6:30, a spunky young woman came in with rain boots on and a whole armload of towels and blankets and said, "Hi, I'm Karla, and I'm here to help you with your shower." Megan's eyes opened, and the prospect of a stand-up shower seemed appealing to her. To date she had been given sponge baths and one shower chair bath. This would be new.

We got her fresh clothes, which consisted of that day's Panther jersey and warm-up pants, underwear, and a sports bra. Karla took us into a huge roll-in shower and used the transfer belt to move "Miss Meg" with skill and ease. She transferred to a shower bench with a long, hand-held spray, and everything was wrapped in towels and blankets. I'll bet we used five blankets and towels, and that would be necessary every morning.

The shower floor was flat, so as water went everywhere, the only thing that corralled it were the blankets and towels, and they also kept Megan from sliding out of the chair. Karla asked Megan questions, tried to engage her, and Megan quickly found a new friend. Karla's spunk and enthusiasm were contagious, and she allowed Megan to try things. When they didn't work, she said, "Don't worry, I'll have you doing that again soon."

Karla was pleased that Linda and I wanted to be a part of the action, and she seemed a little surprised. It wasn't that we were trying to interject ourselves into the process; it was just that we both realized that at some point this would be our new role, so we wanted to know how to do it right. They soon saw how committed Megan's support team truly was. Unfortunately, we also learned that we were the exception and not the rule. We gained the reputation as "the room that kind of runs itself" among our staff team.

The Shepherd Center is special because everyone's first efforts, which are often ugly and painful and harsh, evolve over time. Their efforts help patients develop adaptive strategies that restore lives to immense beauty because of hard work, steady achievements, enhancement of weakened bodies, and the learning and development of new physical skills and methods. The goal isn't always to get back what you had; rather it is the search for what "can be" and the begrudging acceptance of what can't when the facts support that.

In the early days of our journey, I referred to this period as "the hunt for our new normal." Being at Shepherd was part of beginning the discernment process of discovering what can and can't be. That was hard but liberating. Early on, Linda made a comment that still haunts me about the fact that "so much has already been taken from our daughter."

I have struggled with the hard questions of why and how and what isn't coming back. Being the eternal optimist, I never put limits on Megan's rehabilitation. I couldn't. And when we walked into this magnificent place, I knew we were in a place where Megan would have every opportunity to heal, to grow, to find new ways of living, and to remember some old ones. No limits, no conclusions, no preconceived notions of what was possible or not. There was only hard work, long days, focus, and hope—and not one single day when those expectations were unmet.

After Megan's first shower, we began to see that not only was this not the staff's first rodeo, but these people also knew their role and were incredibly good at it. And the day had just begun. Any time a medical professional can deliver hope first thing in the morning is the beginning of a good day.

Soon after shower and meds and getting dressed in her finest Panther wear, we discovered something that would serve us well for the duration of our stay. Apparently, the part of the brain that was keeping Megan from speaking is completely separate from the part of the brain that harbors music, and we are a very musical family. As I was pushing Megan toward the gym for our first morning meal experience, I sensed her fear and quietness, so I broke into song, singing the jingle from an orange juice commercial we had just seen on TV. It's a song from *Singing in the Rain*, and the lyrics are "Good morning, good morning, it's great to stay up late. Good morning, good morning to you." And to my amazement she began singing with me.

I exclaimed, "Hey that was pretty good," and she did her "big voice" guttural "Yeah! Woot, woot, woot!" I couldn't wipe the smile from my face or hers. It made whatever was to come next a little less scary.

We rolled for the first time into a gym that had double doors, a series of tables, and an incredible accumulation of stations and benches, tables and lifts. There was also computerized equipment that looked like something from *Star Wars*. And then there were the people.

We knew no one. Most of these folks had loved ones with them, and many were either in wheelchairs or walkers. Many were severely injured, bandaged or in casts and braces. Others wore helmets. Some wore glasses that had various added attachments limiting view or blocking one eye.

It was an extremely diverse group of folks whose ages covered the gamut, and there were folks older and younger than our Megan. But the thing that was most intimidating and surprising was the fact that we also recognized our own discomfort around these folks, who were significantly challenged by significant illness or injury.

Some were paralyzed. Others were recovering from the same cranial surgery that Megan had barely avoided. It was intimidating to me as a parent, and I could see that Megan was overwhelmed even though she couldn't say so. It was an initial shock and felt troubling, but in retrospect I have no idea what we expected. I can only conclude that as of that moment, we were in denial about the fact that our own child was now a permanent part of that community, as were we.

I am embarrassed and troubled by our discomfort because we as people of faith should be able to accept those who are different from us with love and grace. But what I do know is that this initial shock would eventually turn into amazing respect and empathy for what each person was going through. Each was a child of God, each had a story to tell, and most were far more challenged than what we had faced to that point. We would also soon see that same discomfort from those who encountered us when we went home. But never in that good place. We became community at the Shepherd Center.

Soon a tower of trays showed up, and caregivers went up and retrieved them for their loved ones. Staff distributed the other trays, and meals were time for therapy and staff assessment as well as for getting acquainted.

We realized we didn't have a tray, and a lovely young woman sat down with one and said, "Hi, I am Alexis. I am a speech therapist, and I'm going to do some initial assessments of Megan and how she is eating and drinking, and hopefully we will get her to being able to eat a regular diet. But today we have the pureed stuff." On the tray were oatmeal, applesauce, pudding, and other items that were unrecognizable. I did what I thought I was supposed to do, which in my mind was to get Megan fed.

Wrong! I soon realized that the goal was getting Megan to do for herself instead of us getting good at taking care of her. At this point, we were still not totally sure how much Megan understood, but to this provider that didn't matter. She was determined that Megan be challenged to feed herself as much as she could. The idea was intriguing but difficult for me because I didn't understand our role or how exactly to help her retrain her brain.

Alexis put a spoon in Megan's functioning hand and allowed me to open the applesauce after Megan's unsuccessful attempt. She was able to feed herself but took bites that were too much and resulted in some choking and coughing.

Alexis felt Megan's throat as she swallowed and had her open her mouth to see if she was clearing the thick liquids. She expressed concern and said, "We have a ways to go to get to solid food." That wasn't a surprise, but of course it was disappointing. It set us up a bit for what was to come.

As the day and assessments progressed, the constant, continuous theme was learning how severely our Megan was impaired. What we believed to be cognition was in many cases just lower-level communication and reaction to stimuli.

I am no medical professional, but watching the testing that day, I found it easy to recognize how much Megan was successfully completing and how much she was not. Unfortunately, the latter had many more checkmarks than the former. It once again brought us down low, and I desperately wanted to feel the hope of the day before.

Breakfast transitioned to speech therapy, and Alexis began with flash cards of words and asked Megan what they were. To our amazement, she recognized many and was able to verbalize them if prompted with the initial consonant. There was a process to the exercises, and after each one Alexis made copious notes, so we knew the score was being kept in some form.

That first day, we covered lots of ground and a variety of exercises. Some appeared to give Megan encouragement, but a few quickly reduced her to tears. We figured out that our therapist team was not there to make us feel good; they were there to push and motivate and establish an environment where healing could begin. The moment Megan reached some level of competence, we were off to the next iteration that was harder and more frustrating, but necessary.

The whole team used a common big book filled with exercises and tests that included shape recognition identification and tasks intended to check for vision impairment or even double vision. It seemed to go on and on, and it was obvious that within an hour or so, our Megan was completely exhausted and "over it." We were scheduled for an hour-long break, so we went back to the room and Megan immediately fell asleep.

That hour quickly passed, and we found ourselves having to wake Megan up to get going again. Then it was back to the gym. We spent an hour or so there with our OT from morning shower time. Karla was a ray of sunshine always, particularly those first days. She had her list of tasks to cover as well, and she had Megan respond to basic commands with varying degrees of success. But she made it fun enough that Megan felt comfortable, chuckling at herself a bit for the first time. That was part of Megan's personality before all this.

Karla tested strength and movement in the arm and leg and even in the face. She tried to encourage movement in the limbs that showed no ability to move. All the time, though, she attempted to keep us upbeat and encouraged us with comments about the fact that we are only ten days post stroke, so it was still incredibly early.

As a father, I admit my own angst with every task in which Megan didn't respond or adequately perform, some that perhaps a three-year-old could have done. I confess to a hopelessness that, in my mind, someone of faith shouldn't feel. But at that moment, my mental state was more of feeling that God had abandoned us rather than was interceding on our behalf. It was a lonely, frightening time. Even in a big room full of people, we felt so alone.

The tests ended, and Karla took us to the "cast room," where the OTs and PTs worked their magic making braces and supports. She said, "We need to make a support for her hand that will keep her fingers straight as the 'tone' begins to take over." I said, "Tone? What is that?"

This was the beginning of our education into the longer-term impacts of stroke and how the body behaves.

Karla explained that since Megan's brain wasn't allowing the muscles in her arm to "fire," the body was trying to take over and allow the hand to go to its "prone position," which is like making a fist and pulling her arm close against her body. She explained that our task was to keep everything flexible and working so that as Megan's muscles returned, she could overpower the "tone." Keeping the fingers straight and the hand extended would be desirable.

Karla worked for about thirty minutes, heating polymer and shaping it to fit Megan's hand, complete with Velcro straps that would hold her fingers and wrist extended and straight while she slept. That day, Karla made a brace that Megan continued to use many months later. Her edict was that from now on, Megan should wear this brace most of the time, but particularly at night. Once fitted, Megan seemed content, and we were suddenly aware that lunch was being served.

About that time, our friends Glenn and Sandy Pierce showed up, and what a welcome sight they were.

We got Megan's tray, and once again it was individual servings of gruel with a few bright spots. I knew Megan wasn't likely to touch anything pureed that was green, whether green peas or spinach. That was a non-starter. Pureed ham? Yuck! And then a bright spot: mashed potatoes with gravy.

The spoon didn't stop; she ate every bite of the potatoes. We went to pudding and applesauce, but they weren't as pleasing. Then I realized Megan was using the wrong end of the spoon. When I tried to correct it, she immediately turned it around yet again. I watched in disbelief as she picked up her fork and began feeding herself gravy with it. I smiled at the face she was making, but then I felt the tears rolling down my cheeks as my own emotions took over.

We "declared victory" and took her back to the room for another power nap. As she slept, we had visits from all sorts of hospital folks with forms to complete and lists of meetings and course offerings for family members. The mail got delivered to our room each afternoon, and that first day we discovered that mail even included emails sent to the center. We sat with Glenn and Sandy, who held us up and offered encouragement. But we know our friends and they know us. The quantity of pain and helplessness was enough to go around.

We also got to spend our first moments with Megan's medical team, including her physiatrist, Dr. L. This lovely woman was eloquent, professional, thoughtful, and incredibly compassionate. She assured us of their best efforts and said all the right things to make us more at ease. She explained the process a bit more and how the assessment is used to define a treatment plan and establish an initial discharge date. She told us that once they had done their assessment, we would have a family meeting and discuss goals and longer-term possibilities. And then she was gone.

Our first day was only half over, and at this moment I felt exhausted. Glenn and Sandy brought sandwiches, and we enjoyed a break from what had already been an active morning. But like every day so far, we knew there was so much more to come.

Chapter 12

Assessing Miss Megan

We returned to the gym and met our physical therapist (PT) for the first time: a lovely young woman named Ali. She was petite and athletic looking in her warm-ups. She was relaxed and calm, and said, "Okay, Megan, let's see what you can do."

She used the transfer belt to move Megan into the seat of a stationary bike and strapped her feet to the pedals. "Okay, gal," Ali said, "start pedaling." After a period of adjusting to the seat and pedals, sure enough, Megan rotated the pedals, particularly with her stronger leg. "This will help build the strength in your weaker leg, so we will likely do a lot of this," Ali said. With some newfound hope, Megan said, "Okay."

We moved to other machines that tested strength, flexibility, and muscle control, but not much was there in her right hand, arm, and leg. Megan tried almost anything, but it took a lot of explaining about what was requested of her and how they wanted her to perform. Megan did well with some things, but with others it was as if she didn't understand the request or couldn't make her body comply. She struggled particularly with distinguishing her right and left.

Then to our surprise Ali said, "Okay, Megan, I want to see you walk." I looked at Linda in disbelief, and I think at that moment the PT had our full attention. We rolled Megan's wheelchair to the far side of the room and locked the brakes. In a few minutes, one of the PT interns rolled in a large device that looked like a table with a U cut into it. It had straps and handles and lots of gadgets that could raise or lower it or lock it in place.

They had Megan attempt to stand up inside the U part. They adjusted the table component so that she was standing almost erect.

Her stronger hand held a grip and her weaker hand was strapped to the table using a restraint made of a Velcro-like material. On each side of Megan stood a therapist or intern.

The gym had a number of very short stools with wheels. Shepherd had stringent rules about these stools. Absolutely no one was to sit on them except clinicians or other trained professionals. I admit to having broken that rule early on, at least once, when looking for somewhere to sit for lunch with Megan. I also freely admit that it would have been easy for my big old butt to end up on the floor. It took skill and balance to sit on these, much less sit and roll while holding a patient's leg or ankle or transfer belt as that patient attempted to use severely weakened limbs.

Linda and I sat on one of the training tables with absolute tension in every inch of our bodies. Ali said, "Megan, I want you to stand straight, as straight as you can," and Megan complied. Ali then said, "Alright, now stand on your right leg and take a step forward with your left leg." To our amazement our daughter did take a step, even though it was wobbly, and it was the wrong foot first. But the interns guided her feet to where they wanted her to go. After a few "rewinds," we heard a phrase that would become the norm: "Okay, let's try that again."

Megan put one foot in front of the other for about three steps. It was ugly, and the form was almost frightening, but Megan walked. We noticed that her knee wanted to hyperextend, and her ankle wanted to roll over, but the basic mechanics were in place. "Okay," Ali said, "take a rest for a minute and we will try it again."

They brought in a variety of braces and boots, found one that roughly fit, and strapped it on the weak leg. Megan took it all in, as we did. The professionals did what they do and made lemonade out of some very bitter lemons. With a temporary brace in place, Ali said, "Stand up, Megan, and let's try it again."

Megan steadied herself in the straps of the platform and found that with the weak leg supported, she impulsively took a step forward and then followed that motion with the other leg. She continued what felt natural, with helping hands holding on to her for dear life. Megan took about five steps, almost going halfway across the room.

After a couple of spoken "whoa's," partly from fear and partly from amazement and partly from Megan's blind desire to prove that she could do this, Ali said, "So that's how it's gonna be." She high-fived our little girl for the first of many times to come.

I couldn't stop grinning or shaking. I realized there were tears rolling down my cheeks and my beautiful wife's as well. But these felt good. It was as if a large load had been lifted from our shoulders, even if only for a little while. Hope once more filled our hearts, and we left that place proud, elated, and encouraged that rehabilitation was both possible and under way. We had no idea what was ahead, but we each knew we wanted more of these moments and that the work would be hard, take time, and tire us each day. It was a promising start.

We finished before four o'clock and headed back to the room. We allowed the nursing staff to do their jobs and transfer Megan back into the bed. Not long after her head hit the pillow, Megan was asleep, with HGTV still playing on her TV, as was the daily norm.

A long line of visitors soon made their way in to help acclimate us in everything we could do, the courses to take advantage of as caregivers, and the support groups that could help us deal with our own trauma and personal demons. The Shepherd Center was a "happening place," and there was so much to explore. But to get the most from it, we had to learn. There was much to learn, and we did it quickly and intentionally. We soon began asking staff to help us take on more of the daily tasks of caregiving that we knew we would eventually have to do anyway. The fine nursing staff worked hard to prepare us for even the most basic tasks.

Our first training involved transferring Megan from her wheelchair to the bed, to the toilet, and even to the shower chair. Do it right, and it's a mundane, meaningless daily or hourly action. Do it wrong, and it's a fall or an injured back for the caregiver or, even worse, for the patient. We recognized quickly that these medical folks weren't a bunch of nursemaids cleaning up bedpans or changing soiled linens. Our respect grew each day for these talented men and women.

Within a few days, we were qualified to transfer Megan, to help shower her, and to transport her throughout the building with appropriate sign-ins and sign-outs. I believe in my heart that doing this motivated Megan. To her, it exemplified the promise that we made to her the morning of her stroke. Shepherd's official position is that the families should take time and allow the staff to take care of loved ones. They help train the caregivers later, usually toward the end of the patient's stay.

I suppose we departed from the normal process because we observed that with many of the patients, caregiving was much more basic and much less interactive. Megan was aware and obviously wanted our participation. We were a team of sorts, and she was outwardly attempting to maintain some independence. But for the first time in our lives, we saw doubt in the eyes of this strong young woman. With us at her side, she maintained more of her desire to be strong, and we wanted her to feel at least some level of normal, even though in these days not much felt normal.

And what about the wheelchair? I admit that the wheelchair was initially hard for me to take. We had watched our Megan walk, run, dance, jump, swing, and lift all her adult life. When my daughter and I worked on construction projects during mission trips with our church or around our fixer-upper house, she could outwork me almost every time. She was a physically fit, strong young woman. There was never anything that could keep her down.

One year on a summer high school mission trip, she jumped off a stage the day we got there and twisted her ankle. We spent the night in an emergency room getting treatment for a severely sprained ankle, and she bruised her arms using her crutches because she insisted on getting herself around. Two days later, she strapped on cowgirl boots and danced in a musical production her group had waited months to present to the financially challenged but spiritually rich youth in the coal-mining hills of Kentucky. Megan was and is a tough gal.

So that wheelchair, from day one, took my breath away. No parent wants to see their child in a medical device that they might never be able to leave. It becomes a symbol of what is wrong. I despised the thought of it. I wept bitterly over those initial images in my mind. Then, as only my little girl can do, she said, almost like a child, "Push me, Daddy!" I slowly zigzagged down the hall on the way to breakfast that first morning, and she offered a prophetic "whee" as we went along.

To my surprise, what I saw as "loss" she saw as "gain." The chair meant mobility. There was no more heading for the corner of the bed. As time went on and Megan regained some abilities, she did learn to despise the transfer belt. But she seldom saw the wheelchair as anything other than a means to an end. It was something to be positive about. It was not loss but truly gain.

On our CaringBridge page, I asked the question early on as a person of faith, "Why was it that I couldn't discern whether the glass that represented my daughter's circumstances was half full or half empty?" To me, half empty wasn't good enough. Not only did I miss the portion that was no longer there, but I wanted it back and more.

Unfortunately, sometimes in life it doesn't matter what we want. Even as a person of faith we face challenges that cause us to say, "Where did you go, God? Why did you leave me here all alone?" We have had many of those days. And then a simple "whee!" from my twenty-nine-year-old daughter acting the fool while relegated to rehabilitation two hundred miles from home caused me to notice that God is right here. God is lifting us up, holding us when we can't hold ourselves, and giving us the simple strength to step forward when our broken hearts tell us to fall into a wretched mass of tears and cry "foul."

Megan knew she had work to do, and more than anything she was going to get there one way or another. All we could do was go along for the ride and help where we could. More importantly, we were learning the lesson that this precious child of God had her own developing plans to teach us.

About six that afternoon, Glenn and Sandy said, "Get out of here. Go get dinner, and we will stay with Meh." "Meh" is Glenn's nickname for Megan. Megan has always called Glenn "Glee," and they have a special relationship. We didn't argue, venturing out to Ted's and enjoying a fine sit-down meal. As we returned, we ordered Megan a milkshake to celebrate a good first day. What I didn't realize was that this would begin a daily tradition that would last the six weeks or so that we were in Atlanta. Megan grew to love an evening milkshake, and we enjoyed the joy she expressed in taking the first sips from each one.

Starting our work on a Friday was a mixed blessing. It was an exhausting first day, and the presence of friends made it much less lonely. But we found out that weekends at Shepherd are boring. There wasn't much to do since therapy was only half days on Saturday. Sundays were truly a day of rest. We figured out that exploring the lumbering facility could fill a lot of time and found creative ways to wander.

We spent that first weekend trying to make sure we had what we needed, including clothes and supplies for Megan. We had many visits of an administrative nature, including a required financial meeting with an adviser who helped us make sense of the many resources available to help us navigate this journey. Shepherd helps families with their applications for disability, financial assistance, and other available financial resources. I spent several hours filling out additional paperwork and getting more information about our daughter's work history and financial data to include in these submissions.

Since Megan lived on her own, she had her own insurance and was considered an adult with her own rights, insurance coverages, and obligations. We learned early on that unless we agreed to be responsible for her obligations, we were not legally obligated for her care. In making decisions about care and available resources, this is a significant issue to parents of adult patients. We wanted to limit the negative financial impact of catastrophic illness, so we learned to consult with financial and legal resources early in the process to discern how to get the best treatment we could with the resources we had available. Doing this may keep you from making decisions based on emotion and fear rather than reason and thoughtful planning. Most care providers offer such counseling as part of their services. We strongly encourage anyone going through this to take advantage of those options.

We spent as much time as we could with Glenn and Sandy because we knew that come Sunday, we would send them back to Asheville and spend the next week alone in our new normal. That was incredibly hard during the first full week.

On Sunday we spent the morning watching *Flea Market Flip* on HGTV, and the quiet and stillness of the day, apart from the mind-numbing sounds of the TV, forced us to relax a bit. Stillness in a time of distress is not always a good thing. Your mind runs wild, and sometimes it goes places you wish it didn't.

This day I pondered what was going on at home, in church, with our friends, and with our family. I went down the list yet again about how right now we *should* be . . . dressing for church; attending Bible study; singing in choir; eating lunch with Jeffrey and Brannon. It was surreal and melancholy.

I hooked up my computer and found a network. I went to our church's website, and for the first time we sat and watched the previous week's service, which we had missed as well. It was good to see the people we love and who love us. We had church two hundred miles away. It was warm and emotional and uplifting and heartbreaking all at once. It was what we needed to keep us grounded and looking forward.

That afternoon, Glenn and Sandy came by, and we sent them on their way back to Asheville with tears and jitters. It was like taking the safety net away from the high-wire act. The lump in the throat just wouldn't go away. But again, it was what had to happen. It made us take control one more time and allowed us to anticipate the next time we would have friends and family among us.

As a believer, I found that my faith gave me the charge to seek God and rely on his strength even when circumstances made us feel so vulnerable. The reality is that knowing what your faith calls you to do and being able to do it are often separate things. Over time I began to realize that God and I had some talking to do, because I still didn't understand this whole thing, and to be honest, I was still angry. In fact, I was angry with God.

How could God let something like this happen to those who love him so much? It made no sense. What I eventually figured out is that those who claim God's promises do not have any assurance that bad things won't happen. Claiming God's promises does allow us the assurance that no matter what comes our way, God is there with us, loving us, interceding for us, lifting us up even when everything around us pulls us down.

In these first days post stroke, I must admit that the gift from the Almighty that I sought the most wasn't healing or miraculous intervention. It was simply peace. The turmoil and change caused by any catastrophic illness transforms what surrounds us to something we do not want and cannot accept. The limitations of mortal humans do not afford us the control to restore or change our situations.

For those who believe, the simple restoration of peace allows us to accept that this is still only the beginning of a journey, and whether it results in a reality anything like the life we had before, it is enough. At some level, faith means having to accept the new reality a change imposes on our family. To me, knowing that God was still God was also knowing that although I was angry, I knew in my heart that this would be okay at some point. Having gotten through the initial time when we believed we could have lost our little girl at any moment, we now recognized that we would be content with whatever adjustments we needed to make so that Megan could have a meaningful life. While I would love to suggest that at this moment, I had resolved my fears and accepted whatever was to come, that is not true. The glass still wasn't full, and I wasn't ready to let God off that easy.

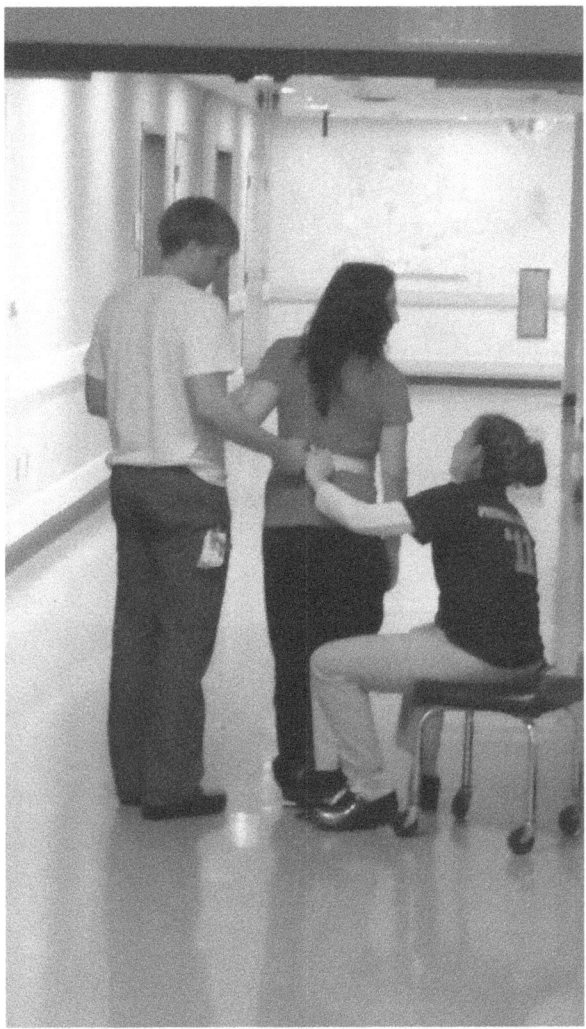

After time and work, Megan began the daily grind of taking steps under the watchful eye of her therapists. Gradually she learned to walk with a supporting brace.

Chapter 13

Quashing Hope

Monday morning came early, and after someone came by to take blood before the sun even stirred, our new friend Karla showed up again to begin our training in shower-ology. The cutest thing that I still love to this day is that she was wearing brightly colored rain boots. We watched and helped and observed and questioned, and at the end of the session, Megan was showered and dressed, with teeth brushed, hair dried, Panther wear on, and the "good morning" song sung yet again.

With meals and meds behind us, we began with a visit from the good doctor that was a little more in depth and evaluative. This time we were told what the week held and what the assessment process looked like. We found out that the entire team treating Megan would meet every Wednesday morning, so no therapy sessions would happen then. We were also told that we were invited to a planning meeting with the team on Thursday morning to lay out our daughter's treatment plan, set expectations, and establish a planned discharge date.

Discharge date. Wow. We often mark our lives with signposts of significant events. Sixteenth birthday, first date, high school graduation, college graduation . . . who would have thought "discharge date" would be one of those? But at this moment, that term had a particularly important meaning that was both something to celebrate and something to dread. To get to that date would signify an immense amount of work, and given the pace at which things were happening, we had no idea how far off that date was. In talking with those around us, most rehab inpatient stays were often between two and four weeks. I felt four weeks would be more likely, but after what we had seen in the first days, I was beginning to believe these folks truly could work miracles.

The next two exhausting days consisted of battery after battery of tests. Everything from PT and OT testing of specific muscle use that involved Megan's entire right side as well as how strong her left side was. They had her using a pencil with her left hand. She played balloon badminton with her left hand to assess balance and eye-hand coordination. There were all types of eye tests to check for clarity, double vision—which is common with stroke—and all sorts of other vision issues. Thankfully those results seemed positive even though Megan had some lazy-eye issues that made focusing a challenge in fast-moving visual exercises.

Then there was speech therapy. I was realizing that our speech therapist was a tough cookie. She pushed hard. There was a book that included individual tests for vision, reading, and multitasking. One had six images of the same shape drawn with single lines, and a single shape would have a subtle difference from the others. I swear that after fifty of them I couldn't tell the difference. This part was hard and heartbreaking. My lovely daughter, who had a master's degree, struggled with almost every page. More maddening was the fact that she knew she was missing them, and it changed her stoicism to emotional strain. She showed signs of being more aware of her circumstances than I had thought.

I again admit freely that when we arrived at Shepherd, I had little idea of just how much was left in her precious brain. The CT scans and all the other tests had left me worrying that coming back from this wasn't about twenty-eight days but much longer. As time went on, Megan reengaged with those around her and became quite good at "fitting in" to her surroundings, limited verbal skills and all.

These first days were creating a trap of sorts where just seeing her attempt things and getting a few tests right offered hope and the uneasy sense of progress. That directly contradicted the notes we had seen as part of her discharge documentation from Mission. Their staff neurologist had written something close to "global expression and cognition impairment caused by stroke." My flesh still crawls every time I recall that diagnosis. I initially thought, "My God, Megan will be an invalid for the rest of her life."

These momentary glimpses at "function" gave me hope. At that point, we grasped for any lifeline that God sent our way. In my layperson's perspective, any improvement was worth celebrating, but that hope would soon be challenged one more time.

On Wednesday morning, the team completed their initial assessment. Megan took a well-deserved rest after breakfast and settled into what seemed like a never-ending "binge watch" of HGTV. We were getting to be on a first-name basis with Chip and Joanna Gaines and the Property Brothers. I love do-it-yourself projects, including anything that involves a hammer. I'm willing to try most anything, and I think I have pretty good skills for an accountant. One of my close friends is a contractor by trade, and when my skills are lacking, he and his crew come and bail me out. Those times prove humbling when he takes apart something I (may) have done and says, "Well, that isn't to code; who did this?" I have yet to claim some of it, but I suspect he knows exactly who did it.

That afternoon the team emerged, and we did PT, OT, and speech. I knew our team had knowledge we didn't have, but I also saw that they were now initiating specific actions. We began working toward certain goals in earnest, and that afternoon they put Megan's leg in a cast.

I did not understand, so our PT explained that the cast would support the leg that had no muscle tone or function and would help her as she built the muscles in her weak right side. She also explained that after a few days they would remove the cast and it would become a substitute brace that she would sleep in along with the hand brace she already had been given. The rule was that if she wasn't in therapy or the shower, they wanted her in this brace, which would keep her foot at the proper angle and bend. It would also provide support for walking. After a while, it became heavy and uncomfortable, but Megan tolerated it with an occasional roll of her eyes.

Speech therapy started with a bang and focused on drawing out more words from her troubled brain. To my discomfort, it was quickly made clear that the prompting I had learned in Asheville was not helpful. No one wants to see their adult child struggle with basic language. I admit to trying too hard to help her communicate by doing way too much speaking for her. I also admit that Alexis, our speech therapist, had my number, and she wasn't afraid to yank my chain, sometimes to the point of ruffling my feathers.

Outside of the sessions, I recognized just how much Megan had begun to depend on her mom and particularly me to speak for her, so I learned to do my best to be quiet. Alexis was tough but encouraging. She said it was important to allow Megan to struggle to speak but not to despair. That took time, and since Megan's expression of emotion was almost stoic, it was hard to figure out when to chime in.

That time came quickly when, to our surprise, she completely melted down in anger and embarrassment one afternoon. It was hard to watch but welcome and precious because as she wept tears of despair, so did her therapist. They hugged, and Alexis promised Megan it would get better and easier as she healed and that she would support her all the way back. That was one of several breakthrough moments we experienced in this high and holy place.

We soon learned another new technical term: *aphasia*. Aphasia is a disorder that affects how you communicate. It can impact your speech as well as the way you write and understand both spoken and written language. Aphasia usually happens suddenly after a stroke or a head injury. But it can also come on gradually from a slow-growing brain tumor or a disease that causes progressive, permanent damage (degenerative). The severity of aphasia depends on several things, including the cause and extent of the brain damage.

The main treatment for aphasia involves treating the condition that causes it, as well as speech and language therapy. The person with aphasia relearns and practices language skills and learns to use other ways to communicate. Family members can participate in the process, helping the person communicate. Often patients struggle for words, but they know exactly what they want to say. It is incredibly frustrating for the patient and the caregivers. At this point, Megan had expressive aphasia as well as some receptive aphasia. She struggled to understand what she was being told and then couldn't respond with what she wanted to say.

The following morning would be our big meeting with Dr. L, Megan's case manager, and the physician's assistant John. We dropped

Megan off in her therapist's care and went into a large conference room, where we were soon joined by our executive team. My stomach was turning flips, and I hoped no one would see how badly my hands were shaking. I had never been that nervous before.

Dr. L is one of those people who presents herself as an incredible technician and amazingly skilled clinician, but her manner is always calm and reassuring. She began by telling us about the process and who had been involved in the decisions. She told us the types of things they had considered, the kinds of tests, and how we would see many of them again as things progressed.

She first told us that as with every patient, they had established an initial discharge date, and our date would be March 23, 2016. I had expected a stay of twenty-eight days or so, and that was significantly longer. She said that would be the inpatient portion of Megan's treatment. She then explained that they would probably recommend an additional eight weeks of outpatient intensive therapy through their Pathways Program. I did the math, and that meant we might not get back home before mid-May. Wow.

I admit that the prospect of being away from home for over three months was a kick in the groin. We were already aware that we were alone and a long way from home. We missed our family, our friends, our jobs and clients, and our church. It was a daunting thought, but that wasn't the hardest part.

After telling us what treatment would look like, Dr. L said, "We do our best for every patient who comes our way, and no two are the same. We are very good at what we do, but we do not make empty promises because that isn't fair to anyone. The diagnosis you received in Asheville is a hard one, and your daughter's stroke was very severe. Our initial assessments support the results the doctors up there reached, and really, we are not sure how much we may be able to help Megan. We concur that she has significant cognitive impairment as well as the expressive limitations. We typically can have a good impact on the expressive part, but with limitations on the cognitive part, it is much harder."

My wife and I gathered our crushed spirits and even protested a bit. "What about the progress we're seeing? What about her expanding vocabulary and her ability to walk with assistance?"

Dr. L's response was that they believed she had the ability to learn and to imitate, but they were not sure how much was "higher-level" brain function. Once again, the air seemed to be gone from the room. It was like a B-grade movie where the hero rescues the heroine from drowning, but after incredible efforts and CPR the victim still doesn't awaken. We were once again on the bottom floor, and the elevator doors were tightly shut.

But then Dr. L pushed the elevator call button and the doors opened just a wee bit when she said, "Listen, I know this is hard to hear, and you folks have already been through so much, but here at the Shepherd Center we believe in prayer and in faith. We know there is much to do and much we don't yet know. But we promise to pray for your family every day, and we promise to use our best efforts to help your daughter."

Baby steps.

We left the room with a plan that was too long, results that could not be assured, doubts about what lay ahead, fear out of our minds, hearts that were still broken, and questions about where God was and whether he even cared. That old familiar lump in the throat and the burning around the eyes came quickly back. By the time we entered Megan's room, we had to put it all on the shelf and regain our composure so we could make plans for how to finish out the day.

It was not until later that night that Linda and I had a moment to talk about what we had heard. Like so much of the other bad news over the last couple of weeks, this was different from what we thought we knew. In Asheville, our neurologist had said that he believed Megan would be an excellent candidate for rehabilitation. What had changed?

In my mind, I could only say that after fourteen days, I knew in my heart of hearts that we had seen Megan begin the trip back. It could not be all imitation and reflex. I know my daughter. I knew she was fighting like hell. I knew she was so over this, all of it. I could see in her eyes that she was still there, that she was struggling to connect, to find her way back, and I knew that she had taken those initial steps.

I stopped being mad with God. I looked heavenward and said a favorite line from a conversation Keanu Reeves has with God in the movie *Constantine*: "I could use a little help here."

We decided that for now, Megan's prognosis was something we could not control, but we could help direct her treatment. We would continue to advocate, support, and see what happened. We would exercise faith. We would pray. We would go forward and look for hope and whatever healing God sent our way. Even if we didn't get back all that was lost, we would get all there was to get. And it would be enough. It would have to be.

Chapter 14

Being Right

While telling this story, periodically I must withdraw from the struggle and try to identify the lessons learned. When I was a kid, my parents expected the daily communication of, "This is what I learned at school today, Mama." Experiencing life events that are this hard, this intense, and this profound only fulfills an intangible benefit if you have the courage and take the time to peel back the onion layers to see what is at the core. Sometimes that is the hardest part to do.

So that the harsh realities will not rob us of any small shreds of sanity that still exist, we should and must try to make sense of it all. Emotionally, none of it makes sense, so my faith is often where I go to silence the "noise" of fear and struggle, treatment and rehabilitation, restoration and hope. "What is" may not be what we want, but "what was" may no longer be possible.

I've mentioned before that often those closest to us do not always have the words, or at least the "right" words, to encourage fractured souls. Their hearts are pure, and their motives are true, but what comes out of their mouths is often a mess.

One such exchange occurred on our first overnight trip home. This opportunity opened due to the kindness of friends and family who came to stay with Megan over the weekend so Linda and I might take care of some things back home. The trip allowed us to visit our church and those closest to us, at least for one Sunday service. It was an incredible blessing with a hint of an excruciating curse. We got to embrace friends, catch up, and listen to good teaching and theology. Those hours allowed us to take a break from our new reality for a short time.

More importantly and more painfully, we were allowed access to the people, souls, and personas that meant the most to us and ministered the hardest and best to us. These relationships are both family in fact and family in faith. They know our circumstance and they know who we are. On that first visit home, all of them were desperate for a recent "word." "How is she? How are you? What can we do? What do you need?" The questions ran together, and the answers and stories were repetitious and almost became rote as we regurgitated responses, almost on demand.

But occasionally, the pain of our friends' minds bubbled up and over. Often, they asked their own most painful and fearful questions. Many times, those questions were almost overwhelming. One conversation involved one of our dearest longtime friends whose service to our church is almost storied. He is educated, both classically and theologically. He is compassionate and kind and has a heart of gold. But on that day his words unintentionally left me bewildered and wounded. His question was filled with concern. His own pain was particularly blunt. He said in a roundabout way, "You and Linda have been through so much, and Megan, I cannot imagine what she has been through. But, Scott, will she ever be 'right' again?"

I was momentarily stunned. I choked up on my response. I simply did not know what to say or how to answer. What in the hell does that even mean? *Right?* How much improvement does she have to make to be categorized as "right"? I think I mumbled something about how much she had improved and the significant progress we had already seen. I tried to assure him that we had great hopes for recovery. There was no denying, though, that our daughter had a significant stroke, and there was much we did not know at that early moment.

I walked away from my friend pricked to the core, saddened, and simply amazed at the blunt inquiry. His comment raised questions that I could not stand trying to answer. One side of me felt that the exchange was terribly insensitive, but my other, more pragmatic side made his question my own. My heart again ached as it had so much up until this moment.

I spent the three and a half hours on the trip back to Atlanta quiet and reflective and honestly a mess, which was not unusual during these days. Questions about what the future looked like were almost "off limits" at this juncture. The reason was simply that I was fearful of the possibilities being raised, particularly after Megan's diagnosis.

The unspoken questions were, "What if he is right? What if our Megan cannot ever be 'right' again?"

Hope plays such a large part in keeping one sane when insanity takes the reality of illness to its conclusion. For us, reality was that we were not sure our lives would ever be the same. I must confess that over the days before and since, I have not known for certain how far back Megan can truly come. Does that mean she is not *right*?

Will a lifetime fighting aphasia mean she is not right? Is she capable of full recovery? And will the improvement we see stay long-term? God, I hope so. But there are times when I have my doubts.

The words of Dr. L's initial assessment haunted us yet again. It is not fair. But I cannot change it except to help fight it, whatever that means. If I live another twenty-five years, if my daughter needs me to, we will continue that fight to get her life back for as long as she cares to fight.

Another dear friend who lived in our shoes for years before our newfound circumstance told us gently and kindly that our search should not be for what was but for that new normal. She offered the idea that before all this happened, we had been on a journey, and before this cursed series of events, we were on the way to Paris. But because of the events of February 2, 2016, we had to change our plans, and now it looked like we were headed toward Venice. It was not the same. It was not what we planned for. It looked very different from Paris, but that was okay because, as she said, "I hear Venice is nice this time of year."

For some reason, that metaphor spoke truth to me. The life we had planned, the benchmarks we expected, and the professional and personal hopes we had for our little girl, all grown up, were now changed. The direction of her life and ours would take a different path. That was not open to discussion or negotiation. Our new journey would require us to repack the car, buy fresh maps, and go through places we had never traveled. But we would eventually arrive at a destination that had the potential to be good.

In our lives there is so much we cannot control. For an accountant who is an admitted control freak, that reality is difficult. But when a medical crisis or some other emergency happens, our best use of time and circumstances is to spend them looking for progress. We change what we can, and then we trust the balance to the Almighty. If you have the courage and the ability to trust, God will take some of your burden from you. You will have to force yourself to lay that burden aside sometimes, even if only temporarily. There will be no easy answers, and some days the problems will seem insurmountable.

On those difficult days, fix what you can, plan for what you can't fix, look for other options that might make things better than they currently are, and then pray about everything else.

There are no guarantees, but to be brutally honest, like our dear friend's inquiry, even if Megan will not be "right" in his eyes, she is still my eldest child, my precious girl, my very dear friend. I am proud of her beyond words, and she is worthy of our best efforts to make her life better than it currently is.

It is simply too damned early to draw conclusions about the promise of her future. To do so excludes the gifts from our faith and the possibilities from a loving God. We will fight on, and if Venice is where we end up, then that will be just fine.

Another extremely hard question that sometimes comes up is, "Did we do something to deserve this?"

Oh my.

This one is likely to hit you and those around you first thing.

Even in the crisis of significant illness, we all seem to need someone to blame. Believe me, I have spent hundreds of sleepless nights trying to grapple with "What could we have done differently? Could this have been diagnosed? If we had only _____ (fill in the blank)." Then it is easy to morph that question into one that seems "convenient" for people of faith. "Are we being punished?"

I hate the thought that somehow our God could choose to seek vengeance for sin by allowing ill to come to one most dear to me. I cannot reconcile that thought to my faith. Earlier I introduced you to my pastor and friend Guy Sayles, who is my age and says the things I often wish I were smart enough to know or think of. He has an amazing mind, a bright spirit, and an incredible intellect. He is also fighting his own extended illness of multiple myeloma. I know that his thoughts about illness and trouble in life comfort me because of his deep, abiding faith in a God of love and forgiveness—a faith we share.

The week before we traveled from Atlanta back to Asheville, Guy posted on his blog *At the Intersection* an incredible consideration of God's role in our hard times. These are his words, but they fit our story and encouraged our faith, so I must share them.[2]

> Jesus taught his followers to acknowledge that the earth does not yet fully flourish under God's gracious rule of justice and peace and to pray that it will. He invited us to join him in his longing for everyone and everything to live in the joy of God's loving ways. The Lord's Prayer makes it clear that God's will is not always done.
>
> Often, people express views about God's will which strike me as fatalism—sometimes an oddly and blithely optimistic fatalism—rather than free faith. They almost thoughtlessly assume that if something happens, it is because God wanted it to happen.
>
> After I was diagnosed with Multiple Myeloma, an acquaintance said to me: "God knows you are strong enough to bear this cancer and give him glory through it." Really? What kind of God singles out people for misery in order to gain ersatz glory?
>
> It's too simple, and it leaves us with a God whom Jesus would not have served and did not reveal, if we say that whatever happens must have been God's will.
>
> "Thy kingdom come," we pray because it hasn't completely arrived. "Thy will be done," we plead, because it often isn't.
>
> I often call to mind this straightforward testimony from Madeleine L'Engle, reflecting on the illness of her husband, the actor Hugh Franklin:
>
>> I do not have to make the repulsive theological error of feeling that I have to see cancer as God's will for my husband. I do not want anything to do with that kind of God. Cancer is not God's

---

2. See Guy Sayles, "God's Will?" *At the Intersection*, March 17, 2016, https://fromtheintersection.org/2016-3-17-gods-will/.

will. The death of a child is not God's will. The deaths from automobile accidents during a long holiday weekend are not God's will. I would rather have no God at all than that kind of punitive God. Tragedies are consequences of human actions, and the only God worth believing in does not cause the tragedies but lovingly comes into the anguish with us. (*The Two-Part Invention*, p. 172)

God's will isn't always done, because, in part, God does not rule by force and fear but by persuasion and love. God knows everything which can be known, but God does not know in a way that abrogates freedom, either the freedom of creation or of human beings. There are some things which are contingent and not yet known, even by God.

Such freedom means that terrible things happen, things God does not intend, and which break God's heart. God suffers along with us. It's impossible to say that God was in Christ and to think that God does not suffer.

God's power is the power of the cross, of suffering and redeeming love. God works ceaselessly to bring everything and everyone to the reconciliation, wholeness, and joy which are God's will. God will not stop offering us the kingdom until God has persuaded us to live in the shalom it promises.

I know far less than I used to know about God's will, but I will trust that Paul was right to say: "I am convinced that neither death, nor life, nor angels, nor rulers, nor things present, nor things to come, nor powers, nor height, nor depth, nor anything else in all creation, will be able to separate us from the love of God in Christ Jesus our Lord" [Rom 8:38-39].

No separation. I cling to that promise.

This process of living through an event that changes your life profoundly offers few absolutes, but the one thing I have gathered and held close through all of this is the knowledge that someone else has walked these steps before us. So, if you look hard enough and long enough, there are supportive words and knowledge available to you that will provide comfort if you take time to search.

I have not asked my friend if our shared health experiences of those days influenced such a timely offering of hope and comfort.

But I do know that it is important as you walk this lonesome road to consider those around you and their experiences. We all hurt from time to time, and shared experiences equip us to withstand the dark shadow cast across our lives when trouble comes. More importantly, shared comfort also helps us find glimmers of light that may yet shine once again.

I can never repay my friend Guy for these words that meant so much to me in those days of terror, but they have become a foundational block of my faith and give me a view of faith that matters—one that will bring me courage as long as this journey goes on.

Chapter 15

The Caregiver

Around this time, Linda and I took on a new title, one we never expected or wanted, one that never gets bestowed with a great deal of pomp or circumstance: "caregiver." We share that title with millions of other folks who acquired it in much the same way.

Even so, anyone with kids or aging parents knows that this title is usually a rite of passage. It signals a significant change in our lives. We have somehow transitioned to a new phase. To quote a friend, "From this point, nothing is likely to ever be the same again." We enter a new normal.

One of the significant takeaways from our time at the Shepherd Center is their perspective that in treating stroke or brain injury or spinal cord injury or multiple sclerosis, you treat not only the patient but also the whole family. Their strategic belief is that treating a patient, for whatever duration their team identifies, only gets you to discharge. What happens after that? If they sent us home without an expectation of what we were facing in our new title and role, they would have somehow failed the patient and the family. Part of their overall process is intentional, specific, continuous, detailed training of families focused on dealing with the new normal, including how to address our own pain and feelings as well as how to care for our loved one. No two cases are alike, so it is always very individualized.

One of the observations that meant so much to me was that many of the staff and volunteers we met had been patients at Shepherd. There is something disingenuous about someone who has never experienced stroke or other illness trying to tell a patient, or their family, how to "go on."

Being around patients who have suffered stroke does qualify, in my mind, as having "experienced" stroke. It's impossible to think of the precious care and gifts that we received in Atlanta and not appreciate the fact that each person who gave Megan and our family that "care" already personally understood our journey. They understood our feelings. They understood just how overwhelming this experience was.

Having said that, I admit that there were folks who intentionally pushed our buttons from time to time. That was an important part of our education. That first week or so, we had the opportunity to join and participate in caregiver discussion groups. We went in expecting to have one of the saddest stories there. We left feeling almost guilty for having it so good. We became aware of our own privilege as well. Many of these folks didn't have the option of choosing to be next to their loved ones as we did. Many had to work, to take care of other family members, to allocate their time when their hearts called them to be here. They had to make hard choices, and many were stressed and stretched emotionally, psychologically, and financially.

Shared experiences quickly touched our sense of empathy and concern and restored a long-standing commitment we have always tried to live out through caring for our neighbors. In "Jesus talk," it is what I refer to as being the hands and feet of God, loving others as ourselves and sharing the love of Christ. It was healing, but difficult healing because every family caregiver had their own challenges and fears. Like us, they had their own feelings of inadequacy, their own doubts about their ability to do what lay ahead.

We were all trying to balance living from moment to moment, trying to support our loved one, and face the fact that our own reality had completely changed. How do we take care of our businesses from two hundred miles away? How will we pay the bills that are accumulating? How do we keep people informed? How do we take care of our other family members back home? How do we cover all the bases without going completely nuts? There was an obvious inequity as well because some of us had resources and support that others did not have, yet we tried to find ways to encourage and hold each other up, particularly in our conversations during non-therapy times.

Several family care group meetings were organized and moderated by a facility chaplain who let people tell their own stories. The intent was to share our feelings and take something back to our rooms that might get us through the next few days. Each family was experiencing dynamic changes in real time.

Linda and I went the first few times the meeting was offered. We listened and participated. It became apparent that one of the key issues we all were dealing with was the dark, painful, sometimes explosive anger over the issues and circumstances that had befallen us. That anger was specific to our individual experience, but we found that its existence was common to every family there, and everyone dealt with it differently.

On one day, a single mother with a son who had ridden his motorcycle into the side of a truck that pulled out in front of him really "went off" on the people I mentioned earlier—the folks who feel led to minister to you but who do not know what to say or how to say it. She was upset over someone who had said to her, in an effort to be encouraging, that she was "strong." That she needed to be strong for her son and family, and there would be time to deal with her own feelings after things settled down and he was better.

To my surprise, most of the rest of the group chimed in with their own lists of things folks had said to them that had also upset them. There was an immense amount of anger in that room. But I truly doubt it was all because someone who was simply trying to help had said something completely insensitive. We all carried this circumstantial anger for different reasons.

The chaplain suggested that we should perhaps "call out" the people who had said stupid stuff and caused hurt feelings. They needed to understand that they had caused us pain. I was amazed to a degree that we all had similar experiences and that we all felt wronged somehow, but I was a bit at odds with the group about how to respond. I expressed my feeling that I could not call out someone who had taken time from their own family, job, or life so that they could minister to my family. I felt like they deserved a "pass" even when what they said or did hadn't helped.

As I said earlier, I had experienced these same feelings from the other perspective many times because, when we go to visit someone who is struggling, for whatever reason, we all have the misconception that we need to leave these targets of our empathy with something—something profound or thoughtful or uplifting or even encouraging.

Now, having been on both sides of this experience, I have grown in my appreciation of those I call "true friends." True friends come and stay, sit with us, meet needs, listen compassionately, tell us that they love us, and give hugs. But most importantly, they come again. I want to be that kind of friend.

I will never again tell someone that God has a plan, or that they are strong and must help others be strong, or that God never gives us more than we can handle (my least favorite). I will do what my best friends did for me. I will go, sit, hold a hand, take cookies or a snack, share a meal, tell them I love them, and just be there—and I will mean it all. Then I will go again. That is what matters.

We decided to reduce our involvement in the family support group and instead focused on learning how to care for Megan. The self-examination did have a benefit, and we found that our anger subsided, and our sense of hope was somewhat restored. But we decided our time at Shepherd needed to be more about Megan, and we allowed our purpose to become our passion.

We all must deal with our own pain and grief in ways that allow us to be a caregiver. Sometimes it is awkward, but the goal in those moments and days is simply to get through the hard part. Often the crisis does not pass quickly. The new normal will come in time, but you cannot force it. Parts of it you will hate. But parts of it will remind you of how things were and will give you enough hope that life is still precious, even though forever changed. It will take time to be comfortable, but at some point, it will happen. As the crisis passes, so does the chaos.

The weekend after the initial assessment meeting, we had several visits from family and friends. The gifts of encouragement and support were a tonic, a bit like Christmas and birthdays all together. One of the first folks to spend the weekend with us was Megan's former roommate and best friend, Jenny Lee. When Jenny rolled in on Friday evening, she and Megan locked eyes almost immediately. There was a connection that convinced me that every word Jenny said "stuck." Jenny said that the old Megan was "in there" because in the Asheville hospital Megan had "booped" Jenny's nose as she left, just as she had done hundreds of times before the stroke.

This time, there was less of the silliness that filled our mornings or got us through the times of exhaustion or helped pass the day between therapies; this was an incredible exchange between two friends. There was excitement, there was an exchange of ideas, there was communication, and, yes, a good bit of it was going one way. But there was reaction and there was emotion and there was joy.

I know what the doctor said, but this convinced me that my Megan was in there. Her brain was functioning at a high level, at least at times, because Jenny was talking about life and prior shared experiences. Megan's broken words had expressions and joy but also inquiries. I am not a neurologist. Hell, I do not even play one on TV. But I know what I see, and what I saw was interaction at a high level. Not imitation. Not reflection. Not impaired cognition. Megan was there, and they were having a conversation with an obvious connection between close friends. It was most present in those first weeks with her closest friends who traveled down on weekends, or during visits with her cousins who graciously took time off from family and jobs and stayed with us for a week at a time.

From that point, we made every effort to add to the therapies a constant ongoing interaction between Megan and many of her friends and coworkers who would and could participate. The socialization that was helping her heal shouldn't have surprised us. Sometimes it is the obvious that makes us whole again. It does not happen overnight, and certainly not even quickly, but it made for obvious progress. Baby steps.

About a week after we got to Shepherd, the mail delivery volunteer dropped by and brought a long, tan envelope. The label had unmistakable blue lettering, and I immediately saw "Carolina Panthers," so I said, "Look here, Meggie, you have mail from your team!" Her eyes lit up. She grabbed the package, looked at the label, and said, "Open it!"

I carefully opened the end of the envelope, and as I dumped the contents out on the bed, her smile, crooked and damaged as it was, lit up the room. Inside was a bright blue Panthers long-sleeve shirt, Panthers socks, a hat, a lanyard, a keychain, signed pictures of Cam Newton and a couple of other players, and several additional mementos of Megan's beloved team.

I checked inside the envelope to make sure I had gotten everything out, and to my surprise and pleasure a sheet of Panthers letterhead fell out. Megan yelled, "Read it!"

It started out "Dear Megan," and it contained a two-paragraph letter of encouragement and support that let Megan know one of her friends had shared about her love of the team. As a result, the Panthers organization took the time to send our little girl good words of encouragement and hope, complete with the predictable last sentence: "Keep Pounding, Megan!" It was signed by Coach Ron Rivera.

We were speechless. There was no better gift that Megan could have been given at that moment and at that place. It was dated the Monday after the team's crushing defeat in the Super Bowl.

We later found out that a close friend, Luann Nelson, had called the Panthers organization and asked what was possible. Mike and LuAnn were already invested in our care through providing rooms in their fine hotel in the Atlanta area for folks who came to visit on weekends. These were and are true friends, and their act of kindness provided a few hours of complete joy during a time in which very little joy had been present for our precious child. Megan smiled her crooked smile for hours, holding each item close and trying to comment on the significance of each.

I know that NFL teams support their communities and fans as best they can and often in amazing ways. I also know that controversies make many folks think less of these highly paid athletes. But if I live to be a hundred, I will always be a Panthers fan. They did not have to do this, but again that one simple act of kindness lifted us outside of the moment and reminded even my little girl that acts of kindness are appreciated and meaningful and healing. Megan did not take off that shirt for three days. The pictures went up on the wall immediately, and the letter sat on her nightstand for all the weeks we were there.

Continuing a theme, her Uncle Bud had rubber wristbands made to share with all who cared to wear them that said, "Keep Pounding, Megan." We wear them to this day.

As time moves on, the symbols of what you have endured begin to become more important because each gives physical evidence of the journey you have traveled. Each of us needs to remember where we came from. The purpose is to simply evidence this minor accomplishment over an adversary that initially had won and won big. Over time, we have begun to wear the beast down. Each achievement, each accomplishment, each simple gift that brings comfort and hope allows us a short, well-deserved moment of celebration. Marking that time allows us to revisit it when the next hurdle we face may also be kicking our proverbial asses.

I have used the analogy of a somehow "new" normal. None of us wants that new normal. In fact, even on the best days, all the trail marks along the way can easily be forgotten. That causes us to return to just how much this whole event sucks, to use my daughter's word. I have often wondered if our momentary celebrations are not window dressing for some weakened thresholds of what an acceptable alternative to "what was" might be. A negotiated settlement, in business terms. If this is our new normal, I still want more. I want it back—all of it.

I often allow my mind and my anger to challenge the periodic gratitude I have felt as I realize that the stroke won't take Megan's life. If I am realistic, the stroke has done exactly that; it just didn't take it all. So I bark like a frightened dog, yapping weakly at the Almighty, but it's wasted effort. Still, it's an acknowledgment that through my pain and frustration and anger, I still recognize who is in control.

In more lucid moments, I still worship and praise and bow humbly to this enormous source of strength. God takes it. I am not sure why, but I am convinced that every word is heard. God listens. And in the far reaches of my mind, God weeps softly and tenderly, as one of God's children suffers in this angry wind and as we endure our own personal Gethsemane.

Megan displayed no anger at that point. In fact, her deepest emotions lasted only moments. An occasional snippet of a sentence began with, "I want "or "Why did?" And suddenly it stopped as soon as it started. Unable to complete that sentence or thought, she moved on.

I still wish for her to engage that sweet release of anger expressed, frustration voiced, pain released. But it slips silently away and quickly falls into the deep recesses of her mind. Soon it is replaced with what is next. In those moments, I am grateful to God that her torment, at least right now, is less or of shorter duration and does not seem to linger. Either her damaged brain or her incredibly positive soul, with the blessed help of antidepressants and mood-enhancing medicines, allows her to look forward, boldly ahead, working hard every day and then collapsing into a late afternoon nap that often lasts until supper. Exhaustion.

Quite honestly, for most of these days, the torment falls to Mom, Dad, family, and friends. Constant concerns include the fears of the financial effects, the questions of "How do we adjust?" and "How can we support the ongoing cost and effort this event will exact on our wallets, our minds, our souls?" The nights allow sleep only in fits and starts, and we often awake to anxious minds that cannot relax and knowing that the punishment on an aging body will one day exact its own price. Then that still, small voice somehow comes through, as if on cue, recalling the words of a dear friend still challenging me to "Look only at today. Let the other days take care of themselves." Good advice, but still far outside my nature and much easier said than done.

Chapter 16

All Therapy All the Time

Fridays were particularly special at the Shepherd Center—reserved for field day, trips, or other special activities for patients who were far enough along to benefit and learn and enjoy. Activities sometimes included going to a restaurant with other patients and therapists to practice "real life," ordering from a menu for the first time since the illness or injury, and trips to the aquarium or the mall. The staff were intentional about building in activities that were not only therapeutic but also fun. It's hard enough for a person to work through difficult tasks that were once easy. For those who know what they have lost or at least are missing, it is particularly hard, and that is where I had concluded our Megan was. While I know that her team still was not sure where she lived cognitively, we continued to see more and more of our old gal. Morning showers were filled with songs, complete with lyrics we had not thought of in years. Sunday school songs with gestures, barbershop songs that she had heard my quartet sing when she was a child, and songs from current artists whose words she could spout off when she couldn't even ask for a hairbrush.

Often during her therapy sessions, she was asked to respond to basic commands and point at the brush or touch the house, and her responses were completely wrong. Linda and I went to every session trying to learn enough to help by supplementing her work. It was troubling, but from time to time we saw improvements. They were slow and hard won, but they were wins nonetheless. Over time, her therapists began to remark on her progress. Megan was making great progress in PT and OT. She enjoyed walking again, even with the aid of a walker or cane. She was engaged and almost curious at her own progress. But along with that progress came a new concern.

One of the most important principles of care at this good place is the need to make sure patients are safe. With Megan's driven, overachiever personality, she was prone to impulsivity, which is common with any brain injury. It's like the typical parts of our brains that keep us from taking chances or acting without considering risks are turned off. Her desire to please and her willingness to try anything new make her at risk for falling, tripping, or otherwise getting hurt, so places like Shepherd have to be particularly careful not to allow headstrong patients like our Megan to injure themselves. They try to work with the patient and their families to draw attention to each process and intentional, planned action. Sometimes that isn't best for a patient's safety. Those who don't practice "safety first" can usually expect to deal with restraints or belts or other types of activity-limiting devices.

One of the reasons I knew Megan was more aware than she was getting credit for was her reaction to attempts to restrict her movements, whether in bed or in her wheelchair or anywhere else. She did not like it. As parents, neither did we. I understood the need to restrict people who were unattended or unaware of their surroundings, but in our case, I challenged staff and management over the need for restraints—mainly because when they were used, it was crushing to the glimmers of hope we had begun to see in Megan. Further, we were with her almost every moment of every day. I requested an informal meeting to discuss the policy and their unwillingness to consider her signs of depression and anxiety over restraints, at least to us.

After conversation and evaluation, our team agreed that while she was in our direct care, we had the choice of whether to use the restraints or not. Don't get me wrong; if we had ever seen her put herself in a position of possibly getting injured, I would have used those restraints without question. But as long as she played by the rules, I wanted to see if we could motivate her toward desirable actions when it came to the restraints.

We told her that the restraints were there to keep her safe and that we would have a say as to their use when we were with her. But we also said if she took unnecessary risks, she would have to use them. Although we had several more singular disagreements over those confounded straps, we never had to put them on Megan unless she was outside of our care, which was almost never. We did split hairs a couple of nights with one wonderful but particularly intense nurse who interpreted the order in a way that, even when I was in the room with Megan at night in my convertible chair, if I drifted off to sleep, he felt that he was to snap her belts. Yes, I did lose it a little when I awakened, and yes, we did have an additional conversation. But most importantly, Megan remained safe.

As time progressed, the Wednesday meetings of the team to discuss progress and treatment options became something to look forward to rather than something to fear. Successes became more apparent, and treatment was quickly altered to accommodate them. The most significant progress was in the area of speech and the ability to graduate from pureed foods to solid foods. While Megan could swallow, she still had some weakness, and it put her at risk of choking or taking fluid into her lungs.

Our speech therapist met with us almost every lunch meal and tried to get Megan to alter how she chewed and swallowed. She had to add a step to clear the weak side of her mouth of unswallowed food. Finally, the day came when she said, "Let's try some solids. I'll start with a sandwich. What kind would you like?" Megan said, "Ham and cheese," and at the next lunch meal she tried her luck with solid food. To her delight, after a lot of helpful instruction and encouragement, Megan ate the whole sandwich, chewing each bite many more times than she normally would and then washing it down with a cup of water, a few sips after each bite. Her therapist critiqued every bite and almost every chew, but Megan learned, and soon her mechanics were in much better form. Success!

It was the beginning of something else that felt a bit more normal. It wasn't without setbacks, but the simple process of feeding herself added one more piece of the puzzle to putting our little girl back together, and she also seemed to feel like she was making progress, for which we were all incredibly grateful. But the truth is that our speech therapist worked with Megan for more than a week, watching her take every bite and struggling with whether this was best for her. Like so many other things, we needed Megan to be able to eat solid foods, but there was still doubt about whether her throat and swallowing were strong enough to support this level of activity. In this situation, Megan finally got to the point that Alexis believed she could safely eat a limited solid diet, which meant no food that is typically difficult to swallow such as potato chips, popcorn, and raw vegetables. Megan can be a picky eater even now. Part of the dieting she had done just before the stroke had set her in motion to limit certain foods, and the stroke did not seem to change that.

Megan had sandwiches, chopped fruits, and some cooked vegetables, but her salvation continued to be Frosted Flakes, pudding, and her mainstay, mashed potatoes. We have a family joke that still comes around each holiday about the "old family recipe" for our mashed potatoes. Linda's family lives for mashed potatoes. No fancy casseroles or Brussels sprouts allowed, so no need to even try. Not having mashed potatoes at any family gathering is a travesty. And thank God, a stroke did not significantly alter that in this little child of God. Bring them on! Add the butter and gravy too.

Meals became something to look forward to once again, particularly as we began to earn privileges that might take Megan away from the trays brought to the gym each morning, noon, and night. The Shepherd Center had a marvelous cafeteria on the ground floor, and once she was cleared for solid foods, we took Megan with us for some of our meals. Often that meant she shared a piece of Boston cream pie or mashed potatoes when the tray that day didn't have any. These momentary pitstops in our nonstop life of "all therapy all the time" soon became something simple that brought release, comfort, and a hint of things normal. Those moments make the journey tolerable, and these were the first glimpses of a return to the life we had and the life that we longed for.

One of the most challenging aspects of rehabilitation in any circumstance is the will of the patient to recover. Often that is connected to a patient's simple "capacity" to recover. But in our circumstances, which involved a highly productive, highly motivated patient with significant impairment of her physical and cognitive ability, it became apparent that the patient was becoming painfully aware of what she had lost.

This is the curse of stroke. Megan was aware of her lost communication capabilities, and that was the most painful realization for her. That came early in her rehabilitation. A secondary event that accompanied that realization was the uncertainty of proper execution of what she was being asked to perform.

Before this event, Megan was as confident and self-assured as any twenty-nine-year-old professional. In a matter of four short weeks, this extrovert with a master's degree was showing signs of a lack of confidence, particularly when it came to speech. Many times, there was sheer panic on her face when she was asked a question she wanted to answer but couldn't. Stroke or brain injury often tricks the brain into allowing the victim to think they are responding in one way, yet another area of the brain might substitute the word they want to say with something totally different.

A perfect example is the fact that once Megan was able to call me "Dad" and Linda "Mom," almost immediately she often called me "Mom" and Linda "Dad." She would soon catch herself, and with a touch of embarrassment she would self-correct. We built a joke in which when she did that, we would call her by her brother's name "Jeffrey." We all would get a good laugh. But her misuse of names continues to this day.

Aphasia is an evil nemesis that tricks the brain and often causes its victim to freeze up, particularly when the person wants to say something important. Megan usually knew what she wanted to say; she simply couldn't initiate the first words of the sentence. Soon the struggle to get that darn word out was replaced with an almost sigh and then an attempt at changing the subject when the word wouldn't come.

Confidence.

How can you even begin to be confident when you cannot trust your own brain to function? Before the stroke, there was no more confident person in my life than Megan, at least about most things. And now, only four weeks later, she looked to me in panic when the words would not come. Her eyes begged for a prompt, a word she just couldn't reach, a thought she already had but could not convey. What could we do? Even if I didn't spend time grieving over the realities of her new evolving normal, the fact that my best efforts to help might not be beneficial was overwhelming.

The takeaway is that when confronted with circumstances that don't provide an obvious option, you must do what brings comfort, provides support, and encourages hope . . . for both the patient and you. None of this comes easily, naturally, or even organically. As you transition through the stages of recovery and rehabilitation, the professionals know what they are talking about. In most cases, patients of stroke will not recall all the details that obviously fill the minds of their caregivers.

Megan still asks us to recall in detail the days we spent at Mission Hospital and Shepherd Center. Those days are not part of her permanent memory except to the degree we have shared. And she has a constant, expanding need to understand all the events she survived and the complex nature of her parents' painful experience, at least to the limits we are willing to share. For whatever reason, those stories bring her comfort and a sense of accomplishment. Hope from despair.

As therapy continued day by day, week by week, we began to figure out that having something to look forward to is a great motivator and mind occupier. We enjoyed those Friday trips. As time progressed, the discomfort we initially felt with the numerous injuries of the folks around us dissipated, and we began to intentionally develop relationships. It made therapy more fun and allowed for regular, friendly competition. Those sessions often transitioned into socialization activities, both with patients and their families.

One afternoon, the Shepherd Center and a local bank sponsored a riverboat casino event. The patients were given chips to use in games that met their fancy. There were slot machines and bingo, blackjack, and dozens of games of chance. Brain injury usually doesn't entirely take away the joy of winning, whatever that looks like. At this event, everyone could win at something, and the prizes were shirts and cups and other treasures from the Shepherd Center. The prizes were nice, but the winning was the real benefit. It was a time of joy and fun, with friends of all shapes and types of injuries playing in one place.

It offered escape for a little while at the end of an already hard day of therapy.

The other consequence was that games that used math, choices, reading, or decisions challenged damaged and healing minds. It didn't take long to see that the ABI (acquired brain injury) patients soon dropped like flies, Megan included, and the spinal cord injury patients gambled on. That afternoon, Megan was asleep in her wheelchair before we left the third floor. We had to wake her up to get her into her bed. She was exhausted. But for the most part it had been a very good day.

On a Saturday about two weeks before we would head back to the mountains, we were told that we would have a special visitor who was a part of the whole Shepherd family. Over time, we had become aware that no one leaves the Shepherd Center unchanged or unbeholden to this magnificent place. It truly is a place where lives are changed, and an important part of the culture there is to encourage all who come their way to give back when they are able.

One facet of that experience is a "peer" program they have established that matches patients with a peer whose experience and injury are remarkably similar. Such was the case when we received our visitor that Saturday morning. We were introduced to a lovely, tall, slender African American woman who had also survived a stroke at the ripe old age of twenty-nine.

This elegant lady introduced herself and explained the purpose of her visit. "The rule is that there are no rules," she said. "I am here to answer your questions, to tell you my story, and then you can ask me anything you like. Nothing is off limits. The only rule is that I also can ask you anything I want as well." Touché.

Over the next three hours, we listened intently and painfully as we heard a story so similar to ours that it was eerie—a similar stroke; the same area of the brain; the same initial result; and the same painful journey. But I swear, to hear her speak I would have never known she had had a stroke. She was an attorney at a large firm in Atlanta and a litigator on top of that. She was a communicator just like Megan. She was now ten years post stroke and had made a remarkable recovery.

After she told us her story, she said, "Okay, now you can ask me anything." Megan to that point had been spellbound. She looked at me and raised her eyebrows as if to say, "Dad, you know what I want to know, and I thought I did. What I didn't know was just how painful what we would hear would be."

I said, "Okay, so how long was it before you went back to work, how long before you could drive, how long before you could live independently?" She said, "I drove for the first time after seventeen months. I went back to work in about twenty-four months. I was able to live independently after a little over a year because I had a close friend who moved in with me here so that I could be close to Shepherd and my therapy, and that was an amazing gift." Then she added, "And the fact is they were all way too soon."

I asked the obvious question: "Why?" She replied, "Because I was not ready. I changed jobs three times in two years. I lost well over half of my friends, and I was scared to death to drive in the city."

She then launched into words difficult to take in but so important for Megan to hear. "I changed jobs because frankly I was not who I had been. I was one of the firm's lead litigators. I was good at what I did, but the aphasia made me anxious to be in front of a courtroom, and I struggled for words, which impacted my effectiveness. I lost my friends because, again, I was not who I had been. Many of my friends were less comfortable around me, and, quite frankly, when you do therapy almost all day, who wants to go out at night? It's exhausting. Dating was impossible. My stamina was severely impacted. I was too tired to have a social life. It was hard.

"But over time things changed, and I began making some new friends. I went back to my old firm, and they reinvented my old position to allow me to prepare cases for court, to train the attorneys to try the cases, and I did all the work that I loved. I still go into trials, but I don't have to face a jury or a judge unless I want to. It isn't the life I had, and I have given up a lot, but I love my life now, and Megan over time you will too."

This lovely child of thirty-nine said all I wish I had known and all my precious daughter needed to hear. She told her that the friends she would lose were not really her friends to begin with. She said that for the near future, the best use of Megan's time would be getting better instead of trying to force a life that isn't complete.

We shared wonderful conversations from about nine in the morning until well after noon, and when the words began to slow, we expressed our profound gratitude. As she gathered her jacket, I asked a last question that I almost wish I hadn't, but now I am glad that I did.

I asked, "So how long did it take you to master your aphasia?" She turned to me and almost chuckled as she said, "Mr. Hughes, no one ever 'masters' aphasia. Over the last three hours I have literally had to fight for every word."

My jaw had to have almost touched the ground. I stammered, "Well, I have to tell you that if I hadn't known better, I would never have known you were struggling or that you had ever had a stroke." She said, "You are very kind, but I have worked hard to get where I am. It isn't what I was before the stroke, but it's good."

Knowing that these events had put us in a place where finding hope to move forward was a challenge, this visit from such a precious person was timely and so important to our journey. It was an emotional rollercoaster made up of a large dose of encouragement tempered with a significant helping of reality. She spoke of her faith. She spoke of her friends and her family, of her parents and their support. And she took a certain amount of well-deserved pride in how far she had progressed. But my gratitude will always follow this young woman because of her own encouragement, nose to nose with our daughter, when she said, "I love my life now, and, Megan, you will too."

Chapter 17

Zero Gravity

Day after day of walking was resulting in a distinct increase in physical stamina. Megan was regularly making laps around the ABI unit, which was no small task. It was amazing to consider that a few weeks before she couldn't even stand on her weak leg. While her efforts involved an increasing degree of impulsivity, which usually isn't a good thing, her PT Ali was with her for each step and each lap. Ali sat on one of the "off-limits" rolling stools. But the way she manipulated it and was able to use her hands and body to form Megan's leg and gait was impressive. It was now becoming important that each step was uniform, the same as the last. This task was hard, partly because it involved a sometimes out-of-control patient whose impatience at recovery was becoming an issue and partly because Megan was so strong on her good side that she could easily overpower her caregivers.

As her strength improved, her consistency and gait were a challenge as she took more steps each week. The answer was a new toy, an incredible device. We went to the third floor and got our opportunity to use what was referred to as a zero-gravity treadmill. These huge devices stood ten feet tall and were large enough to hold a wheelchair. Before Megan got on, they always took her blood pressure and then strapped on a canvas and Kevlar cradle that she could pull on like a pair of shorts. The straps and Velcro tethered her in place firmly and snuggly. Straps with hitches were attached to the treadmill, and she would stand as if supported by a crane. The device had hydraulic lifts that raised her to the point where her body was suspended over the treadmill. The operator of a computer console could control how much pressure her body put down onto the treadmill.

It took five people to run this thing. One ran the computer, two sat in chairs molded into the device that allowed them to hold her leg and foot to assure the proper mechanics. One person stood behind her with hands on her transfer belt at all times, and one person was the captain who made decisions about speed, pressure, length of treatment, and changes to gait. As the machine made its first turn, you could not have wiped the smile off my daughter's face with eighty-grit sandpaper. She was in heaven.

This machine allowed Megan to put one foot in front of the other almost as perfectly as she had done before the stroke. As the techs helped form her weak foot and leg for each step, for the next hour Megan walked. She first walked very slowly and methodically. Then, as her repetitions became more of her own doing, the controller gradually increased the speed. Megan said over and over again "faster," and the staff was quick to respond just to see what she could do.

She took step after step, each one bringing a smile that was a bit crooked but firmly affixed. Over time, the suspension above the platform took its toll, so a break allowed her to relax for a moment. But she would have none of any extended break; she was having too much fun. The more steps she took the more normal she felt . . . until she came back down to earth.

The exhaustion of weak muscles reminded her of how far she still had to go. As the first attempt ended, the melancholy of reality took her spirit a bit as her newfound friend and operator helped her take the cradle off and again took her blood pressure. She stepped into her wheelchair and enthusiastically asked, "When to back?" ("When can I come back?"). Her new friend said, "As soon as we can get you scheduled."

We were becoming increasingly aware that our inpatient time at Shepherd would soon end. Based on our discharge date, we only had a couple of weeks left, and I was becoming aware of the marvelous devices and technicians and rooms that we had not yet visited. I knew there were other things that would perhaps help Megan, so we were constantly talking to our team about treatment and therapies that might have a positive impact. That is one of the best parts of our time there: no two days were entirely the same.

We were allowed and encouraged to try different therapies to see what worked and what Megan found enjoyable. She was more motivated than some of her peers; with most of the brain injury patients we met, there was a significant absence of any real joy, and part of that was likely due to which part of the brain was injured. But rehabilitation is hard work, wrapped in layers of fear and laced with anger and even sadness. It is difficult to overcome the overwhelming sense of loss and the pain of the absence of what was. Each person fights as hard as they can each day, but even with all that effort, words won't come, limbs won't move, memories are hard to recall, and sadness can permeate not only the patient but also those who love and care for them.

In this place of hope and challenge, fear and loss, pain and suffering, only as treatment progresses did the state of transition and hope begin to return for us. Some days it presented as the calm after the storm. No jumping for joy, only a few moments of calm and relief, but welcome nonetheless. With some days it was a beautiful occasional moment of hope or release.

Shepherd uses creative activities to bring restoration. For instance, every board game ever made lives there in Atlanta. Board games use different parts of the brain, and initially some are challenging. But over time, many of the patients progress in ways that can be seen in waiting areas and break rooms as they play card games or board games with math components or simple matching games of colors or faces. While we were there, families enjoyed occasional nontreatment hours through sharing games and activities. Smiles returned to people who hadn't experienced moments of joy in weeks or months. The holes of each psyche were gradually filled with the newness of shared joy and hope. As short periods of success and accomplishment brought well-deserved encouragement, each caregiver had respite from issues that dragged them down and looked forward to the times of gladness delivered by simple activities and games.

Megan had darker moments, but most days she was the exception. From shortly after arriving, her disposition was able to find some *joy*, even though it was sometimes uncontrolled, pure, unadulterated happiness at the prospect of getting better. Early in our time there, she exclaimed with great intention to her Uncle Bud, "I just have to get better!"

Once treatment began to deliver results, most mornings were a time of happiness and relief. The songs of shower time carried us through the morning. The activities of therapy brought distraction, new abilities, and thoughts of restoration. The visits from friends and coworkers reconnected relationships that had been interrupted by the confusion and pain and torment of her brain injury. Megan eventually became the "little Sally Sunshine" of the ABI ward.

She looked forward to most days, her excitement became infectious. Her PT Ali always had her exercise or walk to music, and often it was Pitbull. (I admit that before this time I had no idea such an artist existed.) While constant therapy and those songs motivated her activity, Megan drove our role in supporting her.

The things with the biggest impact were also the things that were most enjoyable to do. I'll bet we played fifty hands of UNO each week. Megan's disposition stayed positive, and most days she smiled through any physical activity. The only thing we tracked more than her smiles were her bowel movements. In a post-stroke environment, regularity dictates everything.

One evening her dear friend JD stopped by to check on her, and after a couple of hours of TV and her milkshake, Megan's favorite nurse came in and exclaimed, "Alright, Missy, you ain't gone in four days, so I brought you a suppository," at which JD jumped up, grabbed his jacket in a dead run, and said, "I gotta go! See you." We laughed for days.

Even initial difficult days of speech therapy became easier as progress grew more obvious. Of all the things I am grateful for, and there are so very many, I am most grateful for the sweet disposition of this precious child of God that made our rehab process bearable. I am not certain I could have gotten through it if she had withdrawn into something more sullen or distant. Megan's ability to smile, laugh, and sing served her well and continues to do so.

One friend wrote in a card that Megan's "indomitable spirit" kept her and all around her clearly focused on why she was there and what she was trying to accomplish. God granted us mercy, and for that we were so incredibly blessed.

I say all of this to make the point that brain injury patients often take their lead from those around them and those closest to them. In our case, if we were positive, Megan was likely to be positive. If we were negative, well, you can imagine. Our number one job was to keep her mentally alert, thankful for her progress, and hopeful for much more. Motivation and positive presence can make even hard days more bearable. That original advice from my dear friend still applied: live in the moment, positively, hopefully, and, when possible, joyfully.

Joy helps because the process of recovery and rehabilitation can be damned hard. An example is that we could never lose sight of just how severely injured some of the other patients were. One morning we were focused hard on therapy. Megan was giving it her best, when quietly and softly a technician stopped our machine and said, "We need you guys to take a break, perhaps down this hallway a bit. We have patient who is having some difficulty, and we need to give them a little space."

A young man had stopped breathing, and a number of staff moved quickly toward his aid. Those familiar words that we heard sometimes twice daily came over the speakers—"code rabbit"—and then the room number. It was always repeated three times, and each time it made us aware that rehab for those most injured isn't just inconvenient; it can be life threatening. We were always amazed at how professional and supportive the staff were. Over time, we all learned to care and be concerned for patients and families around us who shared this common experience.

There were no easy journeys in this place, but the holy work of healing was performed with style and grace. There was nothing cold or institutional about it. I have never doubted some of our doctor's first words that proclaimed the Shepherd Center as a "place of prayer, faith, and hope." I know that institutional medicine may find a desired result, but this place massaged a broken soul as well as a broken body.

One morning our occupational therapist was working with a severely injured young man, and I looked over at her as we waited for our therapy session to begin. She looked at me and said in almost a giggle, "He just spoke to me. I've worked with him for days, and he just spoke." It was then that I detected the tear that she wiped from her own cheek. The joy she shared in that moment made me aware that in doing this kind of work, these good people sometimes get the opportunity to hear a person's first words. And as the events of the other morning had showed us, it is also possible that they may hear a person's last words. It could be both blessing and curse. But how wonderful it would be to come to work and be allowed to see miracles as they occur. There was also something miraculous about our own journey in this place.

The physical work of rehabilitation requires people of special skill and compassion and even faith. It is difficult. We were so blessed to have such a wonderful team for those weeks. We will forever hold them in a special part of our memories, and they will always be important to us. Our lives were changed and made better because of their gifts and encouragement, and we can never repay that kindness.

Chapter 18

Discharge Day

The anticipated date for Megan's discharge was March 23, and it had been our target for some time. We had made plans based on that date. But then her insurer decided that she had progressed so quickly that she didn't need to be "inpatient" any longer. They issued a "termination of benefits" notice two weeks early, saying they would end coverage that day!

Of course, we freaked a little bit. "Where will we go?" What about completing our caregiver training, which was to be a key area of focus during those last two weeks? It was a "Yoda" moment: "Luke, your training you must still complete." Fortunately for us, though, the folks at Shepherd know how this game works. They requested a peer-to-peer conference to discuss the issue. (Our doctor had both an MD and a JD next to her name. These days that comes in handy for her and for us.)

Our case manager indicated that we would likely be able to complete our original course of treatment, although it was remotely possible that we could end up going home early if the conference was not successful. We made the hard decision that we would plan to return to Asheville, whenever that would be, and continue therapy at home with CarePartners and other private providers. This was almost as difficult as the decision to come here in the first place. Our experience had been so profoundly positive and hopeful that now we dreaded that it was ending.

The possibility of going home was also an answer to prayer, and we were excited but terrified. It was the right decision for Megan and for us. She had said more than once over the last few weeks, "I want to go home!" Selfishly, Linda and I shared the same desire. Emotionally, socially, therapeutically, and every other way, we agreed it was time to go home, and with God's guidance it would happen soon.

The transition would take time, and with the patience of Megan and our friends, we would need grace to reintegrate a bit.

Visits and a parade of well-wishers and phone calls would need to wait until Megan's therapies and routine could be established. Food and casseroles were not what we/she needed right then. We needed space. We needed room to get back in town and take a breath. That would be the best gift for now. She still had so much work to do, and that would take time to set up. But we knew without doubt that seeing people again would be healing and welcome as the situation evolved.

Another of the many curses of events like this is the whole realm of continuously changing emotions that patients and care providers face. Those emotions are usually wrapped up in the larger issues of cause and anger, justice and fairness, loss and vulnerability, and the simple and complex queries of why and how this could have occurred.

Why now, why this? My realization has become that through all of this, there comes a time when the human spirit turns to the only thing it can do: try to improve the situation. From the perspective of a patient's family, what "was" is the standard for the definition of normal. But "what was" can seldom be totally achieved. Unfortunately, "what was" is now unattainable, at least to some degree, so decisions about where to spend our energy in trying to effect change are always the harder course.

I had wanted my daughter to be able to speak again, and now she could. It didn't sound exactly as it did six weeks before, but I was amazed and thankful, and we gave praise and gratitude for this accomplishment and gift because when we started, we had lost that.

I had wanted my daughter to be able to walk again, and now she could. It didn't look exactly as it did six weeks before, but I was amazed and thankful, and I knew it would get better still. But for now, we gave praise and were grateful for this gift.

I had wanted my daughter not to have to go through this horrific event and would have given anything to swap places with her, but the stroke happened to our daughter. It is hers to bear. We are a part of the journey, but the journey is hers. All we can do and have done and will do is to try to help, as have so many of our family's friends.

For every gift, every offering of love and support, every effort to help in whatever form, we were and are grateful. Megan is grateful. The emotions of the initial part of this journey were intense and painful, but the results of the help and support and love of others bridged us to what came next, and that was the goal. It didn't look exactly as it did six weeks before, but we were amazed and thankful, and we gave praise and gratitude for each accomplishment and gift.

When we arrived in Atlanta on February 11, our baseline was that Megan could only say "yes," had no movement in her right arm and leg, had trouble swallowing even pureed foods, and exhibited evidence of significant impairment of her cognitive ability to understand her situation, her circumstances, or her environment.

The folks at the Shepherd Center surrounded our family with a focus on love, support, safety, and a desire to help us discern what the future might hold for our eldest child. Our primary doctor didn't sugarcoat the situation; they could only promise their best care and therapies, and even then, the hopes of complete recovery were unlikely if not unrealistic. That initial diagnosis would be hard for any parent to hear. But even in delivering that hard news, our humble, mild-mannered physician told us that at the Shepherd Center, they believed in faith and hope and would pray for us.

In the days after that, our assigned team began working and started attacking the damage one area, one therapy, one session at a time—and almost immediately we began to see improvements. Our team included some of the most amazing young people I have been privileged to be around in my life.

Megan's physical therapist challenged her to walk almost immediately, but walking wasn't enough; she needed to do it well, correctly, intentionally, and safely.

Her occupational therapist challenged her to expect not to simply exist but to live well. She used every tool in the bag to get results, worked on making hard things easier, and urged us not to focus on what Megan would have to give up but rather to expect her to do more, to work harder, and to get every benefit of therapy.

Her speech therapist knew that she had the hardest task, and she embraced it. She challenged Megan to attack even when the frustration became overwhelming and ended in tears and anger and a shaken fist. As the barriers weakened and words became easier (not easy but easier), she allowed Megan a glimpse that with hard work, the upward potential had few limits. It was and is a factor of time and effort, but isn't life that way anyway?

Even those only tacitly involved in Megan's care offered encouragement and hope, and each minor victory was and is acknowledged and celebrated. Her nurses kept her healthy, medicated, clean, nourished, and rested. And they all kept Linda and me sane. The Shepherd way includes one part compassion, one part hard work, one part innovative processes, one part encouragement and hope, and one large part faith. As a result, Megan's words appeared from nowhere one by one, movement slowly returned to her leg and lately to her arm, despair turned to hope, depression changed to expression, and the promise of restoration became a possibility that we continued to embrace as we transitioned back to Asheville.

There is no way to be prepared for this kind of shift in life, yet if we are all honest, this type of change happens more regularly than any of us are comfortable with. But the fact is when it happens to you, it is only natural to throw every tool at your disposal toward the problem. Many of the choices each family must make are based on limited knowledge, advice from others, and to be totally honest, simple faith.

There was no way we could have known our experience at the Shepherd Center would be as positive as it turned out to be. Most people facing significant illness struggle to make even the most basic decisions. And remember, we did not get back to where we were before the stroke after six weeks, six months, or even longer. But when we first started, so much had been taken from us. We were not sure that our lives would ever regain any remote sense of rehabilitation. In those earliest days, our neurologist in Asheville spoke words of truth that were also hard to hear: "If she were fifteen years older, we would be talking about which long-term care facility we would be moving her to. The bad news is she is twenty-nine (because of what she has lost). The good news is that she is twenty-nine (because of what she can relearn)."

We traveled to Atlanta, and we put our best into our time there. The Shepherd Center returned the investment we made with interest that we couldn't have imagined. Many times, I had used the analogy of the glass being half empty or half full. I had said in those first days that I wanted the other half of the glass back. Now this place, with Megan's hard work and a good and compassionate God, was sending us home with our glass restored, though not with familiar content. What was taken is now replaced with promise, potential, and hope. That will be enough for now.

For weeks, we had watched as most of the patients with whom we entered Shepherd graduated from the program. Each departure date was accompanied by a recognition program at breakfast that usually included the person's team saying something about their journey and accomplishments and even what would come next. And for weeks, I had dreamed of what Megan's life would look like from outside the battlefront.

On March 23, after a breakfast of Frosted Flakes, her entourage of supporters and therapists gathered around her and us. Each caregiver spoke kind words of accomplishment and support. For about ten minutes as I scanned each face and listened to each word, it became obvious to me that these folks also struggle with the "disconnect" that medical providers are supposed to maintain. They were addressing family instead of a patient, and it was precious and affirming. Quite honestly, the emotion and love expressed to my daughter and our whole family that morning will stay with us forever.

The tears that each person shed expressed affection for Megan and were acknowledgment and affirmation of how much she had touched their lives, whether through hard work and pushing through difficult tasks or simply the goofy morning songs that helped uplift each person, even on days they perhaps had not looked forward to. Our daughter had touched their lives, and we know what that feels like.

So that day, March 23, 2016, we took home with us the developed love of good people whose gifts to us can never be repaid, whose compassion is administered to each person who comes their way like an elixir of miracle drugs, and whose lives were perhaps made better in some way by crossing paths with our precious twenty-nine-year-old. And for dear Megan, each moment of therapy, each word of encouragement, each goal set and reached made each person we met there a friend, deserving of our heartfelt appreciation and love.

Chapter 19

The Power of Prayer?

"I am praying for you. You are in my thoughts and prayers."

One of the more surreal parts of our journey is the fact that, for more than two years, hundreds if not thousands of friends, coworkers, and even people we do not know well have professed to be praying for us. To be honest, part of that fact makes me uncomfortable.

In those first days, it was said so often that it lost some of the intended impact and encouragement. I wouldn't let it have its intended effect at providing this very tormented, concerned, angry, devastated soul with the intended measure of divine comfort. Through those first days, moments, and hours, I had trouble seeing that I wasn't alone. I could not grasp that God was there, running interference and truly loving us through our own personal hell.

Being the stubborn, type A personality that I am, I wouldn't drop my defenses long enough to let in the offer of support, faith, and encouragement. I blew right past each offer or claim of prayer on our behalf because it was somehow contrary to my perception of our circumstance and was an acknowledgment of the seriousness of our plight.

Some of the most poignant moments involving offered prayers took place on the first day. I have already mentioned my friend Guy Sayles, who prayed over my sweet daughter late on that first afternoon. He said, "Megan, you are a child of God, and God is giving you everything you need to live the life that God wants you to live."

Later that night, another preacher friend, Buddy Corbin, visited our room and Megan's bedside no less than four or five times. His words of comfort and encouragement and simple friendship gave me hope on a night that felt hopeless. I will never know the words that he raised to the Almighty on more than one occasion that night, as my child's life hung in the balance. But knowing Buddy, I also know that there was great respect and reverence as he interceded on our behalf on that difficult day.

My prayers that day were shorter, raw, and pointed. I begged. I pleaded. I searched for words that would not come easily or reverently. I thought *I* had to fix this. I couldn't trust God to be in control; I had to be in control. I was in some kind of damage-control mode, barking commands and working on problems. I didn't have time to specifically deal with God and my faith in any depth. I was busy and panicked. And as I have said before, in those first days I was mad at God.

This is not supposed to happen to the faithful. Except for the death of my father many years before, I had tried to focus on the process and practice of being "salt and light, hands and feet." I hadn't been or wanted to be on the receiving side of thoughts and prayers in recent years.

It is much easier for me to minister to others than it is to accept the help of people ministering to me. I attribute that to a "service"-focused upbringing and my mental manipulation of Scripture, particularly when it comes to lifting troubling parts of Scripture out of the Bible and using them in ways that were never intended. A loose interpretation of Matthew 6:5 says effectively that if in doing good you receive the acknowledgment or praise of those around you, then you have received all the benefit that you are entitled to receive for that act of kindness. You got the credit for your action—as if the motivation for my actions was somehow like "banking" poker chips.

In my troubled mind and soul, I had connected the dots (incorrectly) and felt that to accept the love and concern of those around me was somehow wrong. The strong in Christ should not need support, I thought. We should not need the prayers of others. If we do, perhaps we aren't as strong in the faith as we had thought. And what about the value of being invested heavily in the faith? Was I being punished because my faith had sometimes been too visible or "out front"? Was this putting me in my place for my lack of humility?

It was a warped interpretation in my psyche of "cashing in my chips," and my goal was to add to that chip pile, not take any back. Mentally, was I trying to make this about *me* rather than Megan? If so, it was an arrogant, twisted perspective of faith. My own normal "Jesus talk" would not allow me to admit aloud what you just read. But I am being brutally honest here, at least for now.

Why would I be content to want or accept the prayers of others, even if it is for my firstborn? It was because that would be an acknowledgment that I was not in control and that my daughter's life was in real peril. I told myself, "Where there is life there is hope." I just did not want to live in that particular arena, at least not at that moment. "I've got this," or so I thought.

Deep down, I knew and finally acknowledged that I was in over my head. This situation was serious and life changing, and it was eating me alive.

Up to this point, my prayer life most days was vertical. God was up there, and I was down here, and that was the natural order of things. Suddenly, though, I was cast into a situation where my relationship with Jesus Christ was somehow on trial like it had never been before. As the bad news seemed to come wave after wave, my mind resisted the obvious opportunity to dwell on the "why" question and the "where" question.

Why is this happening to someone who is so precious to me?

Where is God, and why hasn't he shown up yet and done something about this?

All these years, I have been a "good" Christian and added chip after chip to that chip pile, and now that I need to cash some of them in, the dealer isn't around.

My prayers were fragmented and raw and passionate, but they were without form and seemed to go unheard. Simple pleas of "help me, Lord" and "take care of my little girl, Father," seemed to be ignored.

My heart was broken, my mind was tormented, my soul was pierced. What good was this life of faith and service that I had tried to live? I was overwhelmed by the initial prospect that my daughter's life might end or that she might survive this illness so severely damaged that life as she had lived it would be over.

I felt alone and beaten and defeated, and my anger did not fit anywhere else in the room. At times it was directed at who I thought had the power to change things, but that source of power was seemingly disengaged. Where was God?

In the moments of complete disbelief and helplessness, I lashed out at the Almighty. "Where are you? Why do you not hear me? Do something!"

In those moments of the worst that can happen to you in this life, I realized that little was vertical in my spiritual relationship. I was talking to God, sometimes as friend, sometimes as therapist, sometimes as doctor, and sometimes hopefully as my God and protector. And sometimes I was even trying to speak as an angry, disinterested party.

The relationship had become quite horizontal. Had I gone too far? Had I blasphemed the Almighty? Had this hateful event taken all that was important to me, including my faith?

One by one, those well-meaning friends who promised to pray came and went. They hugged and loved on us. They shared stories of their own and listened as we poured out our angst, need, and pain. And they prayed for us. Over and over and over, they prayed.

At times early on, I did not want to hear it. At times it was easier to withdraw into the strange comfort of the dark, quiet ICU room with its beeping machines and blinking lights. I watched and held the hand of my daughter as she welled up with anger and fear of her own, unspoken but continuously evidenced by thrashing and attempts at escape.

Our friend and minister Eddie once again came and spoke words of comfort. "It is okay to be angry, even with God," he said. God has a thick skin and a huge heart and can certainly take anything we have to dish out. Even after all that, God still loves us and wants what is best for us, and even more than anyone else.

Faith makes sense to us when we are in control of what we believe. But when life and circumstances take away the control, it can become a different thing. To question one's faith can be heretical to some, but it is more likely evidence of an active faith. I have come to believe that faith is at its best when we are not in control and we still believe, even when that involves being mad with our God. It is in moments when we are most vulnerable and most honest that our true faith is revealed. If you want to know what kind of Christian you are, look for your faith when the world is crashing around you.

C. S. Lewis wrote *A Grief Observed* after the death of his wife. It explores the processes that the human brain and mind undergo over the course of grieving. The book questions the nature of grief and whether returning to normalcy is possible within the realm of human existence on earth. He begins with, "No one told me that grief felt so like fear."[3]

While our circumstances are different, his conclusions and my humble ramblings share a common series of questions: "Can you reconcile loss, even though losses are all different? Can we somehow find resolution of profound loss in a faith that infers no loss of this life can ultimately have meaning since God wins over death and loss in the end?"

Lewis writes, "The time when there is nothing at all in your soul except a cry for help may be just that time when God can't give it: you are like the drowning man who can't be helped because he clutches and grabs. Perhaps your own reiterated cries deafen you to the voice you hoped to hear."[4] Lewis only partially resolves this dichotomy in the following discourse: "Is anything more certain than that in all those vast times and spaces, if I were allowed to search them, I should nowhere find her face, her voice, her touch? She died. She is dead. Is the word so difficult to learn?"[5]

And Lewis's ultimate resolution of his dilemma is in part articulated when he writes, "Two widely different convictions press more and more on my mind. One is that the Eternal Vet is even more inexorable and the possible operations even more painful than our

---

3. C. S. Lewis, *A Grief Observed* (New York: Bantam Books, 1976), 1.
4. Ibid., 53–54.
5. Ibid., 16.

severest imaginings can forebode. But the other, that 'all shall be well, and all shall be well, and all manner of thing shall be well.'"[6]

When Christ himself was on the cross asking his own questions of the Father, he said, "My God, why have you forsaken me?" During these days, I have asked that same question. And as with Jesus, the Father remained, even when my faith was shaken a bit and wavered.

I usually don't make a practice of arguing with the Almighty, but my respect of the Almighty allows me the freedom through prayer to express my need in ways that might seem disrespectful. We are family relating to family. I know that I have been heard, that my pain is God's pain, and that my life is made better because I believe.

I also know that God's hand was and is all around us each day, even though our pain and anger hid it from us. I also know that the success of my daughter at coming back from her stroke has been affected positively and purposefully because God has been there and has played an incredibly active role.

So what of the friends who said they were praying for me?

I have no doubt that hundreds have prayed and still pray each day for my daughter and our family. My initial discomfort was not because they expressed their concern through their faith, but rather because of events I couldn't control, we needed those prayers. No one really wants this type of intercessory prayer because of the deeper issues it accompanies. But when those circumstances present themselves, knowing that others care enough to minister and reach out in love and, even more, take the extraordinarily personal step of having a word with the Almighty on our behalf, means so much.

It humbles the soul and brings its own "peace that surpasses understanding" (Phil 4:7), because praying for someone acknowledges our own inadequacy to fix a problem and recognizes that in many cases in this life, unless God intervenes, there are limits to human ability. Life is fragile.

As good as the doctors were at Mission Hospital, as fine as the therapists were at the Shepherd Center, as wonderful as our therapist and orthopedists have been since we came home, the comfort

---

6. Ibid., 75.

of knowing that this cloud of witnesses who share common beliefs have interceded on our behalf makes the circumstance better, makes the mind not run quite so fast, makes the heart and blood pressure a little less accelerated. It establishes a common connection that our battle is their battle, that our pain is shared, that our fears are faced with others, and that our combined vision of hope and healing and rehabilitation might be a common goal that seems more attainable.

In Atlanta, we never knew what the afternoon mail might include, but a number of folks included in their cards or letters or packages of socks and coloring books the "order of worship," or bulletin as we called it in the church of my youth. They came from people they had told our story to, including churches from outside our area.

The common ingredients listed in their "calendars of concern" were Megan's, Linda's, and my name. There were dozens of them. The farthest away was from a small church in India that one of our family members had visited on a mission trip prior to February. Word travels fast, as does the love of Christ for other Christians who are in crisis.

Why are there times when I am finally comfortable in my faith? Where else can you accumulate such an army of support and love in one place? There is strength in any event shared, particularly when it is shared through faith. "God is good, all the time. All the time, God is good."

In this family, we argue over everything, but we know that what binds us together is bigger than anything that might drive us apart. Even after all else, we are family. When it's time to circle the wagons, we do that very well. Turning to God in times of trouble is only natural, but the mark of a "better" believer is sharing those harder parts of our faith even when times are good. As we have discovered, good times are often relative to circumstances. Compared to those first days, these are better days. And for each of them we are grateful and give thanks. Part of our faith also calls us to continue being thankful each day, even when days are difficult. I aspire to that although I am still not very good at it. I will still work toward it, though.

As for all the prayers, I know there is power in and from them. Otherwise, we would never have made it this far. There is something healing and encouraging and important about simply knowing that others are "lifting you up."

One important day in the last nineteen months, I received a phone call from another dear friend and minister, David Blackmon. It was a calm day, no material crisis, but these days there are no truly easy days. Every day is a sixteen-hour day, between work and therapy and doctors' appointments and simply trying to provide a life for our daughter that has a level of fulfillment.

On that day, David called to let me know that for no particular reason he and the staff had prayed for us that morning. On that day, the knowledge that others continued to intercede on our behalf gave me a lift; the friends who were there during the most stressful parts of this journey continue to support us. On some days, that is the difference between resignation and resolution. Because of those around us and because of the love of God, given to us all through Jesus Christ, we live a life filled with hope and we are truly blessed.

A dear friend sent this collage of pictures and encouragements shortly after the stroke. The most meaningful content was the two pictures of Megan in happy times just before everything changed.

Chapter 20

The Power of Music

Music has always been such an integral part of my life. I can't remember a time when I didn't sing or hum or listen to the radio or simply relish the lyrics to some stupid love song from my youth. In my life, times of a broken heart were best healed through lyrics written and shared from a common experience.

Now at the age of sixty, I must admit that the lyrics and tunes from my youth make me feel relevant and still relatively hip, if a sixty-year-old can dare to make such a claim. After fifty-five years of singing, choirs, voice lessons, and classical training during my college days, the hours I have enjoyed the most are those times of making music. It wasn't important to me whether it was as a soloist, a choir member, part of a duet with my wife, or even in the barbershop quartet that I invested thousands of hours in as a young adult with three of my best lifelong friends.

Music is a way of life and a way to express ourselves. Lyrics come in the dead of night when all else seems to fail the human spirit. I even dream about music and singing. I can typically find lyrics to fit every emotion that I am feeling, and the hard emotions of these days are no exception.

On one of my earliest posts in Caring Bridge, I wrote the following:

> For those of us that subscribe to streaming music services such as Rhapsody, the recent release of the whole Beatles treasure trove has allowed all those memories back into our lives . . . including some of my favorites like "Penny Lane" and "The Long and Winding Road" and "Nowhere Man." So while passing the hours I have reflected on those important words of the songs of my youth that bring me comfort. For whatever reason, this week in

my mind I became focused on the lyrics of another Beatles standard, "Yesterday." You know the words: "Yesterday all my troubles seemed so far away." I allowed myself a few moments of self-pity, I succumbed to the temptation of a weak faith, and in so doing I watched my own actions affect those around me, including Megan. I have noticed in her recovery process that when we are up, she is up. And when we are down, amazingly so is she.

In the words of Paul McCartney, "Many times I've been alone and many times I've cried, anyway you'll never know the many ways I've tried, but still they lead me back to the long and winding road . . . ," and so "what's next" begins.

"What's next" has continuously involved notes and lyrics from songs across all sorts and types of music. As I mentioned before, for some reason the part of the brain that we use to sing and express music is separate from the part that we use for the spoken word. The philosophical questions this raises are striking. If we believe in a loving God who, as another minister friend says, "knitted us together in our mother's womb," then why is it that God saw fit to separate song from all other communication the human brain is capable of? Such a separation implies that music is a distinct, elevated form of communication, worthy somehow of its own existence. And being a dreamer and an emotional type, this reasoning makes sense because in truth words seldom bring me to any emotional pinnacle unless spoken by someone who holds particular importance.

In most cases, the right song, with its specific and profound notes and lyrics, can usually stir my heart if it is performed simply and offered honestly. Each offering of the same song can bring different emotion or meaning because each of us interprets that song differently.

Case in point: During the first week we were in Atlanta, Megan would wake up and head to her shower, which was a significant production, mainly because of the safety measures we had to undertake each time. Many things are important for any hospital, but none is more concerning or administratively catastrophic than a patient fall.

Take an impulsive, feisty young woman who wants desperately to get better and now add a shower stall complete with a bench, towels, slick tile, soap, and shampoo. It isn't a matter of "if" she falls; it becomes a matter of "when." The shower was her first real physical accomplishment. Our training began with the shower and then the transfer to and from bed as well as using the toilet, all with the dreaded transfer belt. Megan so looked forward to morning showers that her mood improved the moment we started to prepare for it.

For whatever reason, during the first few showers she was so enthused at having once again tapped into something that felt normal that she had to increase the difficulty rating. She began to sing. Initially, it was advertisement jingles off TV.

First and foremost was the "good morning" song from the orange juice commercial. It originated in *Singin' in the Rain*, a Gene Kelly and Debbie Reynolds movie. "Good morning, good morning . . . it's great to stay out late, good morning good, morning to you." This became our theme song for the morning. No matter how tired she was or how sleepy, those lyrics flowed from her tongue when other words except "yes" simply would not come. Rooms down the hall would hear us coming singing to the rafters, and in unison I perceived folks rolling their eyes and saying, "There goes Megan."

Shortly after that came Sunday school songs and youth choir songs one right after the other. "I've got that joy, joy, joy, joy down in my heart (where?) down in my heart, (where?) down in my heart . . . ." And soon after that she would shift into the deep, sultry voice of Adele singing with all the vocal inflection she could muster, "Hello, it's me." There were even spirituals we hadn't sung for years like *"Shut de do' keep out de devil, shut de do' kept de devil in the night, shut de do' keep out de devil, light de candle every-ting's alright, light de candle every-ting's alright."*

Megan's cell phone was always beside her bed. On many mornings, she would reach for it, and to our amazement she would key in her four-digit password and go right in. She would do the "thumb down" as if reviewing emails, and Linda and I had no way to know that she wasn't reading anything.

So, when this music "epiphany" started, I was confused because I knew that she had hundreds of songs saved in iTunes, but for some reason she never wanted to go there. For six long weeks we sang and sang and sang, but not once did she ask for her earbuds or iTunes. It didn't make sense, until one night we were watching "The Voice" on TV and suddenly, here it came. She became an instant fan, and we watched it every night it was on. The music was guaranteed to be repeated the following morning at shower time. In fact, most mornings it became a race to remember the songs from the previous night or even week. But almost every day there was at least one new song. Still no iTunes, either.

While the use of the different parts of the brain didn't guarantee "cross pollination" between music and the spoken word, over time I became convinced that the connection of phrases in sentences she wanted to say were often predicated on lyrics she might remember. It didn't hurt that the singing came so easily even though saying words seemed so much harder.

The music was a turning point because of its ability to help shift a tense moment of loss instantly to an intentional moment of joy. Now, familiarity created joy. There was real joy in each song, and we hadn't planned for that, but we were amazed that something so natural in our family brought motivation and a tool that provided exploration for other therapies.

There were also somber moments of reflection that didn't come often, but they came nonetheless, usually after a particularly hard day of speech therapy. While Megan seldom allowed us to see her express raw emotion, these reflective moments were a window to her soul and the immense pain hidden there. The short moments of angst were usually transformed into a song. It was usually insignificant like the theme song of her favorite mindless television programs of the evening like the lyrics from her favorite show, *Big Bang Theory*. Those lyrics, you might recall, are sung at almost breakneck speed. Megan never missed a word. How can that be?

This young woman, who could not offer a single complete sentence, could rattle off that song at warp speed. How was that possible, and how could we transfer that skill back to conversation? It was maddening.

As our time at Shepherd ended, Megan's graduation breakfast ended with powerful moments of accomplishment and appreciation for the gifts we had received from each wonderful staff member. We returned to her room one last time and gathered her few remaining personal effects that hadn't already been packed into the truck.

Her cousin Lindsay had come to accompany us home. We had already decided that neither her condo nor our home were accessible enough to provide the special accommodations we would need as she continued her recovery complete with walker, wheelchair, and brace. We had concluded that renting an ADA-prepared apartment for a few months as we reinserted ourselves back into the mountains would be necessary.

I located one on the ground floor in a complex less than two miles from our home. It had an ADA tub with a bench, along with everything else we needed, including wider door openings and level ground for walking and exercise. There was even a pool, which we never used.

Friends from church had already set up borrowed furnishings from friends and family and when we got home; all we had to do was walk in and bring clothes and personal items. What a blessing. We knew some of what awaited us back home as we pulled away from the Shepherd Center at mid-morning. Lindsay rode with Megan and me, and to my amazement, Megan grabbed her phone and hooked it to my sound system, and for the next three hours the hits kept coming. It was music I had never heard, but Megan and Lindsay knew every word.

This was a portal into our future traveling arrangements; if Megan is in the car, the radio plays what she wants. I have expanded my listening opportunities to include artists I had never heard of and some I admit I have grown to enjoy: Rachel Platten, 21 Pilots, Bruno Mars, Justin Timberlake, Lady Gaga, Michael Bublé. It was loud and had a beat, and I was so happy Megan's musical interests were suddenly more than imitation and memory. She knew every word, and usually after hearing a new song only once, she could repeat most of it from memory, including rhythms. I was impressed. Often after each new song came a sentence, short as it was: "I like that song."

Life has always amazed me at its ability to change suddenly and without warning. We are asked to change without choice, interruption, or planning, and in most cases, we simply have to do it. No other option is presented. I've always wondered if Christ had occasions of thinking about how hard it was to go with the flow of what happened around him. Did he know that at the end of holy week he would be asked to forfeit his life horribly, cruelly, and on someone else's terms? I know he had more insight into his role, perhaps more than most of his followers do. But did he ever want to say, "No, I will not do this"?

In this difficult journey, I often have questioned why it is necessary. It makes no sense. A loving God would have to agree that it is wasteful to lose the accomplishments and investments of such a young woman. All along the way, I kept saying "no," and all along the way, it made no difference. It wasn't until later, in the times of freedom from recovery, that Megan would ever say the word "no." Even then, she did it in a way that was more creative than I did: "This sucks!"

As a kid, I had a teacher who firmly planted into my mind the old saying, "Mine is not to reason why, mine is but to do or die." Resignation. The task we faced was simply necessary. Megan's words to her uncle Bud from that bed in Atlanta said it all: "I just have to get better."

The song lyrics and melodies that presented her with encouragement and accomplishment and even a look into her past that otherwise was untouchable. Living in the songs allowed her to feel whole when nothing else could. Music became escape and purpose all in one. When Megan sings, her world is closer to what was than at any other time. And when new music and words are offered, they point her toward her new normal.

The frustrations of aphasia require her to fight for almost every word when she speaks. Music demands no such sacrifice, and the sweetness of the words and sounds goes on long after the last note.

Music has been and continues to be a blessing when we find few other true blessings among the hard work of recovery and the cloud of pain and effort that accompanies any normal week.

On the day when we came home to the mountains, filled with sounds sweet and lyric, all the other challenges ahead were placed on hold, and life for those three short hours seemed as it had been before. It was a gift of divine intervention into a story of loss and interruption. But it was also a promise that the words do exist in Megan's brain and can come out if we find the right way to bridge the void that interrupts thoughts and syntax and prevents a sweet soul from fulfilling great potential.

In my mind, I have a vision of the cross, filled with all its pain and emotion, brutality and angst. I see the three crosses and I hear the seven separate spoken words. But sprinkled in during the hours of waiting, waiting for death's cold end, I envision a sound of the humming of ancient songs of faith. Just maybe, Jesus too allowed himself the simple joy of temporary escape to the music of his day that also pays homage to the God we still serve, even when confronted with the most difficult of circumstances.

Chapter 21

Are We Covered?

I do not like insurance and insurance companies but thank goodness they exist. On February 1, 2016, my daughter was a happily employed professional "up and comer" in the children's preschool education field, serving a local nonprofit and helping that agency make the lives of young children and their families better. She had a good job with good benefits, and she worked with wonderful people. She had a home of her own, complete with a mortgage and a car payment. She worked an extra job teaching online undergraduate courses to students in her field. She was the youngest deacon in our church and served in a children's Sunday school class while also working hard to renew the involvement of young adults. Megan was (and is) passionate about everything she did (and does). She had lived a healthy lifestyle, had recently lost weight, and had a significant impact on her family to do likewise.

On February 2, 2016, she suffered an ischemic stroke at the age of twenty-nine and lost her ability to speak, to read, to use her right leg and arm, and to do her job. As a result, she lost her home, her employment, and her independence. But because her employer had provided wonderful employment benefits, including disability and health insurance, she has had amazing care and continues to heal and work hard at rehabilitation.

Without this insurance, her options would have been limited, and I am convinced that her progress would have been a fraction of her achievements to this point many months later. So many people in this country, even now, do not have or cannot afford health insurance. Once again, we are privileged because Megan's recovery will likely continue for a long time to come.

When her employment ended, as it had to do under the law, Megan still qualified for COBRA coverage, which she continued to pay for from the disability income that her employer provided. No misconceptions here: the non-covered cost of this illness has still been staggering, but we are incredibly grateful to her employer who provided these benefits to their employees. That coverage would continue until December of 2017 as long as we paid the premiums, at which time we hoped we would obtain continued coverage through the Affordable Care Act or social security disability. And, on February 2, 2016, my daughter acquired one more significant "bad" thing—a preexisting condition.

To say that the political conversation over health care has been onerous is an understatement, and as part of that conversation a North Carolina legislator implied that families like ours "have caused rates to skyrocket" for everyone else and states should have the ability to effectively "vote us off the island." If we don't like it, in his opinion, we would have the right to move to another state that chooses a different way of insuring its residents.

Another legislator in a different state was quoted as saying that those straining the health care system are doing so because they live in an "unhealthy" manner and therefore they, in his mind, should not have access to the same coverage that healthy folks should have at similar rates. My, what a difference one day can make.

If access to healthcare is only available to those who are "healthy," why even bother? If coverage cannot be provided to help those who suffer catastrophic illness, why have health insurance at all? Catastrophic illness takes not only the health of the individual but also the ability of that person to earn and therefore pay the increased cost of any proposed coverage.

After seeing the amazing capabilities of medicine to heal and restore, I also question the morality of having the "capability" to make life better and productive and then not using that capability, even when the patient cannot afford it. The conversation must involve morality at some point. To take hope away from those who face significant illness and are still motivated to return to productive living lacks that tenant of basic morality.

In the first days of our experience, as a parent and an accountant, one of my biggest concerns was how we could possibly pay for this.

Are we now bankrupt? What portion of this will be our responsibility? How does this work? Am I personally liable somehow? That question stemmed from the fact that in the emergency room at the hospital, someone from the billing department met us in the emergency room and wanted to know how we planned to pay for the services being rendered.

My daughter was lying in bed with no idea of what was going on, maybe not even aware of where she was, and I was dealing with a "collections" person, giving them my credit card to cover the required minimum payment of $400 for ER services. By paying that, had I crossed some legal line? Was I now liable somehow?

For days, the knowledge that we were spending money at a rate that would be staggering scared the crap out of me and weighed on my mind. Once again, a friend with legal experience gave us direction and guidance. Megan was living on her own when she had her stroke. She had her own insurance, and therefore, unless we agreed somehow to be responsible, we had not crossed that line. Megan, on the other hand, might face those bills and medical bankruptcy, which is common in this country. But the financial worries became a side annoyance. My goal was to advocate for the treatment she needed, which we would soon find out was in large part dictated by the insurance company and the service providers.

Right as we were about to head to Atlanta, the first insurance roadblock presented itself. Would they cover the Shepherd Center if it was out of our market? Would they allow Megan to be treated out of state? The process of getting them to approve our choice of treatment took a few extra days, but ultimately, they did approve treatment with the caveat that we would have to pay a co-pay for the ambulance to take her the three-hour trip to Atlanta from Asheville. At that point, it was just one more cost that we accepted, figuring it was adding to a balance we would never be able to satisfy if the bill came.

Then, while we were in Atlanta, our case manager had weekly contact with our carrier. They raised occasional questions, but we had no idea how involved they were in our daughter's treatment. When we got within about three weeks of discharge, we were told that they planned to stop paying her costs because she was making too much progress, and they didn't feel that she needed inpatient care any longer.

I shared that story earlier, but to me that is a symptom of the brokenness of our entire health care system. Isn't such progress the goal? Health professionals fight with insurance providers over care decisions that should only be made by the qualified medical personnel treating the patient. Decisions about treatment should not come from the people in an office three thousand miles away whose priority is not the patient but the profit.

There is a thin line between a life-and-death situation and a cold and callous business transaction. It was an unsavory and somehow perverted environment. We were fortunate, blessed, lucky—whatever you want to call it—because we had good representation, good advocacy, good care, and, if I am "fair and balanced," we had "incredibly fine" insurance coverage and health care providers.

I have never gotten a clear understanding of exactly how much this whole experience has cost to date. I saw our first payment advice for the first few days of care, and it was over six figures (times a couple). After almost two years, our family has never received a single bill from the Shepherd Center. We also stopped receiving bills from Mission after a while. In my crude calculating that I have done based on other charges, I would be amazed if the cost so far didn't exceed a million dollars. If I needed to be personally liable for everything not covered so that Megan could continue to get the services she's needed, I would have done so.

My real question is one that I have heard asked many times during the health care controversy. Is health care a "right" or a chargeable "service"? Our society wants it both ways. When someone simply can't pay because they don't have any resources, we claim we do the compassionate thing by requiring hospitals not to deny services for the indigent, and in some cases the government shares some of those costs through programs like Medicaid.

Why are these the only real options? Health care expense is a higher percentage of the US GDP than in any other highly developed country in the world, yet we seem to think that taking away the benefit of health coverage is somehow right and good or at least allows those who haven't needed it yet not to have to pay it forward a bit. The problem is that we all will eventually need it if we live long enough.

Whether you like the Affordable Care Act or not doesn't matter to me. What does matter is that folks do not walk around thinking that having access to medical help in the future is sustainable as it is currently designed. It is not. There must be a better way. A conclusion of not giving folks access to reasonable care is mean, hateful, and uncivilized, especially in the United States of America. My belief, having several doctors and physician's assistants and other medical professionals as clients, is that the problem isn't that providers are asking for too much. My observation is that the insurance companies, the drug companies, and all the other "middle people" are what run the cost sky high. Too many hands touch each claim. Add to that the attorneys and all their litigation and malpractice claims.

My daughter spent three extra days in Asheville because they couldn't make decisions quickly and efficiently. The system is too cumbersome, complex, difficult, and expensive. The drug companies play the "new drug lotto," and if it hits, they have a gold mine for the length of the patent because that is how long it will be before a generic brand can be allowed into the market. The government has a process to approve new treatment and new drugs, and it takes years and tons of money. In many cases, this process provides some protection, and in others it keeps promising treatments from ever getting to the market because companies run out of money. That needs to change.

If people are given full disclosure of the unknowns, recognize the risks, and are still willing to try experimental treatments, then we should make it easier, not harder. Make it so that if, after consultation, a patient wants to roll the dice, so be it. What we are doing doesn't work; it is too expensive and time consuming and makes healing a game only for the wealthy. After all, the wealthy can go to another country to try a therapy the FDA hasn't approved yet.

Reduce the cost of bringing products to market, and you lower the lifetime cost of a drug. Lower the cost, remove part of the middle folk who have their hands "in the till," and it might just make insurance affordable. All I want is for reason to prevail and a little creative thinking to be used that isn't influenced by someone who is profiting from the decision.

A joke that travels the circles among accountants goes like this: You can have it fast, cheap, or right . . . pick two. That is how it is with health care. There must be a better way.

After a stroke, the care a patient receives over the first year determines whether that patient will be a functioning part of society or a permanent "cost" to be supported by society. Why can we not recognize that and put bigger investments in initial treatment and rehabilitation instead of limiting it in a way that will cost us all more? The cost of treatment is important, and without treatment few will ever "get better," as Megan says.

The cost is only one part of the conversation, because when "medicine proper" runs out of things to try, the family caregivers and long-term providers become the only viable options for offering any semblance of a life for these folks whose lives are changed by illness or some other medical event. Even the care for those whose circumstances are changed because of bad choices or behaviors still must be considered. How is their care to be doled out?

The heartless idea that one's bad actions negate society's responsibilities to care for them seems foreign to the America in which I grew up, yet society and our health care system relegate hundreds of thousands of families to a lifetime of "caregiving" with little support, financial or otherwise. Without the help of dozens of nonprofit support organizations, most families would have little hope of finding a manageable "new normal." Illness takes away the productivity of the victim and the family because we haven't figured out how best to improve the path to recovery, and I of all people understand there are few easy answers. But we must have the conversation.

I pray that those who see this solely as a matter of dollars and cents, or healthy versus unhealthy, are never forced to wake up to our family's new reality of February 2, 2016, and face how little control we have over our own health or the health of our loved ones, even those who try to be healthy. The conversation over health care is only partially driven by the cost of insurance premiums. To fix healthcare, we must answer a myriad of big-picture questions. How do we promote healthy living? How should we compensate providers? What services can or should be covered? How should drug companies set pricing for new medications? What role should insurance companies play in service determination and medical treatment decisions, and how do we dole out such services to begin with? Is the current trend away from the family doctor toward the ER and urgent care the best service model?

We must address the larger issues. Until we have the courage to talk about what is available and how much it should cost without being driven by political influence from either party, we cannot solve the problem for either side. And like most issues that have a financial component attached, solving the problem is not always particularly high on some folks' priority list.

There are no easy answers. For some time now, I have searched for answers. I have found few that don't involve my faith. What I do know is that from that faith, we have a lot in common, including a responsibility to *love each other*. We are, by definition, neighbors.

The whole concept of insurance is that we all pay premiums to cover *our* risk of the possibility (the probability) that our lives may be changed by adversity and that the impact might be mitigated as much as possible by our participation in that insurance. As the political conversation continues, I pray that my country and this damaged system of service doesn't abandon my family and my daughter and all the others whose story is like ours.

Chapter 22

Meet Shepherd

Once we arrived back home, even in our new temporary surroundings, we began again the days of new routines, a lot of established older routines, and of course continued therapy—although in a new place. We met our new physical, occupational, and speech therapists within CarePartners' outpatient program, and to our surprise, and Megan's delight, they were also relatively young, energetic, and encouraging. A significant difference was that, as promised, Linda and I were now the main caregivers, and our responsibilities included filling Megan's other ninety-plus hours per week with activity and purpose.

For Megan, the change was that her days were no longer planned by the hour or occupied by the intensive inpatient therapy. It wasn't easy for me or for Linda to work full-time, try to regain some semblance of control of our mental state and our existing interrupted daily life, and still help our daughter live her best life. Getting up and getting going is two hours of every day, no matter how you cut it. The same goes for winding down the day and getting to bed at night, so that takes care of twenty-eight hours per week. But filling the rest is a challenge since therapy is now only three days a week for three hours each day. For a time, Linda and I split days. I did mornings and she did afternoons so that we each could work, when possible, in a somewhat more structured way. It was still tax season and Linda's bookkeeping load had remained constant and demanding as well.

For those first weeks, we also spent time going to doctor's appointments and getting established with our new medical team here at home. There never seemed to be any downtime . . . ever. I have learned over these months that even a late-fifties parent can still run off adrenaline for a long time, but it comes at a cost. I suspect that I have aged at least five years in these nineteen months. The undeniable signs are there, and over time we have had to try to find ways to decouple a bit from the rigors of caregiving. Neither of us has been particularly successful.

In addition to the full schedule, though, we have been blessed with so many gifts. Our friends and family were constantly supportive, and so many of these intentional moments of respite allowed for times when Linda and I could simply sit for a few hours. Megan was so easy to please. Anything was therapy and enjoyable, whether walking around the apartment complex, going to lunch, or having a pizza dinner with her best buddies. All of it was welcome and exciting and another step toward something more normal.

The therapies were all productive and enjoyable because progress was still visible and apparent. Over time, the exuberance subsides a bit, as do the offers for respite for the caregivers. Part of this fight is very personal, uncomfortable, and increasingly lonely. Try as you may to remain engaged and hopeful, it is easy to suddenly find yourself feeling isolated, down, and distraught. At this point, Megan was the only one getting the mood-enhancing drugs, but we were aware of our own mental pain and unmet needs. The constant demands for care and sustenance, including our own need to make a living, had to take shared precedence.

A common part of any catastrophe is the effort at normalization of the circumstance. In earlier days, it was impossible that Megan could have had a stroke; the shock was universal, and the panic was constant and real to everyone associated. Then time had a way of convincing those around us that our new reality, sad and awful as it was, had become their new perception of us. Folks looked at us differently. Exchanging pleasantries went from "What are you all doing for fun this summer?" to "How is Megan?" We became defined in part by this event.

As caregiver and responsible party and having just dodged the unimaginable possibility that your loved one might not have survived, you are so immensely grateful for the gifts of those around you that you hardly notice some of those close to you pulling away, stepping back a bit, or putting a wall between you and them in order to keep your pain separate from their lives when possible. They want to minister to you, but over time this becomes harder because the relationships must evolve in order to continue. And with some folks, it's just too hard, just too uncomfortable. They desperately want and long for what was, but that isn't an option, so they do the only thing they can to relieve their own pain, which is pull away for their protection, comfort, and peace of mind.

The interesting thing is that no one does this intentionally. I believe it to be an example of how fragile our relationships are and just how much work it takes to maintain a friendship in lives that are already hectic and running wide open. That is our life, and I suspect it is common these days. The addition of an unexpected layer of difficulty injures a relationship, and busy lives can't always accommodate the change. You transition from being friends to being acquaintances, and it happens very quickly.

I've already spoken about Megan's "peer" patient whom our family got to know in Atlanta, and now her words to Megan that day have come full circle: "You will lose half of your friends in the first year, and your other relationships will be stretched as well." That was incredibly hard to hear then and is even harder to live now.

The better news is her next prediction, which has taken some time to happen. She said, "As you progress and as you regain function, you will find that you are developing new relationships, stronger relationships that can withstand just about anything." We have seen that over time, and it is encouraging and helpful. Megan's closest friends have gotten her to this point, but as she gains confidence, she is reaching out again, at least a little, for new friends. We see her establishing some "developing" relationships that appear to be positive, even though many of those are within her care groups and therapy providers.

We have allowed her to drive that process and did all we could to support any opportunities for socialization, but that still left a lot of vacant time that Megan filled with "anything video" that she could find. Netflix became her core experience, and we knew the immersive entertainment option to be less healthy, at least for the long term.

Then one day her aunt Dianne once again suggested a pet friend. At first, I bristled as I had for a while, and then for some reason, even though we were still in an apartment and even though it would be one more "responsibility," in a moment of weakness I said, "Listen, if you were to find a small dog friend who is well trained and would not be a tripping hazard for her, we probably wouldn't say no." Dianne asked, "What other requirements do you have?" and I said, without really thinking, "He has to lick my hand the first time I see him."

In my heart, I thought there was no way this kind of perfect pet would present itself, so I went on to work knowing they might visit the shelters, which had become a normal weekly activity, but not expecting anything more than that.

About ten that morning, I was in a client meeting and my cell phone rang. It was Megan's number. Since the day of the stroke, if my phone rings and Megan's name pops up, I never pass it off. I answered it then, and today would be no exception. When I said "Hello," on the other end a giddy female voice said with glee, "He found me." I asked, "Who found you?" dreading the answer, which was "the puppy." I half-heartedly tried to use it as a speech therapy moment and asked questions for which Megan gave remarkably complete answers. I knew our lives were about to change. With Aunt Dianne's help, she sent pictures of the most adorable, shaggy, tiny two-year-old "rescue" that is part Yorkie, part terrier, and part imp.

I asked if they could hold the dog until we could get there after work, and Dianne replied, "Scotty, there are literally two other folks waiting to see if we want this little guy." They agreed to hold him until Linda and I could get there at lunch, and we headed toward the shelter as soon as we could.

We met them at the Asheville Humane Society an hour or so later. They quickly put all four of us in a privacy room for first meetings, and that cute little brown dog headed straight for me, jumped in my lap, and licked my hand first thing.

Stick a fork in me, I'm done. It was also the first time in weeks that I had seen my daughter smile for an extended period. I realized that joy could return to her life—joy that we couldn't provide alone.

The little dog is precious, and he worships her and seldom leaves her side, even at night. He is well trained, rarely barks, travels well, and loves most other dogs. I am convinced that he is one more evidence of God's good grace . . . a tonic that soothes Megan's soul more than any pill or injection, and he does the same for Linda and me as well. He is a hoot, and they are amazing together.

We filled out the paperwork on the spot, which was a lot of papers to simply adopt a dog. As we went through it all, we found that although this little guy had only been there for a few hours, he had been neutered the first thing that morning. And of all things, the paperwork listed his name as "Fraggle." What kind of name was that for such a cute little guy? The moment we found that out, I said, "Okay, little girl, you are going to have to come up with a more fitting name." So once the papers were signed, she and her aunt Dianne headed to our local PetSmart for some supplies.

The dog spent his first afternoon meeting their big dogs and allowing Bud and Dianne to evaluate his personality and any "needs" he might have. When we got back home, Megan met us at the door and said, "His name is Shepherd." I said, "Why Shepherd?" In broken syntax, she said something close to, "Because I love the Shepherd Center and I love him."

So Shepherd it was!

I could think of no more fitting tribute to our recent home away from home, and the dog's name was a way that we would always affirm and remember those dear friends in Atlanta and the gifts they gave us. Our little friend wears the name well, and to our delight he answered to it almost immediately.

The addition of an animal adds all sorts of new dynamics to everything, and not all of them are good. Along with the initial joy comes the time of getting acquainted, and we soon found that his previous owners had made a less than positive impact on him. Besides the normal "bodily function" stuff, as Megan calls it, he suffered and still suffers with significant separation anxiety. He shakes uncontrollably when you start to leave him. In those first weeks, if we left to go eat dinner, he would stay next to the door and jump, trying to open the door, his little face soaked in drool. He would often be exhausted.

This little guy has an incredible vertical leap—at least four feet. He is ten inches long and weighed seven pounds when we got him. His jumping would take the paint off the door jamb. But once we got home, except for the little pile of white paint flakes on the floor, all was forgiven at least on his end, and he went quickly back into his version of "therapy mode." As the months passed, his issues subsided, but he still does not like it when we leave him alone. The fact is, he needs his humans.

He also thinks he is a much bigger dog than he really is, and he is quick to try to be vocal with animals twenty times his size. Most of those larger dogs ignore him although a few have seemed intimidated, to our surprise. But he also is such a magnet for anyone who remotely likes dogs. People will come all the way across the mall or any street we walk on to ask to pet him, at which he always jumps up on their leg and offers a lick to anyone willing to allow it. Kids are the funniest. He loves them and they usually adore him. Shep loves just about everyone.

He is small, tan, and so cute and perfect. To see Megan's enthusiasm peak with such excitement and joy melted our hearts and showed us that the true way to healing involved opening her injured mind and body to new, unfamiliar (at least in recent memory) experiences of affection and love that would bring order to the chaos of this new reality.

At some level, "healing" meant allowing Megan's psyche to experience new, intense, and passionate feelings that included joy and hope, worth and purpose, and something new to love. This little furball was exactly that. He was a sponge that soaked up all the emotion and angst that we all were burdened with and then allowed us the privilege of sharing relationship and complete affection without expectation or obligation.

Every time we see this little fellow, it is as if it's the first time he's seen us that day. He is excited and loving and genuinely glad to be with us. We—and anyone he encounters—are his new family, and he feels joy at our presence in that moment. There are lessons to learn from a pet just as there are lessons to learn from every relationship. The lessons just seem easier to consider when they involve something that gives so much love and worships us without demanding something other than an occasional scoop of food and patience when walking him on any day that ends in Y.

I realize that taking on another personality when facing the challenges we already faced could have been a disaster. Linda fretted about that a lot when we were deciding whether to take on this new dynamic. And to be honest, Shepherd is another variable to consider in day-to-day decision-making. But in our case, this one dog has brought with him little downside and an immense amount of love. His contributions to Megan are undeniable. He still, to this day, hovers over her. He sleeps on pillows above her and watches her every move. He greets her at the door every time we leave and jumps with delight when she walks in the room. He has a way of offering affection at the exact moment we need it. He is now family, and we have accepted that.

Oh, he has left "presents" from time to time, but that is minor. We also discovered quickly that PetSmart, among others, offers training events that are helpful. Megan and I have been through two such seven-week events, and although Shep's attention span is often overruled by his excitement at anything that distracts him, he has learned a lot and is remarkably well behaved.

When Megan's mood is down for whatever reason, this little guy senses it, walks up to her, curls up in her lap, and puts his head on her. They are joined at the heart, and the hardest challenges are easier with him by her side. No matter whether we are out at dinner or shopping without him there, it is always inevitable that at about the halfway mark of whatever we had planned, Megan will shift gears and say, "I miss Sheppie." We almost plan more around his life and needs than we do around hers. And that's okay. We have discovered every dog-friendly restaurant in three states, and those folks get our business about 90 percent of the time. We love our sweet animal.

This entire journey is about doing whatever is necessary to regain the semblance of a life that has purpose and similarity to the life we had before the stroke, but which can never be exactly as it was again. This little man is now implanted into the middle of the journey and has made it better and new. We are richer for his being here, and it has become difficult to imagine life without him. In this new reality, we have absorbed him into our lives, and he seems incredibly glad to have found his new humans as well.

We have grown to love this little animal. If we had to go through the stroke, I am glad to have this little ball of joy on our team and in our family. It is an easier journey with Shep. He is a gift that we could not have anticipated, and we are grateful that he came our way.

This was one of many walks during our days at the apartment complex, which had a small dog lot and many helpful benches.

Chapter 23

The "Mental" Part of Brain Insult

In the past nineteen months, my daughter has made an incredible initial recovery from a stroke that almost took her life. But incredible doesn't mean complete. Participating in her recovery process has been a remarkable privilege. She is not who she was, and neither am I. Nor are we as a family.

Each day is a separate specific experience, and I rarely know what to expect. Linda and I work hard to provide structure and purpose, but I am disappointed that so much of Megan's existence involves Netflix, *Say Yes to the Dress*, *Big Bang Theory*, *The Voice*, *Dancing with the Stars*, and HGTV at this point. We continue to work hard to alter that reality.

If one measures success, the days also include a significant amount of puppy therapy, surfing the web for specific content, texting with voice command, Pinterest and sports, as well as speech and PT and OT when we have insured visits available. We have tried a variety of alternative therapies as well, including hyperbaric chamber treatments. This therapy was suggested by her speech therapist, and the theory is that by forcing oxygen into tissue and blood cells, you provide those areas the ability to heal. Oxygen helps the body and its cells heal. Thankfully, we have seen observable results from these therapies, some more quickly than we did with much of the traditional PT and OT in recent months.

I have often said that progress comes in "fits and starts," and it does. When we see appreciable progress, it is celebrated and acknowledged and represents another step on Megan's journey. The problem is that the "journey" is only in our minds. This is the harsh reality of a life interrupted by illness and injury, or "brain insult," as our neurologist called it in those first days.

Dressing it up as a fun trip down memory lane is something I did to keep from crashing into rock bottom on the challenging days or weeks when life, circumstances, and rehabilitation ran headlong into each other. It gets easier only in small degrees that often aren't measurable, at least in any way I can recognize. There is an obvious, undeniable impact on a caregiver's mental health.

Some days, you allow your mind to go places that it should not: *What if?*

What if it doesn't get better?
What if she can't ever work again?
What if independence isn't achievable?
What if something happens to one or both of us as her primary caregivers?
What if she is miserable and we are only making her more so?
What if this really is God's punishment for the sins of my youth?
What if God isn't a God of love?
What if I have burned my last bridge with the Almighty and my own obstinance keeps me from the "life God calls me to live"?

Megan's words in circumstances like these are often "I hate this," particularly in times when important words simply won't come to her. But Megan, as I said before, has an amazing ability, recent in its genesis, of being able to shift focus away from events or circumstances that are too difficult to accept or deal with. It's what I perceive as some form of self-distraction. When she was released from OT the first time, it was effectively because she was no longer making progress. Her reaction was, "Yay! I am done with this. I still can't move my hand, but at least I don't have to do this stuff that I don't enjoy."

Through it all, Linda and I spend a lot of our time trying to figure out what we should do next. One of my biggest fears has been what will happen when we reach that point, that finite moment when Megan realizes, as do we, that this is all there is. This is all we can or will accomplish. We are done. We have spent all we have, done all we can do, and no one else has any hope to dangle in our faces, offering the carrot of creating life and presence that is better than what we have at this moment.

I equate this to a degree of what we grew up calling "playing chicken." We intentionally aimed our bicycles at each other from opposite ends of the street and then peddled as fast as we could directly at each other, trying to figure out who was "chicken," which would be the first person to alter their course to avoid the head-on crash.

Right now, we face this adversary and pedal at breakneck speed toward every new opportunity for healing, and in truth we can't turn the handles. We must win at all costs. No flinching, not an inkling of willingness to veer, and at some point, at that final moment, I fear our "journey" will end in a heap of twisted metal and bruised bodies and additional catastrophic injury. And then what?

It's been said that "Life is a succession of lessons that must be lived to be understood."[7] The hardest part of this is what we don't know, and there is still so very much of that. But we keep searching and we keep hoping and we still find new opportunities for lessons.

The continuing constant is that Megan will not give up. She can't. She meets each day with courage and a relentless spirit. When I allow myself to sink into the questions and quagmire of uncertainty, she still helps us find joy, even if only for one moment at a time. When we falter, and we do quite a bit, as is always the case in this human existence, we look for something else to help us focus once again on the possibilities. Notice I didn't say anything about *probabilities*.

The year I turned twenty-four, my dad contracted renal cell carcinoma. From the day of his diagnosis in May, he would fight valiantly but still succumb in November 1981. I have often told friends that we lived more in that summer than we did in the twenty-four years I had with him before that diagnosis. When it became apparent that he would not likely survive the disease, his oncologist suggested treatment to keep him comfortable. Comfort measures.

---

7. This quote has been attributed to Thomas Carlyle, Ralph Waldo Emerson, and Helen Keller, among others.

As to any kind of treatment used to fight the cancer, the only option was aggressive radiation. The doctor didn't think it would work, and it might result in less time. But he indicated that if Dad wanted to try, he would order it. My dad said he wished to try it.

When we got home that night, I experienced one of those rare times when we watched TV but also talked. Dad was a man of few words, but when he spoke, it was usually worth listening to.

I said, "Daddy I don't understand your reasoning in deciding to do the radiation. Why risk hastening your death if its potential for controlling your disease is that unlikely?"

Dad sat there for a few minutes quietly, and then he said, "I know son, but a feller has to have something to hope for."

There may be greater wisdom recorded somewhere in the writings of the world's philosophers, but those words from Dad still mean so much more to me, particularly now. Sometimes you just have to have something to hope for.

In these days, I have leaned into his words more than once. There have been many dark days during the last nineteen months, but when we have tried things that had no understandable reason to work, we have often felt closest as family and most alive. Those are the things that have given us hope, even when the results are not completely successful. Just the action provides a hint of progress even if infinitesimally small. If it is recognizable, it is progress nonetheless.

Another lesson of those days was the fact that after the initial battle against cancer, my father's most difficult adversary was his inability to have strength when he needed it most. It was humbling and frustrating.

Thirty-five years has changed very little. Disease has the upper hand when it wins an initial battle. Megan's decreased stamina is her biggest frustration and impediment to making progress. She still can do much physically, but after an hour of mental challenge she is as weak as a pup. The stamina is unpredictable and often exhausting to the point that only sleep will restore function. At other times it results in almost a catatonic state that includes watching TV but not seeming to be connected to what she is watching. It is almost daydreaming. Her neurologist said that Megan's brain will continue to heal for several years after the stroke, and the variations in stamina are often an expression of that continued healing.

The most potent weapon against a brain insult is breaking the elephant down into bite-sized pieces. (How do you eat an elephant? One bite at a time.) The first battles and the first fights typically yield the most real estate. So, from the initial event, we began the intensive process of measuring how far back we have come. As a percentage, from zero to sixty percent we observed that renewal is quick and gratifying. After that, each additional percentage gained has been hard fought and physically and mentally exhausting. But our goal has been to achieve continuous effort with variations in therapy and innovations in treatment methods, and we have determined that this is hard to accomplish and eventually becomes an elusive goal. It is what we seek, but it is difficult to achieve. We continue to fight for each percentage point. With God's help and grace, we still climb that scale, although more slowly.

And what about caregiving? How do we as laypeople and full-time caregivers and advocates innovate and keep Megan interested and focused? We continuously look for new information and opportunities. The National Stroke Association (which was folded into the American Stroke Association in 2019) has been a constant source of materials, ideas, stories, blogs, and other resources, particularly for the task of caregiving, or "care-living" as they call it. They stated their mission as "to reduce the incidence and impact of stroke by developing education and programs on stroke prevention, treatment, rehabilitation and support." As I looked for guidance in those earliest days, I tripped on the following from some of their printed materials that describes the journey succinctly:

> Stroke recovery is not a linear process. The stroke survivor's needs may change, and as a caregiver, your role will change along with them. It is helpful to be open to these changes. As the stroke survivor regains strength and independence, your role may lessen, but it may also increase if new challenges arise. Keep open communication with the stroke survivor to make sure you are tuned in to their changing needs and concerns. Over time, you

and the stroke survivor may need to re-establish boundaries and figure out new ways to communicate.

This resource and many others like it provide perspective and grounding because the reader understands that unlike them, someone else has experienced this process before. Whoever wrote these words understands the journey and the process, but being open to the changes is easy to write and much harder to live. Find your support where you can, but looking for sources with experience and reasonable authority is the best place to start. There are many blogs set up by folks who are walking their own journeys, and one I became fond of is hosted by Abby Maslin.

Her post, "The Not-So-Secret Confessions of the Caregiver" (*brainline*, December 2, 2013, www.brainline.org/blog/reinventing-our-family/not-so-secret-confessions-caregiver), allowed me to view what lay ahead from the perspective of someone whose journey preceded our own. One of the most difficult parts of this process is the fact that those around you don't always "get it." Your life has changed from simple responsibility for yourself to planning and organizing every waking moment of your life and the life of your loved one. "Caregivers rarely get a moment to themselves," Maslin writes. "We often feel as though we are living a life sentence of solitary confinement. We wish people could see beyond the brave exterior. We wish we could better articulate our own needs. We wish everyone in our support system could understand the tough choices we've been forced to make. But at the end of the day, we're simply too tired to explain ourselves."

She spends the balance of the post offering her description of what her life is like taking care of her husband, TC, who experienced a traumatic brain injury. The post does a marvelous job of explaining the day-to-day stresses and frustrations. It also addresses the ways others often respond to our new circumstances that illness or injury has caused among families. Two profound points she makes speak of the long-term nature of the changes they face and how others perceive them. She writes,

Brain injury doesn't go away. Trust me, I get it. Some people may be tired of hearing about our brain injury woes. Believe me when I say I wish those days were behind us. But even with a remarkable recovery like TC's, there are lingering health concerns, psychological issues, and fears. Our life will never go back to the way it was, and neither will we. Over time friends and family will have to adjust to a new way of interacting with us. We hope you'll like us for the new people we are, but we understand if you miss the old us. We miss us, too.

Making lemonade from lemons is an art form. Over the course of the past year, I've fielded a few off-hand comments about our lives being "ruined." I must admit that word "ruined" stings a bit. Our lives are different now, but I refuse to accept the idea that brain injury is a life ruined. If anything, brain injury has provided us with the challenge of living better than we were before. Living better is a goal TC and I practice daily, and it requires some serious mental stretching. We may not be able to put this attitude into action 24 hours a day, but it's certainly what we're working toward.

It's easy for caregivers to bottle up their frustrations. With such a demanding role to fill, we are apt to put our own needs last. And as much as we sometimes wish others could read our minds or occasionally walk in our shoes and feel these demands themselves, our only real option is to stay honest with the people in our lives.

It's my hope that in sharing our secret caregiver confessions, we can strengthen the lines of communication, benefiting everyone affected by brain injury.

I am grateful to have had access to Abby Maslin's words during our difficult days. It allowed us to know that others had felt what we were feeling. And as I said before, hope keeps us all going, but hope is difficult to sustain. Our expectations and desires often impede what Maslin refers to as "living better," particularly when we spend so much time looking backward, desiring what was and not what is or what can be. What can be is not something we can control.

When given a success, we sometimes conclude that it looks different than before and therefore isn't as good. But success is success; it means that Megan can perform a function she couldn't do before, and that is success. The problem is that those supporting us often don't agree if it isn't a complete success.

Remember my friend's comment about will she ever be "right" again? Right in whose eyes? Those around us seem to expect "what was." We spend our days trying to achieve "what was." But life grants to each of us only "what is." *What is* consists of some parts that are necessary for a reasonable life and other parts that are, well, negotiable. I'll call that "what can be."

With our Megan, as time has progressed, we have continued to focus on the absolutes. But we are not as focused on those other parts" as we were when we began. We attempt to achieve, and when the absolutes won't come, we simply will not accept defeat. Instead, we do our best to trust in our hope. That hope often leads us to other options, and when necessary, we move toward a measure of acceptance. Our focus sometimes needs to change more toward achievable adaptive options. Sometimes "what was" just isn't possible, as painful as that can sometimes be. We retain hope, though. Hope leaves the door open.

Hope keeps us going, and as the Scriptures remind us, "those who hope in the LORD will renew their strength. They will soar on wings like eagles; they will run and not grow weary; they will walk and not be faint" (Isa 40:31, NIV). The questions remain. The fits and starts remain. Some days we do see progress, and on other days we don't. But we won't give up, we won't change direction, and we won't lose hope. Neither will Megan.

Chapter 24

What's Next?

As a baby, she rested her sweet head on my chest and was comforted by the rhythm of my heart beating joyfully because of the blessing of a new life given to Linda and me. She always knew how to get her old man to do what she wanted. I remember an NSYNC concert with three of her friends in Greenville, South Carolina, that left me completely void of any ability to hear high-frequency sound as a result of 10,000 middle school girls screaming their delight at Justin, Joey, Lance, and the boys. I had enjoyed life before kids, but I again admit freely that the addition of our two has made our lives full and rich and joyful. I know that as a parent, my greatest fears involved the helpless times of not being able to keep our kids safe or well.

Our kids were active and accident prone. When our son Jeffrey was three or so, he went running through the house and tripped into a Jenny Lind table. It sliced his eyebrow wide open, and after an initial trip to our family pediatrician's office, we still ended up in the emergency room since the cut was on his face. They didn't want to just stitch it up.

My, how times have changed. My brother Bud sent our swing set seesaw directly into my upper lip, almost separating it from my nose, and as I recall as much as any three-year-old can, they stitched me right up. Of course, I have worn a mustache for decades to hide the scar.

But with little Jeffrey, as we arrived at the emergency room, we had to go through the normal intake process on a Friday night that was also a full moon. I held Jeffrey with a compress on his little eye, with Megan nearby, while Linda sat answering the intake person's questions. As we sat there, the ER was like a beehive. In came two separate gurneys from two different ambulances with older adults having heart attacks. There were cuts and scrapes and bruised limbs, and as a young parent I was oblivious to the impact that this "horror" was having on my little girl, who was already traumatized by the injury to her little brother.

As we continued to wait at that desk, her little body snuggled up tight next to mine, and then I realized she was trembling. I turned to see her staring at the entrance in which a man was walking in with paper towels and dabbing at the blood coming from dozens of pellet wounds from an apparent shotgun injury.

I grabbed Megan, threw her on my other shoulder, hid her eyes as much as I could, and asked for a phone to call our friends the Pierces to come bail us out and take Megan home while we dealt with the healthcare system before it was the juggernaut it has now become.

To this day, I worry about all the times I lacked the sensitivity to be the kind of parent my kids deserved. I worried that Megan might carry emotional or psychological trauma because of my parental ineptitude. I think all parents worry about that. But despite having to find our way through parenthood, no one loved their kids any more than Linda and I did. We have always been family, even during the terrible twos and the terrible teens, which really weren't all that terrible. As life goes on, the love we share as family changes to accommodate growth and distance, but it remains one of the few constants that I can still recognize.

Life changed significantly for us when our kids went off to college. I still remember the summer Megan first went to UNCG. That whole summer was filled with excitement and anticipation, and when the day came for us to take her to campus the excitement continued in earnest . . . until the moment when we had to say goodbye. The lump in the throat that has been so prevalent during recent times got one of its early workouts on that day. It was so quiet as we left and headed for home. That is one of those moments in which, as parents, we all wonder whether we have done enough. Will our family be forever changed by the normal progression that takes our kids into the life God calls them to live? Will our child settle in and find her calling? Will she find happiness and success and all those things we all wish for each of our children?

Those first weeks were filled with phone calls, emails, texts, and the usual finding our way with anything new. But Megan found her way and soon was wrapped up in her first year, and our visits were welcome but increasingly less necessary. She carved out relationships and purpose and did well academically. She grew into her own, and in our pride, we realized this was a person we recognized and appreciated for many reasons.

As Megan moved toward being an adult, we were increasingly involved in Jeffrey's high school experience as we became all-in band parents. Our local high school had an incredibly successful band program that was tops in the area most years, and Jeffrey was more introverted than his big sister. We did all we could to help him find his way as he grew more outgoing and began to develop relationships of his own.

Megan and Jeffrey were close but in a very interesting way. I think Linda and I both expected Megan to find the love of her life before Jeffrey in that she was so extroverted, and Jeffrey was so introverted. When Jeffrey took off for Western Carolina University, we were floored soon after when one of our friends asked us who Jeffrey was dating and we responded, "Say what?" We began internet stalking and found pictures and other "evidence," and soon our knowledge was confirmed. Life has a funny way of sneaking up on you sometimes. Brannon became a part of our vernacular and our lives, and she fit in as if she had always been here. We were amused at Megan's response to the whole thing when she quipped one day, "Well, I'm happy for them, but if they get married before I do there will be hell to pay!"

After years of dating and graduations and new jobs, Jeffrey came to us one evening and said, "I think I want to ask Brannon to marry me." We asked the obvious questions about money and living accommodations, jobs and all the rest, but we all agreed that this was right and good. And then Jeffrey bought a ring and they set the date, and we spent the summer of 2015 planning and executing a lovely and wonderful wedding.

One of many precious parts of this whole experience is the fact that Brannon had respect for Megan even before her decision to become part of our family. Knowing that Megan was talented in so many things, Brannon immediately asked her to be her maid of honor. From then on, this wedding was Megan's passion and purpose. She put her heart and soul into making it something sweet, special, and memorable.

Those days were only months before the changes of 2016, but when we talk about the importance of "what was," this is a significant part of it. One of my favorite pictures of that remarkable wedding day was an "after" photograph in which the whole wedding party attempted to jump in unison and hopefully catch most if not all of us at least a few inches off the ground. For whatever reason, it worked, and we got one of the best pictures of the whole day. Megan, in her bridesmaid dress, was easily three feet in the air doing an almost split with the biggest grin in history.

When I had to decide what picture of my lovely daughter to post to her CaringBridge site, I struggled a bit. But once I found an electronic version of that picture, I immediately cropped it to be of Megan alone and posted it, for many reasons. Not the least of which was the fact that at the moment of posting, so much of her precious face and body were so damaged and different. But *this* was our daughter. This was "what was," at least physically. And this was what we would aspire to and aim for throughout rehabilitation.

As I mentioned, we have spent so many countless and perhaps wasted hours wondering whether the stroke could have been detected or even prevented. One of the moments that stirs doubts and brings us questions involved a day when Megan and Mom and Dad were all working hard to lose weight and be healthier. Megan decided to give blood at church on the same day that we also had an extended evening choir rehearsal.

About an hour or more into the rehearsal, Megan fainted and went down hard. I was on the back row, and suddenly people were motioning me down to the lower platform where she lay motionless. Before I could get to the floor, at least three folks had dialed 911, and I tried to get her some air and elevated her legs. I thought for sure that this was a result of her overdoing it right after giving blood without eating a reasonable meal.

When EMS got there, Megan was coming around. They checked her out, and her blood pressure was at rock bottom. Megan had no intention of being transported to the hospital. She said she was fine and just needed to eat and wanted to go home. We kidded her about the fact that the whole EMS crew were big, strapping boys about her age, and that she just didn't want to make a bad impression.

We let it go. Would her PFO (the hole in her heart) have been discovered if we had gone to Mission that night? It's doubtful, but who knows. We went home, got her fed, and she seemed to recover completely. I remember being offended when one of our friends suggested she had had a "seizure." But in remembering that night, which was a long time before the stroke, I still face my demons.

Even though Megan saw her doctor and followed up, from now on I plan to change my own beliefs, at least for my family. If any medical event involves being unconscious or even being disoriented, do not self-diagnose. I would even go one step further. Do not try to direct the decision-making process of your doctor. Doctors are human, and they can't help sensing and being influenced by the desires and beliefs of patients and their families. If it involves anything outside of a snotty nose, don't take the chance, and don't allow your strong-willed children to overrule you, particularly if they get their strong-willed nature from you.

About three months after we got back to Asheville, our neurologist referred us to Asheville Cardiologists Associates for evaluation of whether it was time to close the PFO. Megan was tired of being "stuck" all the time to measure whether she remained therapeutic regarding her Coumadin blood thinner. I admit that I never got comfortable doing those international normalized ration (INR) tests, seeing how long it took her blood to clot, and having to prick her finger to take a few drops of blood. But you do what you must to make sure your child is safe and therapeutic. We met a wonderful young cardiologist/surgeon who immediately seemed to take an interest in Megan.

He ordered a series of tests, and as a result we returned to a consultation in which our doctor said he was comfortable that the PFO was likely the source of the original stroke. There were treatment options, he said, that would permanently close the opening and might not involve open heart surgery. A new device is now available that is much like a stent commonly used to open closed arteries. This little device, which looks something like an umbrella, is implanted in the opening. A second piece is used to create tension from the other side that ultimately covers the hole with mesh.

Over three months, the body allows tissue to form over the mesh and permanently closes the opening. We talked for several days about this, but fearless Megan was adamant that closing it and being allowed to discontinue the use of Coumadin was what she wished for most. Although her sentences were rough and tumble, her passion and desires were unmistakable. We scheduled the procedure for two months later on August 12.

The thought of entering that hospital again brought dread, fear, and nerves that had nothing to do with the level of care that this good place dispenses. It was about the fear of having to subject Megan, who had already gone through so much, to more procedures, more pain, more invasions, and more angst. But at least this was on our terms. We had a say. We could have said no. But it had the potential, at least in our minds, to end the likelihood that Megan might face the devastating effects of another stroke. Of course, we were going to do it.

We arrived pre-dawn and watched as needles were inserted and questions were asked over and over and over. We walked down the hall with Megan to the surgical suite, and we told her we loved her and sent her into the hands of our surgeon along with the one who originally discovered and diagnosed her condition several months before and would now complete the task of correcting the defect he had identified.

Once again, we sat with our friends in a different waiting room and the hour-and-a-half surgery went on for nearly two and a half hours. The nurse finally called us to the desk, and we talked with the surgical nurse, who said all had gone well and that our doctor would soon be out to talk. By design we knew we would only spend one night in the hospital, and soon we went home with a new addition to our story that ultimately has done its job.

Three months later, we went back to Asheville Cardiology Associates to have the follow-up that would determine the success of the procedure. After an hour of tests, we met with our doctor, and he said, "It looks great. No bubbles and no leaks." It was a complete success.

Megan and Dr. P had become good friends as well as having developed a healthy doctor/patient relationship. They had connected early on as soon as she found out that he and his wife had young kids. As we got our final instructions and follow-up plans, he indicated that Megan would be discharged and could return if need arose.

He put his arm around Megan and said, "Okay, gal, so what are you going to do with the rest of your life?"

His simple question made us all pay attention.

Megan stopped for a minute and realized that this was the first time she was having to consider making longer-lasting decisions about what came next. She rubbed her chin between her fingers with her newly developed "let me see" move and said, "I don't know yet."

He said, "I think you have a bright future, knowing of your spirit and spunk. I'm proud of you for how far you have come." Megan smiled that crooked smile.

He then did something we were amazed at and so appreciative of: he took even more time out of his busy day and walked us all the way out to the reception area. He gave her a final hug and a wave goodbye.

Another chapter closed in this wondrous ride, but one that had made Megan consider the possibilities. As a result, not all of them seemed quite as shadowy or ominous as before. For the first time in months, Megan felt that she had options, and that was a gift from a new friend that blessed us all.

This picture captures perfectly what we referred to as "what was." Although so much has changed, despite the altered physical changes, this is still who she is and who she will always be.

Chapter 25

Saying Goodbye to Some Things

The return home was something we so longed for over the weeks we were in Atlanta, and we knew better than most that what we returned to would be different from what we had left. Things had changed, and practically speaking they had to change a lot more to accommodate what we were calling our "new normal." The early experiences of rehabilitation had begun to bring us glimpses of change and accommodation and, yes, limited hope. But the constant cloud over our lives wasn't going anywhere. We knew that the excellent medical "help" we were getting had a huge financial price tag to address, although we had no real clue how that worked or what the true impact would be.

We also knew that Megan's employer had already been gracious to her by allowing her to share in a personal leave bank that meant her salary continued until the end of June. The benefits she was provided were very much appreciated. But the unspoken question finally needed to be addressed. The reality of that conversation brought the future into clear focus. Under the law, Megan's employment would end at the end of June. In these cases, there is little that anyone can do, and we of all people understood the basics of the employee/employer relationship. As an accountant, I advise clients about it almost daily.

Having that knowledge does not make it any easier to accept. I'm now sixty years old, and in evaluating the day in the not-too-distant future when I will walk in knowing that it will be my last workday, I view it as both daunting and, at times, frightening. But to set that date as a twenty-nine-year-old, knowing that a stroke has taken away your ability to earn a living at least for now, seems stark and final. Just weeks earlier, Megan's professional possibilities had appeared to be a virtual red-carpet ride that trailed off into an exciting future, beckoning her onward to reaching new heights and achievements over a career that was just reaching full speed.

I know that the seeming unfairness of this adds layer upon layer of disappointment, and that is how we first felt its proverbial sting. There is a finality to this "life interrupted" that seems perverse and hateful and is difficult to get past. But much of it is simply fact, hard as it is to accept. That is how we have tried to make sense of it. Our attempt at trying to deal with "what's next" involves one of many discernment processes that we are party to. They all "suck" to a degree, but each has a purpose and an intent.

Megan wants to work again, but her hopes of being in front of a class of adult childcare providers have transformed into a fleeting hope of some type of work that will have purpose but needs to bend and reshape or completely morph into something brand new. Our family does not yet know what that might be. As in so many things, Megan has a positive spirit, but she can't help but occasionally comment that she wishes she could once again _____ (fill in the blank). The list includes the ability to drive, sing from a hymnbook, read for pleasure, date, teach, live independently. . . . The list is painfully long. But it is also appropriately filled with hope and a plan of how to get there, at least for some of the desires.

In our last days of being in Atlanta, Megan and I had a blunt, unplanned talk about what we all were returning to. I asked the question that I had dreaded most: What should we do with her house? Megan never even blinked. She immediately blurted out, "Sell it; we have to sell it." I said, "Don't you think we should hold on to it at least for a while?" But that person, about whom everyone else wondered whether she understood her own circumstances, showed absolute clarity and reason when she said, "Why? I can't afford it anymore."

So not long after we got back, one of the early things she wanted to do was go to her home. She walked through every single room and picked up her stuff and gathered a few things she wanted for the apartment we were living in. She sat down on her own sofa and covered her and her mom with a throw and watched TV for a short while. And again, as we drove back to the apartment, she said stoically, "Sell it."

She was the one giving up her dream, and in that moment, it was our hearts that were once again breaking. God, I hate this.

The following day I called a friend of ours who is a real estate broker, and we listed the townhome for sale. While it was being added to the multiple listing service, the next weekend Megan and I went there again to finally complete the subway tile backsplash for her new kitchen in what would soon become someone else's dream home. It was the right finishing touch, and Megan approved wistfully.

In less than four weeks, we got a contract, and within a few more weeks it would be time to hold the closing. As those last days approached, Megan wanted to drive by Union Chapel more and more often. For fun one Friday night, she wanted to host a movie and game night with her buddies there, so we ordered pizzas and drinks, and then Linda and I disappeared. They had a wonderful evening of "just them," which felt normal and fun and eventually became emotional and painful, as we expected.

As we went over to clean up and take out the trash from the evening, we walked into the conversations of Megan and her friends planning a moving party to help her pack up her things and move the significant load of furnishings that she had accumulated over just a couple of years. There were tears and hugs, compassion, empathy, and absolute understanding. To our amazement, it was Megan holding us all up as she approached this huge change with determination and an underlying foundation of hope that I have yet to understand.

Moving time drew near, and we and dozens of her friends, including Glenn, began packing boxes and separating things to store from things to sell. One Saturday, we held a garage sale, and Megan sold a lot of her stuff for not a lot of money. Our conclusion was that anything that sold, even for a small amount, helped us save money on storage fees for whatever time storage would be necessary.

From the stuff that did not sell, she gifted to those dear young friends of hers a few of her possessions. They seemed thrilled to get them, and she was so proud that they found her tastes appealing. We consigned some furniture at a local consignment shop and stored the remaining items in a rental unit.

Then there was her massive accumulation of clothes, particularly shoes. To say Megan is a "shoe diva" is like saying Donald Trump can be "controversial." Megan had dozens of pairs of shoes, including what I call "skyscraper heels." As she began to pack up her clothes, the emotions finally overtook her. And for one of the few times thus far, she sat in the middle of her bedroom floor where the stroke first happened and wept bitterly. It was as if the whole event fully hit home, and it went on for a long time. She had large black plastic bags for separating her things. In that fit of painful emotion, she began tossing shoes toward the "dispose" pile. Almost all of them. I interrupted and said, "Whoa now, sis, let's don't get ahead of ourselves here. Don't you want to box them up for now?"

The words she uttered didn't communicate what she felt. With tears in her eyes and animation in her face, and with a voice that to that moment we had heard very little, she pointed at a lovely stiletto heel and then pointed to her brace-covered leg and said, "But I can't . . . ." The words stopped, but the meaning and passion found their target and pierced our souls once more.

I had another "dammit" moment and said, "Okay, let's do this instead. Let's pack up the ones you think you might be able to eventually wear and those you like the most, and we can decide a year from now, if need be, about the rest. I want you to have something to work toward, and wearing some of these may not be out of the question."

Megan looked at me as only she can with an expression that said, "Dad, are you completely out of your mind?" But she gave in and finally said, "Okay."

So we boxed and separated, and after what seemed like weeks, the house was finally empty. We cleaned and touched up paint and polished floors, and then it was the day before closing. As we came home from dinner, I already had the car aimed toward Union Chapel, and Megan asked, "Can we go?" We went to 17 Union Chapel Road one last time. We had gathered all the keys we had and left them on those lovely granite countertops.

Megan walked in through the garage and climbed every one of the thirty or so steps from bottom to top. She stopped and methodically walked through every room and every closet. She looked in every cabinet. Linda and I followed for a time and then realized that this was her way of saying goodbye, so we hung back.

When things got too quiet, we walked upstairs and found her again looking out the window with tears streaming down her face. We left her alone though we couldn't hide our own tears. Megan came down those steps one last time, walked through the kitchen, and rubbed the subway tile. She said softly, "Looks nice." She walked out on the deck over her parking lot that looked down onto Reems Creek Road and quietly focused on the setting late summer sun.

We turned off the lights for one last time and got into the car and headed back home. The sale closed the following day with the receipt of a certified check in place of her dreams, but not without the hope that at some point those boxes and storage units might again allow our sweet child the opportunity to spread her wings once more—even though the physical layout and new location would likely need to be modified to accommodate her "new normal."

The first part of any journey is often the hardest, and this one is no different. Hope keeps us moving forward. Faith keeps us looking upward. Reality keeps us firmly rooted in what can and cannot be achieved. But somewhere along the way, every person who goes through this must face that reality. It hurts and is hard to do. The sooner you face it, though, the more likely you are to make decisions that lay a foundation for positive change. That helps encourage the soul and establishes initial goals that are reasonable, hopeful, and motivational and are therefore attainable.

I've already mentioned Eddie Morgan, who is a family and spiritual compass of sorts. Eddie is married to Martha, and she is an educator whom Megan often looked up to as she has tried to effect the same positive change in childhood education. After the stroke, Martha approached Megan about coming back to teach at First Baptist. Martha had taken on the task of leading the infant class, which was increasing as young people were once again starting families within our church.

Megan showed a bit of trepidation at the prospect, but to our surprise and delight, one Saturday night she said, "I need to get going early in the morning. I'm helping Martha." And once again Megan looks forward to giving back and has done so with grace and beauty. I observed with interest how the parents of these kids would react to the new Megan, and I know that in those first weeks they unintentionally watched her a bit closer and gave a few more instructions and checked back at times when they hadn't the previous weeks, but in a short while, Megan's return to children's ministry became normal again.

Her interaction with families outside of church had always been an act of love and encouragement, but since the stroke it was obvious that some folks and even some kids were unsure of this "new" Megan. She wasn't as she had been. Her smile was a little crooked, she walked a little funny, and her words were a bit uneven, but her joy and exuberance were the same. The kids brought her personality back out of the shadows and allowed most of the previous relationships to resume at some level. They are not the same as they were, but they are good, and seeing Miss Megan is something they look forward to.

In my experience, children are exceptionally good judges of character and trustworthiness. Kids require encouragement to simply "share relationship" with someone outside their day-to-day environment. Megan has always gone out of her way to connect with kids, and now she works even harder at trying to make those connections, both with the kids and their parents and siblings.

Megan's previous talent for outthinking and outworking everyone else is right back where it belongs, even though on a simpler platform. She is working hard to find a way to use what she knows but still has trouble communicating. As part of her speech therapy, Megan has started reading children's books so she can read them aloud to her classes as she did before. The aphasia doesn't give her a break for good intentions, but she beats it into submission over a period of weeks. This is a significant part of her "getting better." She is pouring into that half-empty glass a drop at a time. It is different, it isn't what she or any of us wanted, but to resign or give up isn't in her DNA, and so the children help her see a future that is still important and possible. Miss Megan loves those kids, and ultimately that is what matters.

Over the months I am finally beginning to understand that in so much of this "production," the stage on which the play is performed is like a blank page, but the words have not been written yet. Megan continues to formulate them. She knows what she wants to write just like she knows what she wants to say.

Even though I desire to put the pen to the page for her, the story isn't mine to write, and it never can be. Only she can do that. And to my delight, she is again picking up that pen a little more often. Aphasia will not win all the time.

Chapter 26

Lessons Learned

One of many difficult parts in this "journey" is the intense, overwhelming pressure brought on our family by Megan's illness that propels us into a constant search for "relief." Relief from stress, relief from pain, relief from anger, fear, depression, hopelessness, and particularly doubt. Doubt plays an integral role in all of this because so much of what we are going through appears impossible and insurmountable. This villain we fight has all the tools it needs to keep us off balance and make us question everything. Even when we are making progress, the doubt makes us question things in a way that is hard to control. An earlier chapter I wrote was titled "I Don't Know," and from the first hours of each day as I drive to and from work, when I seek to address my only constant in all of this—my God—I often start each petition with that phrase, and then I can't add anything meaningful to it. Saying "I don't know" is often beyond my control. It is out of my mouth before my brain can catch it. At times I wonder if God thinks I am a complete idiot or worse, if there has ever been anyone of less faith and courage than I have.

Then I look to others whom I consider my heroes of the faith and think about the challenges they have faced. On most days, I catch a glimmer of hope because the human condition that God placed on mortals has us all wondering, all questioning, even all doubting, if we are truly honest. During the Easter season, our church often puts in the order of worship the line "The Assurance of Pardon." This moment usually comes right after the time when we confess our sins and seek God's pardon for all that we have done wrong. We are of such curious incompetence as Christians that we usually need someone to remind us of God's promise that when we humble ourselves and truly seek forgiveness, our transgressions are simply eliminated from any record of wrongdoing kept by the Almighty, totally forgotten. In these days as I lack the courage, faith, hope, and certainly confidence, it has taken someone else to remind me that even when I am lost on the journey and have trouble finding my way, God is there. God is always there . . . and has been this entire time. Oh, I have fussed at God at times and I have tried to blame him when I'm talking with others, but as is usually the case when those we love have to suffer through the sometimes harsh challenges of life, the first target we all seem to aim at are those who love us the most and those who have, through their exhaustion, already given us much more than we deserve. And they will continue to do so long after any barb or attack is sent their way. Our pain and mindless spewing of venom is forgotten and forgiven as soon as it is spoken. That is how love works. But that doesn't make it fair, and those of us who are the seeming victims of injustice need to take note of that. Don't bite the hand that feeds you or, more importantly, the hand that loves you.

As we have worked our collective way through these days, I have longed for life to regain an ebb and flow that remotely looks like anything we had before. For Megan, that former life is all but impossible; her life is so significantly changed that to expect the impossible is folly. I have prayed for miracles since that Tuesday morning, and God came through. We have gotten so many more miracles than anyone can expect in this life. Our daughter lives! I praise God for that each day. She walks, she speaks, she has an amazing perspective most days, she loves . . . particularly one sweet little animal that we didn't even know existed before this happened. It is easy for me as a father to fret over what has been taken, what has changed, what has not returned, and what will likely never heal. That is the burden I carry as a parent, and that is the source of an ongoing personal fight that seems to be headed at least in part to some type of stalemate if not failure. I started this book as a guide for others to follow when they navigate the treacherous waters of recovery, healing, and rehabilitation. But what does success look like? I see glimpses often, and that is wonderful, but who is really winning? We win occasional battles, but who is winning the war?

I want my Megan to win. She deserves to. No one has fought any harder, and no one should have to endure what she has been through. "It isn't fair."

Bingo! "It isn't fair." There is the obvious truth in all of this.

In an earlier chapter, I mentioned Abby Maslin's blog that has helped anchor us and allowed us to share and understand common challenges. Recently, though, I was fortunate to read a different caregiver's account of their journey on a similar website. It is a journey of some fifteen years that has also resembled what we have felt for much of it. A mother expressed incredible frustration at having to appear to be strong, blessed, and grateful, especially now that her family's experience has come to a point when they send their loved one back into a new chapter of added independence and hope.

But in a post of absolute honesty, this mom unloaded paragraph after paragraph of pent-up emotion and exhaustion over trying to maintain hope of reclaiming the life they had before their event took place. It is brutally honest, refreshingly transparent, and simply put. She finally says, "I can let down the mask and say what I really feel and perhaps be a little selfish as to what I plan to do with the rest of my life," although the task is not over but simply changing phases yet again.

So much of what any family experiences in this type of event is simply that. What has been taken from our daughter has, in differing ways, also been taken from us. A red-hot burn pierces the heart of each person close to the center. And in trying to respect those who watch us from the outside, we all sometimes live in a more public eye, and most of us try to put up a front that isn't real, isn't honest, and isn't sustainable. Those around us hold us up as examples or evidence of something that we didn't want or ask for, and all too often we do not feel competent to fulfill it.

Injustice demands that we respond and make a stand, but in fact there is no magic cure that can restore the whole. What has been taken from my Megan has also ripped much from our souls, and even now we lie in pain, crumpled on the ground on many days. And we selfishly, angrily, intentionally want it all back. It isn't fair. But it is where we live and will live until the time comes, if ever, when we can rip our lives away from the jaws of the beast that illness often becomes.

While Megan's needs are still so important to me, so is the relationship I have with Linda, and to be honest we have let that bond suffer and be sacrificed far too much. The time we have spent sitting on the couch with our daughter watching *The Voice* or *America's Got Talent* or *Fixer Upper*, I might like to have spent with her doing other things. But for now, we do what we must to be family, to survive, to find relief, and, when possible, to make progress.

A few months after we returned from Atlanta, Eddie Morgan asked a question that made me smile, but it hit close to reality: "So what is it like having a sixteen-year-old at home again?" I have had to add that it may have similarities to a sixteen-year-old, but to be honest, Megan has a thirty-year intellect but with filters that she has trouble applying.

We have learned so many lessons from this experience. My hope is through telling our convoluted story, another family might find these lessons helpful as they travel the uneven path toward Venice. If you were to find yourself in similar circumstances, as you go through the hard days of extended loving service, fulfilling an uncomfortable role that you some days resent and simply do not want and don't feel competent to fulfill, there are several things you can do:

- *Allow yourself to grieve.* No matter how significant or insignificant the event is, failing to grieve discounts what has happened and doesn't allow you to process the byproducts of the insult. Those byproducts include anger, depression, irritability, fear, and so many other difficult things. To heal, to survive, you must process these and find a way to deal with what you, your family, and your patient are feeling. Take time to grieve. Also try to understand your grief, which may require help from a counselor, pastor, or competent friend.
- *Recognize, acknowledge, embrace, and, as you can, "put down" your anger as your story unfolds.* Anger is normal and unavoidable; you will experience it, particularly if the cause of the event is in some way attributable to someone else or something else. Anger will not restore your loved one. Anger will not remove the burdens of the injustice.

Anger will only breed anger, keep you from healing, and separate you from and likely frighten your family and friends. Anger will damage lives if allowed to run loose. Anger will damage your own health, and it will keep you from the faith you claim and the God you serve. It is not an answer and usually does not help after a reasonable time of grief. It is also difficult to get rid of completely. But put it down when you can.

- *Advocate for your loved one from day one.* Even if someone with a lot of letters after their name tells you they want to do something to your loved one, feel comfortable to ask, "Why is this necessary?" A close friend said that if you ask "why" four times in succession after any premise or statement, you will likely get to the real answer to the question you have asked. And if after being asked, someone gets mad or pushes back, ask for another opinion. Don't be a jerk, but do, intentionally, be an advocate.

- *Say "thank you" a lot.* There is something healing and inspiring about appreciating those who treat your loved one, those who visit your loved one, and those who will be there for you and your family throughout this long journey. On the days I struggled the most, being grateful allowed me to find balance. The pain was/is still there, but the expression of gratitude motivates you to keep trying, to keep fighting, and to keep loving you and your family.

- *Be intentional about trying to maintain your entire family dynamic.* You aren't the only one hurting, and your moments of encouragement may be a lifeline that your spouse, mother, father, son, daughter, or friend may need to support and love you. We have spent much of this time passing around and sharing the responsibilities or being the "keeper of all the sanity, love, knowledge, and wisdom." You are strong for as long as you can be, and then you let someone else fight for a while, particularly in the early days. Don't be a hog. Pass it on, take a breather, and then pick up and carry the load again when necessary.

- *As this "battle" moves to future phases, you will find that non-family relationships change to accommodate circumstances, treatment, life, work, and choices.* Some relationships will grow, some will die, and some will be particularly hard. With us, not everyone could go to

Atlanta, but that didn't mean our friends were any less interested or invested. And honestly, this journey truly is a marathon. Banking support is valuable and necessary. Some folks believe that our lives even now are where we plan to stay. They have concluded that we don't need them to come around as much or that they should perhaps move on because our lives have too much drama or too much pain. In some cases, we no longer seek their friendship since our lives even now have little extra time for anything other than work, patient care and support, and occasional personal maintenance. This relational change hurts, but it is sometimes necessary. It is one of many regrets you may have to face. What you will discover is that in many cases, you were doing all the work in some of those relationships, which, in the words of a brilliant young Atlanta attorney, suggests that there was no deep friendship there to begin with. There was only a relationship of service. What I have also found is that as some friendships change, others expand and grow as we nourish them. When you get to Venice, you will still need friends and relationships. Hold your truest friends close. In crisis, those relationships will help you survive. As your new normal gets closer, many of your other friendships will find new life, nourishment, and an appropriate place in your new world.

- *Learn how to have faith again: to pray, to seek God, to share your experiences, and to express your faith in ways that aren't completely wrapped up in what has happened.* I have struggled to teach Bible study again because, try as I may, my faith now is inextricably linked to these events. That makes offering perspective that is meaningful to others, without seeming to evoke their concern, much more elusive. After a time, even though your pain is still there, some people may conclude that you seek attention by bringing it up, and perhaps we sometimes do. But I will never be the same, and, honestly, my faith will never be the same either. Just like Megan, things may look different. They aren't exactly as they were, but they can still be good. I spend time looking for Venice. I also have work to do on my faith. But I am sure that God did not, has not, will not abandon us in all of this. So "I just *have* to learn to get better" at being a Christian. I have a long way to go, but my faith has gotten me through many, if not most, of the hardest days. There was redemption in allowing God to cradle my less damaged brain as I prayed for God to heal my daughter's severely damaged brain. God has and continues to answer those prayers. We continue to be transformed. That is an amazing gift and truly is enough. It is well.

- *Find the ways to forgive perceived offenses from others.* Over the years, I have observed firsthand that the hard and harsh things that happen to or within families dealing with crisis seem to linger for a lifetime. I have often heard folks say, "I will never forgive _____ for what he/she said, did, didn't do" during a crisis. Don't make the mistake of compounding an already difficult situation. Instead of trying to "divide," look for what can "unite." Make forgiveness a frequent stop on your road to Venice.

- *Learn all you can about what has happened to your loved one.* You cannot positively affect something that you know nothing about. The resources are there, and you cannot make informed decisions about treatment, rehab, or anything else if you don't understand the problems. Don't make decisions without conversation or consultation. Find the book; read the book. Always try to respect what you believe your loved one would want. If things get too hard, step away for a few moments when possible and revisit the issue when decisions can be made in calmer, more thoughtful moments.

- *Never give up. Never ever give up.* (Thanks, Jimmy V.) Even when things seem hopeless, find the energy, the love, the knowledge, and the hope to fight on. Besides your love and faith, tenacity is sometimes all you and your loved one have as a resource. There will be times when you don't want to have to make certain decisions, but unless you have reached the point where going on makes no sense, find the course of action that you believe gives your precious loved one the possibility of healing. If healing isn't possible, then find the course that brings hope, comfort, or peace. And do not question your previous actions. As my wise Momma often said, "Son, you did the best you could." Crisis events take on their own path. Maybe you can find one, but I never found a crystal ball that was reliable. There will always be things you will question or wish you could have done differently, but that is all 20/20 hindsight. Accept what is done, let go of your regrets, be informed about the decisions you will make when possible, and pray *at all times* for wisdom and hope.

- *Take care of yourself.* You are of little use if you reach exhaustion or are confused by too many days at the ICU or rehab room. Take care of those around you as well. Find time to relax, to eat, to exercise your mind and body, and to share relationships with family and friends who minister to you. Be intentional about celebrating even the smallest accomplishments or successes. Find a way to laugh at least daily, even if it is at your own expense. The small successes will release the tension, drop the shoulders, calm the moment, prevent the meltdown, and unite the circle of family and friends. Find new ways to be family. During our times of rehab and renewal, we found that games, reading, and movies allowed us freedom from stress and the ability to feel at least a bit more normal.
- *Hug. A lot.* There is something about an embrace that releases tension and emotion even between big, tough men. And it should continue even when things calm down a bit. I still hug my buddy Jon after sharing a meal or playing a round of golf. It has become a symbol of our shared experience and our respect for each other even when life is challenging.
- *Finally, be grateful.* So much of this process is filled with what is gone, what is wrong, what is missing, and what has been taken. Over time, the list of what is present, what is restored, what is improved or "better" grows for many of us. Hope is the central source of our ability to go on, and finding it isn't always easy. But hope has a way of sneaking in through all the bad, all the darkness, all the angst. When things are hard and hopeless and dark, our natural tendency is to withdraw or give up. We at some point conclude that our situation is too hard, too unjust. But usually there are reasons for hope. Something shows promise no matter how small. Healing begins. And for those glimmers of restoration, rehabilitation, and recovery, and a new evolving normal, I have been able to show gratitude. It is my nature, which shocks me to a degree. I really thought I was a curmudgeon. Sure, I have too often been angry, sullen, distant, hopeless, and depressed. I am especially good at anger. But I cannot ignore the gifts that gave us hope, the treatment that began addressing the damage,

and the incredibly hard work of others helping us survive . . . and for all of that, I have an immense feeling of gratitude. You can be grateful to the caregivers, the friends, the doctors, the co-workers, and, if you are a person of faith, you likely have to give thanks to God. What has been taken causes feelings of sadness, but the expression of gratitude to one friend, to one caregiver, to one other person, to God changes your perspective from darkness into light. I prefer the light. It is the light that provides healing. And for that I must always give thanks.

The search for Venice is a journey along various terrains, and sometimes the trek is all challenge. But if you allow yourself to grow, allow yourself to learn, allow yourself to be tested, getting there is its own reward. Parts of the trip are disappointing and sad, but if you focus on the journey and work hard to stay motivated, you will find your destination. It is not where you planned to go, it is not what you planned when you started, and it doesn't look like what you expected and hoped for. But in its own way, it can be just as sweet, just as beautiful, and just as filled with promise. After all, I hear it is nice in Venice this time of year. I want to experience that. We all deserve to experience that.

Chapter 27

The End?

Typically, when you get to the last part of any book, the story concludes, "The End." But in this case the end does not seem apropos, and likely the end isn't even in sight at this juncture. You see, Megan has not slowed down in all these months, and neither have we. There is a part of "the end" that I long for—the end speaks to conclusion, resolution, or perhaps even successful completion. But at this point there is only more work in sight. Each day has its own purpose and plan. Each night as I tuck my thirty-plus-year-old daughter into bed, her question is usually the same: "What's the plan for tomorrow?" Sometimes on a Sunday night, she asks about the coming week.

In these first months, even in a recovery as remarkable and successful as Megan's has been, we must acknowledge that we are not done yet. In our hearts, there is much more to do even though some of it has not revealed itself to us. We have not completed the course originally laid out for us. A business associate asked in clinical terms, "How much longer will your partners be comfortable allowing you the latitude to take care of your daughter?" My response was, "As long as it takes." Truthfully, they do not have much of a choice if they need me as a partner. Megan must be our primary focus, now and for the near future, and my good friends in my firm know of my commitment to this task.

We are grateful for the many ways our friends and associates and doctors and family have altered their ways to accommodate our new reality. "What is" requires modification almost every time when "what was" is no longer possible. When "what was" becomes impossible, we must reevaluate our needs. Like Venice, it can still be nice if we are willing to attempt to live by the words of Reinhold Niebuhr, pastor of an Evangelical & Reformed Church in Detroit in the 1920s, who wrote what has been called the Serenity Prayer. It goes like this:

> God grant me the serenity
> to accept the things I cannot change,
> courage to change the things I can,
> and the wisdom to know the difference.
> Living one day at a time,
> enjoying one moment at a time
> Accepting hardships as the pathway to peace,
> taking, as Jesus did,
> this sinful world as it is,
> not as I would have it,
> Trusting that You will make all things right
> if I surrender to Your will,
> so that I may be reasonably happy in this life
> and supremely happy with You forever in the next.
> Amen.

"What is" requires us to lean into the idea of surrender and trust and acceptance. This allows us to experience a reasonably happy life in full knowledge that this is not all there is but is rather a prelude to "what will be." I do not believe God never gives us more than we can handle, as some of my well-intentioned friends have offered as guidance. The Bible in 1 Corinthians says that God will not allow us to be "tested" beyond our strength (in a context of not worshiping idols). I do not believe this means we cannot experience loss or sadness beyond our ability to cope, at least for a time. Our world is filled with rampant mental illness and conflict, and the thought that God would regularly push us right up to the edge, to the breaking point to test our loyalty or faith is particularly un-Christlike.

The God I have grown to know and recognize is with me through whatever comes. In many lives I have observed over my years, some believers have been pushed way over the line of what I think any one person or family can stand or should have to endure. I cannot believe that God caused these events as some kind of test.

I also believe God was there every day, every hour, in every hard and challenging moment. There have certainly been days when I went way over that limit, and those were the days I lashed out and railed uncontrollably at God. What I believe fervently is that my faith makes me different because I have the support and belief that even in the direst circumstances, God gives me the ability and perspective to positively affect others and myself, forgiving my misdeeds, giving me hope for things unseen and un-promised, and offering a perspective that allows me to work toward hope, justice, mercy, and love, even when none of those are present in the events of that particular moment.

Even in moments of despair and disaster, Christ called on the name of the Father. He lived a life of complex service and raised the dead, healed the sick, and interceded on behalf of the thief whose plight was like his own. He sought comfort for his mother Mary and commended his existence into the presence of God when he had given all he had to give in this life.

Authors for years have tried to address why a loving God allows good people to experience horrible things. So many try to tie a pretty bow on some piece of Scripture or observation or revelation that they believe speaks to the circumstance. I think some of them miss the mark completely. Recently I heard a friend offer a sermon that asked the same questions and presented possibilities but settled on something that gives me the hope I have lacked: "Perhaps the reason prayer so often seems to go unanswered is the possibility that there is something else to be learned."

In these post-stroke months, our family has gone to school, and the lessons we have learned are painful but of spiritual worth. None of us wanted this advanced degree. But if there is one thing I am certain of, it is that with each step we have taken on this mental and spiritual journey, the lessons we have learned and are learning have been specific, often painful, important, and beneficial. These lessons have allowed us safe passage thus far. I submit that there are more lessons to learn, so we will stay in school.

I also believe faith calls us to works—not just to good deeds but to "get your hands dirty" intercession that makes better the lives of those with severe needs. If I live another twenty years, I am glad to spend it providing a home of love for my daughter if that is what is necessary. I will plan for her security as well when I am no longer here, although at this moment I do not know what that will look like.

I realize that the world is not entirely ready to embrace this place of hope for wayward and damaged souls the way I envision it. These days, I am offended at the mentality that drives people to selfish motives and self-centeredness. But I also admit that in the terms of the world, we are privileged. We are still part of that "one percent" when we compare our financial circumstances to those living in other parts of the world. I told friends early on that when I was confronted with the question of "Why me?" my response had to be "Why not me?" We have good jobs and savings that we can use—more than we need in the grand scheme of things. But in my perhaps warped perspective, I do not consider those who have much to be damned to hell for eternity if we are willing to use what we have for the glory of the Almighty.

I also understand and fear to a degree the Scripture that says it is easier for the proverbial camel (a person of wealth such as myself) to go through the eye of a needle than it is for a wealthy man to enter the kingdom of God. Even so, I am still not convinced that God calls us to a life of a complete lack of means or resources. It comes down to how we choose to use what we have. Do we own what we have, or does what we have own us?

The life I wish to live would have me using any wealth I have for good and for justice. I am by no means wealthy in US terms. I have two mortgages and a 401k. If I could retire to take care of Megan full time, I would have done that by now, but my uncertainty about what that entails financially makes me hesitant. Also, in current dollars, just continuing our health insurance requires us to keep a job until we reach sixty-five, when we can currently plan to qualify for Medicare. What I want and what may be required may be two different things, and Megan's needs will be our priority as long as hope exists, and even after. I will continue to take each day as it comes, and those decisions will resolve themselves as long as our current treatment can be sustained.

What does Megan want? I do not know all of that even now. Megan still embraces her original conversation with her uncle Bud when she said, almost emphatically, "I just have to get better." I was proud of Megan before any of this. She was my shining example of what is good about the next generation. She has her faults, as we all do. But she was doing it right, living by the rules as she understood them, and trying to live a life she felt had purpose and hope. She still obviously wants that. We do as well.

Our collective goal is not perfection or recovery or even "what was." We simply plan to work hard to go as far as we can. We will follow the technology and the therapies, and wherever that leads us will be fine. There are no preconceptions, only the goal of "getting better"—whatever that ends up meaning.

As part of that trip or journey (in my mind), the recent words of Megan's cardiologist weigh on us. "What is it that you want to do with the rest of your life, Megan?" One of our biggest challenges will be motivation should the therapy plateau. How do we stay motivated? In my mind, this gift of family and friends will continue to bring us hope and encouragement. The walls to insulate pain grow slowly when it comes to family, and they fall just as quickly.

Megan recently indicated that she wants to take a trip, maybe to New York again. Broadway shows are always something to look forward to, and the exploration of life presented with drama and music will keep tunes and experiences in the forefront of a life still trying to find its way back. We will continue on the road we started down, and I believe God is still calling Megan into a life that is abundant. We have to find that life, and we have great hope that it is within reach.

At the Shepherd Center, one of my greatest struggles was realizing that I carried an unintended fear of and discomfort around the many patients whose catastrophic injuries and physical circumstances were difficult to watch and even harder to accept. In those days, many amazing things happened as my perceptions of their circumstances turned out to be wrong. I could not accept them as they were because they were different. Along the way, I learned lessons about the lives of the sick, the injured, the physically challenged, and the mentally challenged, and I realized that we all sometimes struggle with anyone we perceive as different from us.

One of the most poignant lessons of my life so far was taught to me by a young man whose body was gnarled and twisted by weeks in a coma and physical weakness from lack of use after injury. I observed this young man as if he was absent any true purpose, function, or capability. He was someone to be pitied, someone to observe and comment on arrogantly with comments like, "Oh, how tragic." I quickly learned that physical appearance in his case or limits of expression in Megan's case do not define the person.

Over several weeks, I watched as day by day these wonderful young people worked hard to move and stretch individual muscles and joints. This particular young man eventually became able to function, moving his hands and legs on his own, and on one sweet day he spoke for the first time and commented to his caregiver. His journey continued, and day by day, session by session, he was gradually restored right before our eyes. Somewhere along that trip my focus changed from "how tragic" to "how incredible, how wonderful, and how amazing." I have no idea how far his journey will go, but it does not matter; his journey is already a success. He was and is being transformed.

My point is that none of us are who we truly want to be. We all are trying to be different; we want to be healthier, skinnier, more beautiful, more faithful, or perhaps less awkward. We might try Lasix or Botox, a cleanse, the gym, or therapy to change everything from our looks to our psyches. We are all on that journey, all going somewhere. Observing the young man in Atlanta showed me that some of our journeys are elective, and others are of necessity. We have to change just to be able to live or to continue to live.

Pity serves only the conscience of the observer. If you want to help a person, it requires action, investment, and communication. Not one patient or family we met in Atlanta wanted pity, but all appreciated conversation, encouragement, smiles, and shared hope. None of us knew what was to come; all of us knew we needed help.

Finally, those of us who wonder whether the glass is half empty or half full are missing the point. The glass in many cases is refillable.

Megan's journey is not complete, but it is successful already. Every so often, that journey must change direction to accommodate what has yet to be restored. We can all make our lives revolve around our own deficits, but if we want true happiness, we should not lose sight of what we already have and believe we can attain. Do not judge where someone else is in their journey, because you really cannot tell. In Atlanta, I started off feeling sorry for someone I perceived as having needs far greater than ours, and that young man's progress was underway long before we even got there. My pity did nothing to help him.

Do not measure someone else's circumstance with goals that mean something to only you. Measure progress based on the goals established for each damaged life and celebrate with them because their success is your success. The beauty of healing appears differently to each person who sees it. Even though to some it is painful to observe, it is pure, remarkable, wonderful beauty nonetheless.

Somewhere along the way, Megan picked up a bumper sticker that says, "Aphasia—loss of words not loss of intellect." She doesn't want pity; she wants to be able to tell you what is on her mind.

Not even Megan knows where this is going and where or when it will transition to "what's next." We are simply along for the ride. It is important that we never lose sight that this journey, part mental but all real, is more than a means to an end. It has its own purpose and content that we attempt to use to "fill" our half-empty glass with what makes us whole.

When we take time to embrace the changes these events force on us, we can finally let go of the burden and once again take up the yoke of living, different as it may be. When we become more comfortable with our new circumstance, we can also acknowledge and recognize the old and familiar, although it is framed in a new context of reality that requires acceptance with purposeful evolution. "What was" becomes "what is," and we all live out our collective journey toward "what is next."

Baby steps.

Although we had to adapt one of our two adult trikes to accommodate Megan's needs, it's amazing what you can do with a coat hanger, some electrician's tape, and a role of wide Velcro.

Epilogue

As I write this, it's been seven years since Megan's stroke. It seems like more. These have been busy, challenging, difficult years—but good years. I know I've seen Venice a couple of times by now.

I've made several attempts at getting this book to a publisher, and each time I have allowed someone to read it critically, it has been a bit like running naked through Walmart. (It may not be the worst thing you see there on any given day, but it is still uncomfortable for us and for those who get the glimpse of more than they wanted to see.)

I think the reason I have held off, to a degree, is because everyone who has read it wants to know how Megan is doing now. So much has happened since those first two years, and I feel obligated to add one more chapter so that everyone suffering through the beginning stages has an idea of how far a person can come in a remarkable recovery like hers. And do I have more story to tell.

I know I resisted the original advice that "this is a marathon, not a sprint." But it's true. Part of this journey requires simply using all we can get access to in order to beat the stroke into submission. Megan's work ethic has helped her circumstances because she's been willing to use every device as a weapon to defeat her nemesis. Sometimes it has been incredibly hard work. Sometimes it has involved letting go and allowing others to drive. And sometimes God has simply intervened by offering options that weren't available previously. Often it has required us to accept that "Venice" has many streets or canals, and sometimes we just don't know what exploring those unknown paths might offer.

The damage done by the stroke impacted the physical, mental, social, and spiritual aspects of Megan's life. In trying to find things that help her and work for her, we have had to blend a variety of therapies for each affected area. By far, speech has been the most difficult area of recovery. It still is. Remember that speech includes swallowing, communicating, and even reading. Megan still struggles with these functions, particularly reading.

We have seen continuous improvement in the areas covered by physical and occupational therapies. While Megan's ability to walk showed improvement over the months after the initial time covered in the book, we learned that physical therapy will usually plateau when it comes to breakthroughs and relearning. We also learned that the damage initially caused by the stroke takes its toll on other parts of the body.

Though Megan improved her gait while working hard to walk again, some of the muscles in her leg, hip, and arm have not returned. Muscles not being used tend to atrophy. Since Megan's calf muscle would not fire, it began to decline and grow smaller. Everything is connected, so as that muscle got smaller, the Achilles tendon shortened and made her foot point down. That changed her gait, and she began having to kick out her foot to take a step.

Our medical team referred us to another new physician friend who is an orthopedic surgeon. Megan's issue is called "equinovarus," according to Dr. H, who introduced us to the likelihood that surgeries may be necessary in the coming years to help with the impacts of changes in gait and stress being put on joints, back, hips, and other places.

Dr. H suggested a procedure called a SPLATT. When he explained it, I admit my initial reaction was, "Oh no, you won't." But as I did my research, we quickly got comfortable. Of course, Megan was on board from day one, but Dad took a little longer.

I developed a bias toward ortho guys. Who thinks up these procedures? It's like working on my old car. I have a mental picture of two or three docs sitting around a bar table wearing brightly colored golf shirts and drinking beer. Their conversation begins with the last putt and transitions quickly to something like, "No, hear me out, what if you zigzag cut the Achilles tendon and extend it? That would raise the foot. Then you take the tendon that goes to the big toe flexor, split it and wrap one of the halves around the bottom of the foot, and attach it to the outside of the foot, so when the patient raises the toe, they raise their foot. It could work."

You can't make this stuff up. That is what a SPLATT procedure essentially does as I understand it. And it did work. I am glad that some of the most qualified innovators in the orthopedic world occasionally play golf and drink beer. Their innovation made my daughter's post-stroke life much better. It is thoughtful creativity, and for it I am grateful.

In fact, her walking and gait were so much improved that Megan has recently been able to give up the leg brace, at least for now. She still hyperextends her right knee with every step she takes, and her walk is very different from her pre-stroke athleticism. But thanks be to God, she can walk, she is mobile, and we have options to consider when other issues take their eventual toll. Also, she now wears two shoes that are the same size. No heels yet, though.

Baby steps.

As for the ongoing struggle to communicate, we received yet another gift from a conversation with our friends at the Shepherd Center when we decided to return one spring day to share a meal with Megan's A-team therapist friends. In conversation about us looking for new resources with a specific focus on aphasia and the havoc that it wreaks, Alexis happened to mention a few graduate school programs that are both innovative and reasonably accessible. One of those is the program at the University of Central Florida in Orlando.

We reached out to the director of that program and immediately found website information about the Aphasia House. It is remarkably simple in concept. Take the brightest and best graduate students in their speech therapy program, which happens to be the largest in the nation. Add their most qualified instructor as the person directing their efforts and planning the testing and types of therapy to be delivered. Then, every semester, bring in a handful of patients for six weeks of intensive daily therapy and allow them to interact and share their experiences and circumstances. Additionally, charge them enough to help cover the costs of the program but far less than would be charged if these patients were receiving inpatient services in a rehab facility.

When we heard about this and checked it out with the resources we had developed, Megan, as usual, was "in" long before we were. Once again, traveling from North Carolina to the Orlando area and having to pay for services, travel, lodging, and food in the middle of tax season seemed a bit much. But since there is so little aphasia treatment available that is truly innovative, we saw this as the gift from God that it was.

We applied and within a short time received a call from Dr. E, the program director. We had a lot of good conversation and arranged to make a whirlwind trip for Megan to be assessed for their program's admissions process. That happened around Thanksgiving 2018.

Megan and I flew from Asheville to Orlando late Monday afternoon the week of the holiday, arriving around eight at night. We stayed in a local hotel and drove to campus the next morning in our rental car. We got there around ten in the morning and spent time getting introduced to the facility and program. They began their assessment tests, with me present, and initially that throat lump made a classic reappearance. As Megan quickly tired, it became apparent that her hard-earned verbal skills were still limited. I was concerned that her limitations might prevent her from being accepted, and Megan quickly recognized how far away she still lived from anything mirroring "what was."

Dr. E was encouraging and supportive and sent us on our way to catch a five o'clock flight home with a promise to get back to us quickly so that we could plan to attend in the spring semester if the testing indicated she was a good candidate. Megan and I shared frustrations and a touch of sadness because we both knew how hard she had continued to work to restore her communications to a more functional level. Now the testing took the wind from our sails.

In early December I received a transfer of a call at my office. I noticed that my mouth was dry as I answered the phone. The upbeat voice on the other end of the call said, "Scott, this is Dr. E. How are you?" I responded, "I'm doing fine. How are things in Orlando?"

After exchanging pleasantries and talking UCF football a bit, she got to the point.

"Scott, we want to extend an invitation for Megan and you guys to come to Florida for several weeks to see if we can work with Megan on her aphasia. Megan is not the normal patient we typically get to work with. I want her to come to UCF because I really do think we can help her as she learns how to live with aphasia. But if I am truly honest, I also want Megan to come to UCF because of what she can teach my students."

All these months I had been so focused on getting help for our Megan. I was again realizing that through this horrible experience, Megan is always a gift in her own right, to us and to others. Her willing spirit and positive attitude make her therapeutic treatments a learning experience for her providers as they offer her good therapy. We committed to this opportunity, and Megan was elated even though at that moment she had no idea what she was committing to. All she knew was that she had connected with these people in her first encounter. But more importantly, she recognized that inaction offers no opportunity for improvement and action at least offers potential and a tinge of hope. Megan always will be about action and, therefore, hope.

We scheduled our five weeks in Orlando for mid-March to late April 2019. The school had a professional connection to a hotel chain that offered a discount to participating families, making our lodging more affordable. Amazingly, they offered a pet-friendly option, so Shep was able to go with us. Asheville had a low-cost flight directly from Asheville to Sanford, Florida, which was only fifteen miles from the facility. It was cheaper to fly than it was to drive, since driving was about nine hours.

Megan and I drove to Orlando that first weekend and Linda flew down later in the week. We got checked in and settled and began getting familiar with the area, including pet-friendly restaurants and entertainment. It was reasonably easy to get around, and the hotel had a great internet connection, so I could work from there as I finished tax season remotely yet again.

The first day, we all walked in and got the tour of the facility and the various treatment rooms, which were small office/classroom settings. We met with Dr. E, and she introduced us to our team of four young women who were at the top of their classes and would serve as our therapists. Each would focus on a specific area of treatment, and we would have each for an hour daily along with a group-therapy hour with all four of the other recipients. This would allow for socialization and a time of recovery between the intensive therapy sessions. We wasted no time getting started. It all began that day.

As we went through the sessions, we saw that each student therapist had spent significant time developing strategies and plans for what would be covered, so we didn't know what to expect. At each session, Megan got to know the person and figure out their personalities and style. All were good fits, and each brought an interesting perspective and attitude. Megan came to love them all. On that first day, we got to the third session and Megan had breezed through whatever they had offered. We concluded that she was obviously further along than they had initially thought. At the last session, all four therapists along with Dr. E were at our table, and Dr. E said, "Megan, we think we have underestimated where you are and want to talk about the things you need in order to progress." She spent a few minutes asking questions about our observations related to her weaknesses and her specific needs. With each comment we made, they took copious notes.

Dr. E had them take Megan into another room and identified a couple of other tests that they administered over the next hour or so. While that was going on, we discovered that once again the uneasy balance between cognition and expression was the source of why Megan had been underestimated. They had focused on expressive therapies to help Megan be able to communicate more. As I understand it, the problem was that the source of her inability to communicate was significantly impacted by her inability to understand what specific communications were about rather than her formulating particular responses.

When the providers returned, the testing confirmed that. So now these young people's planning and efforts to prepare for Megan went out the window. Dr. E said they had work to do, but by the time we returned the next day they would have a plan, and therapy would pivot to respond to the newly identified focus and needs. We were a bit confused by all this, and over our late lunch we heard Megan express doubt about whether this would be beneficial. We took Shep out for some fun and returned to the hotel later in the afternoon.

The next day, we came back for day two, and each therapist explained their new tasks. They were totally different. One focused on multitasking, one focused on reading and spelling, another on math and time management, and as Megan began, Dr. E came into each session and evaluated what was happening. After the first session of multitasking, Linda and I knew they had found the buttons to push. Megan had to keep up with the time of four separate activities and call time, then tell the therapist what activity was next and participate in it. The second was reading a paragraph over and over while timing herself to measure improved speed. By the end of the third session Megan was showing signs of being tired, which is evidence of her brain being truly challenged. When the day was complete, we went to get Shep and had lunch. Megan was quiet and had difficulty keeping her eyes open.

We soon headed back to the hotel, and Megan curled up for a nap, which lasted for over five hours. We knew that the folks in this good place knew what they were doing and had found therapy and treatment that would have an impact. Megan knew it too.

Each day we went with Megan to each session and saw what was happening so that we could use these methods to help her improve her strategies in dealing with aphasia. So much of it was a bit heartbreaking because we now understood more specifically that the damage to Megan's brain was foundational. Among other things, we were now learning how to help her relearn individual letter sounds and the connection of how letters can make differing sounds as they form words. She began using tiles with letters to help her learn to spell words that she could already say. She uses those tiles even today.

We saw improvement but in small doses. Improvement takes time, and the stroke beast has to be worn down. As we had seen in Atlanta, the words she struggled the most with were the little connectors like *a, it, the, he, in, at, of, as, to,* and so many others. Other sessions had her singing Broadway tunes and working on her independence. And then on day three, through normal conversation the name "Shep" came from her lips.

Dr. E halted the session and had about a fifteen-minute conversation about Shep with Megan. We found out that she too is an animal lover. Dr. E asked, "So why aren't you bringing him to the sessions?" We had no answer. Dr. E said that Shep is an important part of Megan's therapy and support team. In this place, he was welcome, and she emphasized that they would love for him to be there if we would bring him.

The next day he was with us, and he came every day for the rest of the program. In typical Shep form, he sat quietly most days and focused on his "peeps." He was a magnet, and the therapists and patients were drawn to him. The following day, Dr. E had prepared a pet bed, complete with toys, for him to relax. Shep was and is a rock star. His interaction with others added puppy therapy to an intense setting, and all he connected with felt their shoulders relax and stress quickly vanish.

The days at the UCF–Aphasia House are another of those watershed opportunities that profoundly helped Megan take significant steps toward Venice. Like the Shepherd Center, this place offered high and holy days that gave our daughter goals and skills, friendships, and hope. The relationships developed there continue today as those young people have graduated and gone on to careers in speech therapy. Dr. E shared that one of the lessons Megan offered was causing each of her providers to have to consider the fact that they will likely get attached to patients even though they are called to maintain the patient/provider relationship. You will not find that in a typical classroom, but these stellar students got an object lesson that will serve them well as they search for what is next in their own lives.

I know that we all learned something over those five weeks and that this good place profoundly improved our lives. Like the

Shepherd Center, they began the journey to improvements that we otherwise would not have found. We will always be in their debt, and we will always consider them dear friends.

Our experience at UCF also led us to a similar program at our own Western Carolina University. It is a smaller program; their clinic is similar in methodology but is once or twice weekly for an hour. Megan continues to participate each semester and still benefits from the wonderful work they do, which was continued throughout the Covid pandemic on Zoom.

Megan also works as a volunteer in the First Baptist *First Kids* program, which is a half-day childcare program offered during the school year. Going back into the classroom was not what she had planned, but it has allowed her to stay in the profession, and she has had a positive impact on the kids that she helps serve.

Megan applied for and eventually received Social Security disability, and that lengthy acceptance process now qualifies her for Medicare. The disability income helps financially cover her health insurance supplement through Medicare as well. The financial impacts of a stroke are profound, and we are fortunate to have these resources to take care of some of her living expenses. Megan still has hopes of living independently eventually. But for now, sharing space with Mom and Dad and Shep is where she is comfortable. Who knows where this will go, but for now it is good.

Another of Megan's life-changing experiences was her desire to drive again. We struggled with this mightily and had our doubts about whether she was a candidate or if the idea was even reasonable. Shortly after we returned to Asheville, her local physiatrist, Dr. D, planted the seed that he could see Megan driving again in the future. To appease Megan, we allowed CarePartners to test her, which isn't free and, like so much else, is not covered by insurance. It is a test that lasts a couple of hours, assessing her ability to operate a console set up like a car but also her reaction time and her ability to multitask in a dynamic environment.

To our surprise, Megan functioned very well on the operational piece, but she fell far short on the multitasking. That was a deal killer and resulted in the notification that "we do not believe Megan is a candidate at this time." It was one more "gut check" that crushed yet another of her hopes to be "normal."

Since much of the multitasking is directly impacted by cognition, we wondered, and she wondered, if her improvements achieved at UCF that focused on cognition might result in an improved retest. Dr. D made a second referral to their staff and the test was arranged. Two years after her initial test, Megan was as nervous as we had seen her. To our amazement, she went through the steps of the test with significant improvement. Nailed it!

The instructor indicated that if we wanted to proceed, the program was a couple of months long, included significant driving instruction, and would require Megan to pass the driving portion of the DMV test and the signs test. The nice part is that the instructor would go with her to the DMV and observe and support her. It was intimidating even for Megan, but we agreed it was something she wanted to do and that we had to try.

Oh, and her car would need to be modified for a left-foot gas pedal and a multifunction programmable spinner knob for steering so that she could control signals and wipers and such with one hand. Insurance wouldn't likely help with the $6,000 cost.

That had little impact on the decision, though, because we knew we were going to do this. Megan had the money from the sale of her house, and she said, "I'll pay for it." Megan really wanted this.

We traded Megan's car to get one with the new safety monitoring systems that identify cars in your blind spot and warn of lane departure, which was suggested by the instructor. We found a nice Subaru Crosstrek with low miles, and they sent us to a vendor that converts vehicles. It was a chunk of money, but they did a great job, and she had her adaptive car so that she could take the test upon completion of the course.

She scheduled driving day appointments, and the first one came quickly. CarePartners has a driver training vehicle that can be configured to fit a variety of disabilities, so her instructor spent several minutes setting up the car for Megan's needs. And then they were off into the parking lot for a first jaunt. To our amazement, they then made a right turn and were on the busy road.

In thirty minutes or so, I saw the driver training car turn back into the parking lot and Megan was still at the controls. When they parked, I chatted with her instructor, who told me that Megan was a good candidate for the program, and she looked forward to continuing Megan's training. Within a few weeks, the time came for Megan to take the driving test at the NCDMV.

We all were a bundle of nerves, but Megan did well, and while she was out taking the test, her teacher told me that from the first day she knew driving was in Megan's future. When Megan returned, she and the officer were all smiles and went to have her picture taken. The hard work paid off; the anxiety was replaced with joy. These days, joy is still always a good thing.

On the road once more!

Of all Megan's accomplishments, driving has been most transformative because it gives her independence that nothing else has. She has driven to the coast more than once, and having ridden with her several times, I believe she is a safer driver now than she was prior to her stroke. Her lead foot that was inherited from her father is still sometimes a temptation, but she does well in practicing safe driving. It is another success that she is grateful for.

These days, when someone sees the difficulties of her new normal, Megan still puts the hard stuff aside and says with acceptance and just a bit of determination, "Such is life." To me that is her lesson learned among so many lessons. We all face difficulty. It is a certainty. Such is life.

So much more has occurred during these days. Megan lost her Nana, which was another profound experience that reminds us of the brevity of life even though she lived to an incredible ninety-two years. We also moved yet again to be near Bud and Dianne. Megan's former roommate and best friend had a child and adopted a preteen. Linda's dad, Walt, passed away only fifteen days after Nana's passing. Change once again has exhibited its dominion over us all. God is still God, and we are not. And life goes on. For that we are immensely grateful.

You have honored us by taking the time to read this journey down a crooked road with no brakes, no guide, and often no guardrail. Thank you. So much of the travel has been uphill, and I know it was sometimes hard to read. We are not who we were when this detour started. Paris was firmly in our sights, and Megan was on cruise control to a life filled with promise. But life happened, and our world changed.

We have since found our new normal, and it is good. It is more of what we planned for, it is different from where we started, and it is what we have worked like hell to attain.

Understanding sweet Megan before all this is key to recognizing and understanding the grief that we all carry around regarding what was lost. The version of Megan that we have right now is nonetheless incredible and even miraculous. But that doesn't take away the grief we feel over what was lost and the future that she will not have. I still carry that grief even now. But it doesn't mean we don't honor Megan as who she is right now. We believe it is possible to both be grateful for Venice and still be devastated not to go to Paris.

For those of you searching for how to deal with difficult things, I hope our experiences were helpful, and I hope they give you ideas on how to approach your circumstances. I hope you find God's good grace in your journey, as we finally have. I also hope and pray that you find your new normal. Venice is a great place to visit, but don't plan to live there. Life is calling, and you must get on with it, different as it may be.

As for us, after everything we have been through, Megan is still able to travel. We just got back from New York, but we still haven't seen the Eiffel Tower, and I hear Paris is nice this time of year.

Sweet Megan (and Shep)

www.ingramcontent.com/pod-product-compliance
Lightning Source LLC
Chambersburg PA
CBHW071329190426
43193CB00041B/1041